MORE CRITICAL PRAISE FOR
LOVE, RUTH: A SON'S MEMOIR

"An intelligent, heartfelt, and often deeply touching account of an unveiling. Lovett's search for reconnection with the mother he was forced to let go makes for one of the most compelling tales I have ever read. When a loved one is wrenched from our grasp, we must find a way to reassemble that person, to take her back into our arms and hold on as long as is necessary, and then— and only then—to release her. *Love, Ruth* tenderly chronicles one such victory."

—Christopher Noël, author of
In the Unlikely Event of a Water Landing–A Geography of Grief

"With elegant style, Lovett writes of searching for the unknowable: the essence of his mother who died when he was two years old. In a swirl of facts, news clippings, visits to former homes, and interviews with friends and family, Lovett looks not so much for the great-granddaughter of the Coca-Cola founder in order to display his genealogy, but to find the feeling person, the one who might have written him a letter had she been well enough, the one who certainly touched his face and smiled at him with adoration. *Love, Ruth* is a moving portrait of the need to fill space when it is emptied of form."

—Phyllis Barber, author of
How I Got Cultured, A Nevada Memoir

Love, Ruth
A Son's Memoir

Ruth Candler Lovett
1935–1964

LOVE, RUTH

A SON'S MEMOIR

Charles Candler Lovett

The Callanwolde Guild
Callanwolde Fine Arts Center
Atlanta
1999

A portion of the proceeds from the sale of this book will go to
The Callanwolde Guild in support of the facilities and programs of
Callanwolde Fine Arts Center.

Additional copies of this book may be ordered for $17.00 plus $3.00
shipping from: The Callanwolde Guild, 980 Briarcliff Rd. NE, Atlanta,
GA 30306; or by phone at (404) 872-5338; or on the Web at
www.callanwolde.org

Copyedited by Michael Welch.
Designed by The Snark.

ISBN 0-9672040-4-6
Library of Congress Catalog Card Number: 99-74424

First Edition

Chapter epigraphs and quoted published material from: Annie Dillard, *An American
Childhood* (© 1987 Annie Dillard, published by Harper & Row); A. S. Byatt, *Possession*
(© 1990 A. S. Byatt, published by Random House); Jane Austen, *Mansfield Park*; Pat
Conroy, *The Prince of Tides* (© 1986 Pat Conroy, published by Houghton Mifflin); Russell
Baker, "Life with Mother" (© 1987 Russell Baker, published in *Inventing the Truth*, ed-
ited by William Zinsser, Houghton Mifflin); Asa G. Candler as quoted by Charles Howard
Candler in *Asa Griggs Candler* (© 1950 Emory University); William Shakespeare, *Ham-
let*, Act I, Scene v; William Maxwell, *So Long and See You Tomorrow* (© 1980 William
Maxwell, published by Random House); J. Milton Richardson, letter to Ruth and Bob
Lovett (19 September 1955); Ruth, I:16-17, Authorized King James Version; Eudora Welty,
The Optimist's Daughter (© 1969, 1972 Eudora Welty, published by Random House);
Paul Auster, *The Invention of Solitude* (© 1982 Paul Auster, published by Sun Press);
Lewis Carroll, *The Diaries of Lewis Carroll* (© 1954 The Estate of Charles Dodgson,
published by Oxford University Press); *Cumberland Island A Challenge in the Golden
Isles* (© 1966 National Park Service); Steven Millhauser, *Edwin Mullhouse* (© 1972 Steven
Millhauser, published by Alfred A. Knopf); E. M. Forster, *Howard's End* (© 1910, published by G. P. Putnam's & Sons); *Random House Unabridged Dictionary*, Second Edition (© 1993 Random House); *The Book of Common Prayer of The Episcopal Church*
(1928 and 1979 editions).

For Lucy
Who inspired & shared the journey.

ACKNOWLEDGMENTS

This book would not have been possible without the help and encouragement of so many people who knew Ruth Candler Lovett and who remember her. To all of them I owe a debt a gratitude.

I would especially like to thank those who corresponded with me: Tom Allen, Charles Howard Candler, III, Betsy Candler, E. Dudley Colhoun, Jr., A. Robert Cordell, Beverly Holliday Cresse, Jane Lee Taylor Crockett, Nannette McBurney Crowdus, Richard A. Denny, Jr., William B. Dillingham, Kathleen B. Edens, Louisa Candler Eldredge, Aurelia Eller, Sandra G. Epstein, Austin Ford, Patsy Cathcart Fordyce, Glenn Fuller, Jane Pinckney Hanahan, Alice Gray Harrison, Fritzi Herring, Virginia Olsen Horton, Sonja Olsen Kinard, Bingle Lewis, Gene Linton, Susan Lovett Coleman, Bettye C. Maddox, Russell Major, Gail T. Minier, Fran Oliver, Elizabeth Millis Ormsby, Nancy Osborne, Ward Pafford, Ruthe Yeargan Proctor, Louise C. Scranton, Marge Sosnik, Constance Wilson Treloar, Henry Valk, Katherine Massengale Walter, Jake Ward, Catherine Candler Warren, William C. Warren, III, Floyd Watkins, Chappell White, Emily Wilson, Harvey Young, Jane Young, and Joanne Taber Young.

Anne Sherow and Clarece Martin of the Westminster Schools Archives; the Emory University Alumni Department, Library, and Registrar's Office; Patricia L. Wright at the Sweet Briar College Library; and the Registrar's Office of Sweet Briar College all provided valuable information on Ruth's education. Liliana Major of St. Luke's Episcopal church, Atlanta, and Milly Kitchene of the Winston-Salem Junior League provided information about Ruth's participation in those organizations. Thank you to Tom Shanks of SunTrust Bank for providing a copy of Ruth's estate tax return. Elizabeth Lovett was especially helpful in finding materials relating to Ruth's life.

Thank you to Bobbie Randall for providing Ruth's handwriting analysis, and to Rand Lee for his gentle kindness in leading me though unfamiliar territory.

Many friends and family spoke to me about Ruth, and I am grateful to them for all they shared with me. To Wight Crawford, Don Harrison, Wilson Sneed, Catherine Candler Warren, Sonja Olsen Kinard, Sam O. Candler, and especially to Glenn Candler Fuller and Betsy Denny Candler I extend my thanks. I also owe a great debt of gratitude to Bo and Betsy Candler for hosting Janice and me on Cumberland Island.

Bob Lovett participated willingly in the project from the beginning, and my thanks cannot begin to repay him for hours of conversations, both in person and on the telephone, that form the core of this book. He also provided access to much archival material that gave me important background information. Miriam Lovett patiently contributed her thoughts and counsel, and for this and so much more I am most grateful.

I would also like to thank those who read the manuscript and shared their reactions with me: Michael Welch, Rob Roberge, Diane Lefer, Walter Wetherell, members of writers' groups and workshops in Kansas City, Montpelier, and Santa Fe, David and Elizabeth Lovett, who kindly shared their thoughts and memories with me, and especially Chris Noël. Chris encouraged me to embark on this journey, and his constant support through the months of research together with his thoughtful criticism of the early chapters gave me the firm footing I needed to see this project through to its completion.

Thanks to Lisa and Ron Newham for their frequent hospitality on my visits to Atlanta.

I thank my wife, Janice, for her support and patience, for sharing my enthusiasm and many of my travels, and for figuring out how to open the trunk in my grandmother's attic. Thanks to Jordan for telling her creative writing teacher something that made me feel like a real writer. And thank you to Lucy—for showing me how important a parent can be, for patiently and excitedly accompanying me in Atlanta, and for inspiring me, with her inquisitive mind, to answer the questions I had always been afraid to ask.

Finally, to all those at Callanwolde who had the vision and confidence to take on the publishing of this book: Sonja Kinard, who has been an encouragement almost since the project began; Samuel Goldman, executive director of the Callanwolde Fine Arts Center; and especially Jeanne Pearson, president of The Callanwolde Guild, whose leadership and enthusiasm saw the project through to fruition.

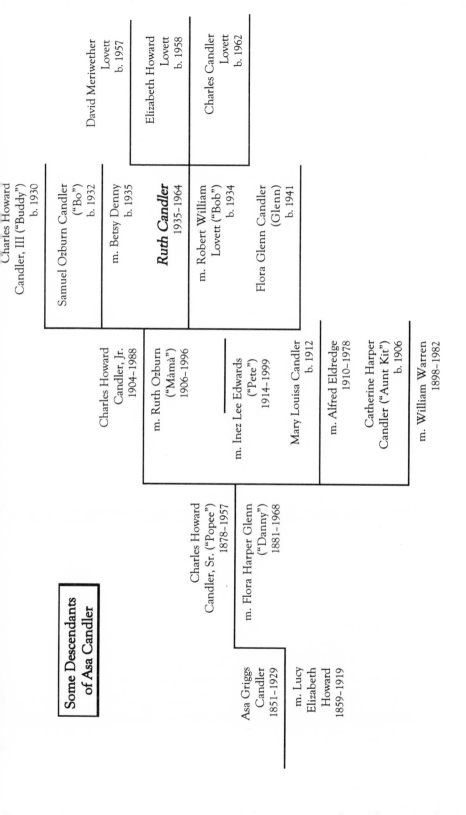

Some Descendants of Asa Candler

Asa Griggs Candler
1851-1929

m. Lucy Elizabeth Howard
1859-1919

Charles Howard Candler, Sr. ("Popee")
1878-1957

m. Flora Harper Glenn ("Danny")
1881-1968

Charles Howard Candler, Jr.
1904-1988

m. Ruth Ozburn ("Mama")
1906-1996

m. Inez Lee Edwards ("Pete")
1914-1999

Mary Louisa Candler
b. 1912

m. Alfred Eldredge
1910-1978

Catherine Harper Candler ("Aunt Kit")
b. 1906

m. William Warren
1898-1982

Samuel Ozburn Candler ("Bo")
b. 1932

m. Betsy Denny
b. 1935

Ruth Candler
1935-1964

m. Robert William Lovett ("Bob")
b. 1934

Flora Glenn Candler (Glenn)
b. 1941

Charles Howard Candler, III ("Buddy")
b. 1930

David Meriwether Lovett
b. 1957

Elizabeth Howard Lovett
b. 1958

Charles Candler Lovett
b. 1962

I saw the angel in the stone, and carved to set it free.
—Michelangelo

I

A young child knows Mother as a smelled skin, a halo of light, a strength in the arms, a voice that trembles with feeling. Later the child wakes and discovers this mother— and adds facts to impressions, and historical understanding to facts.

—ANNIE DILLARD

At ten o'clock he makes the call. It is late September. The heat has broken and the windows are open, but the air that shifts through the room comforts no one. She sobs, begs, moans for anything to stop the pain. Her body convulses from beneath the sheet and she grasps blindly for the table by the bed. Drugs, painkiller, morphine, more, anything. Her cries come like the surf, crashing violently as the pain builds and drifting away not because the pain eases but because her energy is exhausted. The intensity of each outburst is unpredictable and just when she seems about to slip into sleep she erupts from the sheets again driven by what eats her from inside. "The pain—I can't stand the pain." What must the neighbors think?

Her mind has been invaded and then conquered by the morphine; her body, bloated where the cancer flourishes, but sunken elsewhere, screams at her and she screams at him or anyone who will listen. More morphine. More. More. And he knows he can do no more, that in this bedroom in this house on this street she will only hurt herself, or someone else, or scare the children. So he makes the call at ten o'clock. The woman at the other end must hear her cries, must know.

At ten o'clock, on Wednesday the twenty-third of September in nineteen hundred and sixty-four, from the phone by the bed in the master bedroom at the end of the hall on the second floor of the house at 1943 Robinhood Road in Winston-Salem, North Carolina, my father, Robert

Lovett, calls Baptist Hospital and asks the woman who answers to please send someone to pick up his wife so she can die. It is a sunny morning with a slight breeze, and the air is tinged with the promise of fall. In driveways up and down our block, other mothers load infants into cars for the morning shopping. Three miles away, in their classrooms at Summit School, my brother David and sister Elizabeth stare out the windows at the playground. In the red brick house with white painted siding on the second floor, I am passed from father to uncles to grandparents. I talk to them in my evolving two-year-old speech. I show them my favorite toys. I sit on their laps and listen to stories of Curious George and the Cat in the Hat. I serve as their distraction from the events in the master bedroom at the end of the hall on the second floor, until I have eaten my fish sticks and my Spanish rice and someone takes me up two flights of stairs past the shut door and to the attic for my nap. By two o'clock I am asleep.

She's too weak to walk and the stretcher cannot make the turn at the top of the stairs, so they carry her out strapped into an armless chair with a black vinyl seat and a cane back on a wooden frame.

. . . A chair I have sat in innocently countless times over the years, never suspecting it was anything other than a chair. A chair that still sits in my father's study at the mountain house. I sit in this chair after I discover its secret—that outside of a hospital bed it was the last piece of furniture my mother ever touched. I try to feel something of her in it. I close my eyes and try to imagine being bound and carried by two strong men, at a slight reclining angle, out my bedroom door, down the hall, down a flight of stairs, through the front door, down the four brick steps into the front yard and out to a waiting ambulance at the curb. I try to imagine this chair taking me away from my family, my home, my children, my life. I feel chilled and sober, feel frightened and alone. But I do not feel *her*. . . .

She leaves the house at three o'clock and gradually the uncles and grandparents drift back to the Howard Johnson's by the interstate to wait. When Daddy brings me down from my nap, the door, which has been so often shut in recent days, stands open. I look in, and see the empty bed.

"Where Mommy?" I ask. And he tells me she has gone back to the hospital, and I never say anything else about it. *I never ask about her again.* Until now. And now I wonder: Would it have made any difference, if I had had a chance to say good-bye?

When I turned thirty, my investment counselor talked me into buying life insurance. To qualify, I had to pass a physical—blood test for AIDS, urine sample for smoking and drug use, stethoscope against the chest for general purposes. Turns out I'm disgustingly healthy. The exam concluded with the usual interminable list of questions about my medical history.

"Ever had diabetes?"

"No."

"Chest pains?"

"No."

"Hepatitis?"

"No."

"Father still living?"

"Yes."

"Age?"

"Fifty-eight."

"Mother still living?"

"No."

"Age at death?"

"Twenty-nine."

The incantation stops. The doctor, a stocky Hispanic man who has been smiling and making witty remarks, looks at me for the first time. Not at the body he has been hired to inspect, but at *me*.

"I'm sorry," he says in a voice I have heard many times before, a voice that could convey no more shock or condolence if I told him my mother was just hit by a bus in his parking lot. Dr. Olmos's voice recognizes not only my loss, but his own mortality and ultimately his inability to perform his job, to hold off death.

I brush off his sympathy.

"It's okay," I say, "I never knew her."

My family rarely talked about her. Her parents and siblings never spoke to me of her. To me, she seemed to inhabit the list of subjects that Southern gentility forbade. The family, which was nothing if not Southern and genteel, simply didn't talk about certain topics. Money was among these. My grandfather, Ruth's father, once listed two others as the Scotch was being poured; "We can talk about anything but religion and politics," he said.

If politics, religion, and money were clearly off-limits in conversation, the forbidden included another topic I never heard stated outright—pain. And the loss of my mother eclipsed all other pains. In my presence, at least, she was avoided, as if she never existed. But she did, and I am proof.

My father mentioned her on occasion, but his stories told late at night around the fireplace in the damp cool evening of early summer in the mountains revolved not around her life, but her death, and were so fraught with pain that they made me shy further away from the topic. In his tears I saw the very reason for the rules of avoidance. Now, though, I am ready to find out who she was, if it's not too late.

Why do I start this search now, in my thirty-fourth year? Certainly there has been a series of failed catalysts—moments that might have spoken to me to search her out. My marriage to a woman with adoptive parents who knew less about her mother than I; my passage through the age of twenty-nine, the age at which my mother died and that had loomed like a mystic barrier; the birth of my daughter, Lucy, when I began to see the strength of the bond between parent and child; my second marriage to a woman whose mother died at forty-eight—she *did* know her mother and understood her life. Any of these might have been the time, but none were.

Lucy has passed her second birthday, and I look at her and see how much of a person she is at two, how full of the life of both her parents. She is not a baby who would ignore the disappearance of a parent, but an individual who understands her parents as permanent, immovable, and supremely important forces. She is what I was in September of 1964, when my mother, hysterical with pain and hallucinating from damage done by morphine, was carried out of my house strapped into a chair while I slept in my crib. I awoke, looked inside her room, and asked my father, "Where Mommy?" and he explained that she had returned to the hospital. All this I can understand, and I do not doubt that my daughter would do the same if her mother were whisked away at nap-time. But I never saw my mother again, and, as my father has told me, I never, after that first question, said another word about her. She slipped from my life and from that moment I grasped, as if by instinct, that she had entered the realm of the forbidden. And it is for my daughter, as much as for myself, that I now choose to remove her from that list, to ask the questions I never asked, to discover this women who bore the pain of my birth and the pain of her own death. I ask the questions so I will know, but also so my daughter will not wait until she is in her fourth decade to open the box that contains her past, her creation, her identity, and to discuss what is forbidden.

I hide emotions and avoid conflict. Ask my shrink, or my friends, or my parents. Do not ask those who have known me for only a few days or a few months, because I am also an actor. New friends doubt me when I confess that I'm a shy person.

I feel desperate to hide myself here, for the part of me that seeks after Ruth is the most secret part of me, one I refused to open, even to myself, for so long. How, then can I possibly open that part up now?

My mother's name was Ruth Candler Lovett. As I write this, I cannot tell you the date of her birth, though I believe the year was 1934. I cannot tell you the date of her death, though I know it was late September of 1964. I can tell you a few facts about the twenty-nine-year span of her life. I can show you the two houses she lived in as a child growing up in Atlanta. In one of those houses, I can introduce you to her mother, whose years have thrice exceeded those of her daughter. The other, I drove by once. I know there are others—places she lived with my father and with her older children, my brother and sister. I can show you the house she moved to in Winston-Salem when I was two months from being born, a house I grew up in without her, a house my father and his second wife, Mim, the woman I have always thought of as my mother, are moving out of this month. I can tell you she was a member of the Candler family—that her father owned a farm, her grandfather built a famous mansion, and her great-grandfather founded The Coca-Cola Company. I can tell you that she attended Washington Seminary in Atlanta, Sweet Briar College in Virginia, and Emory University in Atlanta. She had three children, and she died of cancer. These facts I know.

I have some vague impressions—that she loved music, and perhaps played the piano; that she was beautiful; that she and my father had the perfect marriage; that she was a good mother.

It is remarkable what I do not know. What did she major in in college? What were her favorite foods? How did she dress? Did she read the newspaper every day? Like to go for walks with the children? Go to the movies and eat popcorn? Whom did she vote for in 1960? What magazines did she subscribe to? Did she watch a lot of TV? What did her voice sound like? Who were her friends in school? Where did she travel? Did she do volunteer work? Was she a morning person or a night owl? A beach bum or a mountain lover? How did she feel about God?

None of these questions can hope to get at who she was. Together, their answers would make up nothing more than a personals ad. But I don't even have that.

My time with Lucy is limited—six or seven visits a year, and never more than a week at a time—so I maximize it, even if we do nothing special. I try to be constantly aware of her presence, to notice and record everything she does. I lend a special significance to this time and to her actions. Am I more blessed than Ruth who didn't know that her time with her children was limited? Did she take our presence for granted, believing she would have a lifetime to spend with us?

When I write about my mother's death my hands shake. I cannot concentrate for long; I have to get up and pace after every sentence or two. I might be sweating at the end of a paragraph. But as I begin to investigate her life, I feel no such emotional attachment to my work. It is a research project, like many others I have undertaken. I approach it with the curiosity and distance of a biographer, not yet fully absorbing the fact that the baby near the end of the story is me.

I ran a secondhand bookstore for six years with my first wife. I loved the constant treasure-hunt for new stock, the ever-hovering possibility that the next person through the door would bring in a gem. Often families called on us to buy a lifetime of books from the home of someone who died.

Once I spent a week appraising and ultimately buying nearly six thousand books from a run-down four-room house. Every room had bookshelves on every wall, even covering over the windows. The man who had read them lived alone. His only friends seemed to be the local library staff. His remaining family lived far away, and seemed not much interested in either him or his estate.

In that week of working in his house for ten hours a day, I got to know him perhaps better than anyone had in life. I saw how his passions changed over the years—books on Greece published in the fifties giving way to books on jazz published in the sixties. I followed his life through boxes of army manuals and playbills, articles torn from magazines, and thousands of books. His life was words, and I could have recreated that life in the pages of all those books. It is uncomfortable to know a dead stranger so intimately.

Leaving the house with the last of some two hundred boxes of books, I thought about my mother, and how I didn't know the title of a single book she read.

When I stand in the side yard of my grandmother's house in Atlanta the smell takes me back twenty-five years. It slips around when I try to pin it down, but it's something to do with the slate-gray smell of ivy, wet leaves and mulch slow-burn rotting, and the hint of pansy blossoms early in spring. All these smells float like the best parts of a gumbo in a dank humid broth that nearly drowns them but really brings them together—the fuzzy green-brown smell of the magnolia, not the blossoms or the hand grenade seed clusters or even the glossy, glassy leaves but the subtlety of the tree itself. It is a smell that not only exceeds but differs from the sum of its parts.

That smell brings back Easter egg hunts with pastel-dressed cousins reaching under holly bushes and into ivy, walks in the woods to the vegetable garden in a clearing at the foot of the hill, and summer afternoons drinking Coke on the screen porch.

The house is set far back from the street behind a wooded hill, and the lot is so large and so heavily forested that no other homes are visible. The sounds of the street disappear. Even though I'm only a mile from the frantic pre-Olympic traffic of Peachtree Road, I could as easily be standing in the same spot fifty years ago, when my mother moved to this house as a child.

At eight I walked the grounds with my grandmother's second husband, a retired rear admiral named Carl Stillman. Carl had, I believe, a mental condition (perhaps "pose" is a better word) that disallowed his accepting commonly held truths. This led to incessant lectures on the evils of fluoridating water, on healing nearsightedness with eye exercises, on why modern medicine had nothing to offer him, and so on. To the adults in the family, these pontifications fluctuated between annoying and amusing. I didn't understand about eccentrics.

"You know," he said, "your mother's not really dead." This sounded interesting. I'd been shutting out his discourse on vegetarianism, but the mention of my mother smacked of the forbidden.

"When a person dies they get reincarnated."

"What's that mean?"

"Well, they come back to earth and become a person again."

That was all I needed. His mention of a Hindu principle, provided without context or explanation to my eight-year-old ears, needed no verification. He was an adult. If he said Mommy was alive someplace, she must be. For several days, I wondered if I might meet her. Was there any way to search for her? Would she remember me? Did she live with some other family now? I pictured bumping into her on the street. "What a coincidence—so nice to see you again."

What amazes me about this incident is the matter-of-fact nature of my thoughts. I did not long for her. My heart did not leap at the possibility of getting her back. I was curious. I found it interesting that she still existed. Two weeks later, back from my visit to grandparents and sitting at the dinner table, I announced that my mother was still alive somewhere because she had been reincarnated. I have seldom seen my father deeply upset. He spouts off about this and that, argues with Mim, yells at his children on occasion, all the things any father does, but rarely is he angry in his soul. But that night I saw his fury, and felt it. I even felt that he was mad at me. I had mentioned a forbidden subject. Easy for me to believe that his anger had to do with that. But what he said had nothing to do with me, or Mommy, or even Carl.

He said, "*We* don't believe that." Even at eight I realized the discussion had turned to religion, a topic I had not associated with my statement. As before, I did not question adult authority, particularly my father's. If he said *we* didn't believe in reincarnation, then it must not be true. The discussion ended. I never brought it up again.

How, at age thirty-three, do I feel about my inevitable death? My mother died at twenty-nine—I feel vulnerable. My mother died at twenty-nine—I feel invincible.

I have always attributed my silence on the subject of Ruth to my adherence to a family ethos of avoidance, but looking back, I detect in my younger self another element—a blind and total acceptance of fact unique to little children. Despite their reputation for asking "why," children are much more likely than adults to accept facts without question, without explanation, without justification. Adults yearn to understand why a young mother would be taken from the earth. But a child whose acceptance of an adult's statements about reincarnation is as total as his rejection of those same statements when repudiated by his father, such a child, when told that his mother is not returning, might just say, "Okay, thanks for telling me," and go on with his life.

"I remember that there was a mother," wrote my older sister Elizabeth, "but not what that mother was like. It upsets me how few memories I have."

David, the oldest of Ruth's three children, who was seven when she died, also has no clear memory of Mommy. "I remember specific events when she was sick," he said. "Mommy getting a shot in the rump at home, seeing her in the hospital lobby, finding her prosthesis in the bedroom and having her explain to me what it was . . . but none of those recollections include memories of her face, her voice, her touch."

One year when I was in college, my parents gave me my life for Christmas. It consisted of report cards, school pictures, letters I had sent home from camp—all the documents and records that one might expect to accumulate in twenty years. But this life they gave me began when I was four and entered kindergarten.

Lucy lives in North Carolina. I live in suburban Kansas City. She visits for a week here and a week there, but I am generally far removed from her two-year-old life. Yet she knows me so intimately. She does more than recognize me when I come to get her, she loves me with an outward enthusiasm adults have forgotten. Her adoration is, for now, unconditional. How much stronger must be the bond between a two-year-old and a parent who lives with him every day.

When Lucy is here, I lie next to her while she sleeps and breathe in the aroma of her freshly washed hair, her sweetness. I can only describe my feelings then as a swelling of the heart—some combination of pride and joy and pain.

When she is not here, I sniff her bottle of shampoo to inhale the memory of her and I expect to cry, I want to cry, but tears do not come.

Shortly before I turned three, Daddy asked me what I would like to do for my birthday. "But I'm too little to have a birthday," I said. I couldn't remember turning one; Mommy had been in the hospital having exploratory surgery and getting bad news the day I turned two. The only birthdays I had seen celebrated were David and Elizabeth's. Birthdays looked nice, but I felt much too little.

When I was growing up, we had one picture of my mother in the house. I hesitate to use the word photograph, because it was so unrepresentative of reality. It sat on the dresser in my sister Elizabeth's room, in a gilt wooden frame. I can only guess that Daddy granted Elizabeth possession of this picture because she looked most like the face in the frame.

Now I have a copy of that image in my office. It is one of those black and white airbrushed photo-portraits like one finds in college yearbooks in the 1950s. Her shoulders are draped in a wispy fabric and her body gradually fades away above where her breasts would be. She wears large white earrings, and her dark hair, with its perfect wave, is perfectly in place—so much so, it looks more like a solid unit, like the plastic hair of a cheap doll, than like a collection of individual strands. Her skin is smoother than anyone's skin at any age, her nose small, her lips full, straight white teeth peeking out, and chin protruding just the right amount, rounded in a gentle curve.

This photo taught me, visually, what I later learned with my ears—no one speaks ill of the dead, especially those who die young. Ask many who knew her about my mother and they will describe her as "wonderful" or "kind"—meaningless words. Likewise, this picture showed not a human being, but an image of how the memory might imagine a human being after that person had died, with all the bad things forgotten, airbrushed away.

For years, this photograph was the only evidence of my mother I ever saw. It pervaded my image of her so much that she became something other than human to me, and perhaps that made my losing her easier. Certainly it made the task I undertake now, of trying to humanize her, harder. That photograph shaped me in odd ways.

Its portrayal of a young dead woman, combined with its unrealistic beauty, placed it, and therefore her, in the realm of the angelic. How easy to see my dead mother as a guardian angel with this portrait the only image of her I knew. Through this angelic image she became for me, on occasion, the sort of intercessor Mary is in the Catholic church. The thing that made it easiest for me to believe in the afterlife was her death, because I found it more difficult to believe I would never know her than to believe I would see her in heaven. Her image was, after all, not human, but heavenly.

I was the one who named Lucy's blanket "Woobie," taking the word from the Michael Keaton movie *Mr. Mom.* When Lucy's grandmothers returned from shopping for her a few days after her birth, I christened the whole pile of receiving blankets "Woobies." As months and then years passed, the pile got smaller, and finally one was chosen by her as *the* Woobie, that piece of soft-worn cloth that would seem as important to her, for a time, as mother or father.

She came to visit in the spring, when she had just turned two, and Woobie was her most prized possession. I began to think that convincing her not to drag it around in public places might not be such a bad idea. Spring can be blustery in suburban Kansas City, where nothing stops the wind coming off the seven hundred miles of plains that separate us from the Rockies. That week, Lucy helped me clean out my car. She took trash to the trash can and carried cups inside. When we were all finished, we started to look for Woobie. By the end of the day, I realized she had taken Woobie out of the car and set it on the driveway, where it had blown away. I began to panic, but with no prompting from me, Lucy concocted a story right out of García Márquez. The wind, she said, had carried her Woobie up to the moon, and when the moon was full, she would be able to look up and see her Woobie. Maybe one day it would come back. Maybe not.

Later, her mother gave her a scrap of an old receiving blanket to serve as a Woobie. On the next visit Lucy told me her Woobie had flown down from the moon into her room where it had left this piece of itself before flying back out into the night and up to the moon. But even that first night, when all of the Woobie was on the moon and Lucy was without her security blanket, she slept well and happy.

This, I thought, is how my two-year-old deals with loss. She offsets it with her imagination. And how much of a leap is it, really, from imagining your Woobie on the moon to imagining your mother as your guardian angel?

I have, in thirty-three years, accumulated nine pictures of my mother, which I spread out on the carpet of my office.

In the oldest Ruth looks about three, standing in front of a tree with hands clasped behind her back, looking like my sister's daughters did at that age. In the most recent she sits by my father in a picture of her generation and their spouses taken on my grandmother's curved staircase at Christmas 1963, nine months before her death. She wears a plain red dress with matching heavy lipstick and her hair is poofed out on all sides—no doubt specially styled for the holiday visit with family. My father's arm wraps around her back, his hand resting on her shoulder. She looks healthy.

The snapshots are still slick on the front, and some have rough deckled edges. They have a smell that is not quite musty, not quite chemical—something between old books and moth balls. Of those taken before my birth, all but one are black and white. I run my fingers along their edges and bore into their images with my eyes, hoping to bring them to life.

Ruth Candler, about three years old.

One color picture of Ruth in blue shorts and a T-shirt holding an exit sign in front of her house in 1951 has yellowed badly. Another that might be from the same period shows her cross-legged on her lawn, but the print is marred by the white lines of a fingerprint. In three shots she poses with my father—once at a dance, a corsage on her wrists and Bob's arms around the flowing taffeta of her dress; once in casual attire, the two embracing firmly, turning to face the camera almost as if it were a disrespectful intruder; once on a mountaintop, their arms around one another's waists. I have no

pictures of the two of them
that do not involve at least the
suggestion of an embrace.

She is a large woman—not
overweight, but with a healthy-
looking, childbearing frame.
Standing next to my skinny father, even in flats, she is only
two or three inches shorter
than his 5' 11". Her hair has
the same curls and wave mine
has, and she usually wears it
short with a sweep of curls
above her forehead on the
right-hand side, the same way
I wore mine for thirty years or
so. The contrast between the
picture of her at sixteen and
those of her as a grown woman
is not surprising. Her arms get
thicker, her shoulders broader,
and her hips wider. In the one
picture where she's caught

*Ruth and Bob along the Blue Ridge
Parkway in 1954.*

from the side it is evident I inherited my lack of a chin from her—something the angel-photo managed to conceal. The one thing the angel-photo
got right was her smile—it is soft, gentle, and natural, and black and white
or yellowed color does not diminish its message of zest for life and love for
my father.

I have three pictures of Mommy and me. One shows me just under a
year old, naked, sitting on the top step of the swimming pool at my
grandfather's farm. My brother floats behind me on a inflatable raft and
Mommy sits at the very edge of the frame, her hand outstretched in case I
topple toward too-deep water. The other two are of me as an infant. One
shows me lying in her arms, but her head, except for the tip of her nose, is
cut off by the edge of the picture. In the other she stands in front of the
house in Winston-Salem and holds me up for the photographer to see.
Her face is nearly out of the frame and mostly in shadow. Only my head is

visible, and I look no more than a few days old. It seems an awfully tenu-
ous connection.

My wife, Janice, and I are taking her daughter Jordan and my daughter
Lucy to the zoo. We feel like any two parents with their two children. Over
the course of the morning we have progressed from "What do I wear,"
and "I don't want to get a hair wash," through snacks and seatbelts and we
stand in a hot parking lot putting on our sunscreen. I smear the lotion on
Lucy's bare arms and carefully apply it to her face. Then I put a hat on her.
I have read an article recently that says severe sunburn received as a young
child can lead to skin cancer decades later. And so I take these precautions to protect Lucy, realizing that the smallest things I do for her can
affect her future in enormous ways. She is two.

In 1967, three years after Ruth's death, my father married Miriam Möller,
whom her friends called Mim. This was a convenient appellation for her
stepchildren as well—close enough to "Mom" to sound maternal without
creating psychological confusion. I hesitate to use that word stepchildren,
for Mim has never been less than a mother to me. I never, in the course of
growing up, referred to her as my stepmother, or to my younger brothers,
Peter and John, as half-brothers. I was just shy of five years old when Mim
became my mother. I can recall no other, nor do I have any clear memories of anything that happened before she and Daddy were married. My
childhood was happy, and Mim was an important part of that happiness.
She assumed the role of mother of three at the age of twenty-three—just
thirteen years older than my brother David. When I turned twenty-three
I was freshly married and hardly ready to assume the role of baby-sitter for
an evening.
      Mim may also be part of the reason I have waited so long to seek out
Ruth. I had some fear that Mim would see my search as a rejection—that I
was somehow attempting to replace her with acquired memories of Ruth.
Perhaps more significant, though, Mim was, and is, a good mother. I never
felt any great absence in my life because I had lost a mother. Mim was my
mother, and I felt no need to seek out any other.

When Lucy was a sleeping baby, I would tiptoe into her room and stand
silently next to her bed. I held my breath and listened for the sound of

hers. Sometimes I placed my hand on her back, my fingers running the length of her spine, and felt for the steady movement that would let me know she was alive. Each time I finally heard breath or felt her chest expand, it seemed like a miracle. Each time, I reassured myself she was breathing and stepped back out of the darkness amazed. I wonder if Ruth did the same to me.

I imagine this: A square of white granite, small enough for me to pick up if it had not settled into the green earth, sits at the bottom of a hill in Westview Cemetery in Atlanta. I see it gleaming in the sun or gray-streaked with rain, dusted with snow or covered with orange and yellow leaves. I see myself standing over it alone, hands thrust into my pockets, eyes locked on its simplicity. I feel the wind at my back and the snow or rain or leaves blowing past my feet. I hear myself speak to her, as if the nearness of her remains provides some conduit to her soul. I smell the air crisp or damp or cold and I hear a bird or cricket or the traffic just over the hill—or silence. I see, at last, the stone alone behind me as I walk away. Alone with the red rose that I lay across its whiteness. Alone.

II

Letters are a form of narrative that envisages no outcome,
no closure. . . . Letters tell no story, because they do not
know, from line to line, where they are going. . . . Letters,
finally, exclude not only the reader as co-writer, or pre-
dictor or guesser, but they exclude the reader as reader;
they are written, if they are true letters, for a reader.
                                                    –A. S. BYATT

When my grandfather, Charles Howard Candler, Jr., died in 1988, some family member, after cleaning out his files, sent me a slim manila folder of the correspondence between Ruth and her father. I skimmed over the file the day it appeared unexpectedly in the mail. I read the last few letters, and glanced at others looking for news of myself, but then the phone rang, or I had an appointment, and I stuffed the file in the back of a drawer or the bottom of a box. Now the Kansas heat of early July 1995 has sequestered me indoors. Most of the letters that have followed me around for the past seven years and now lie on the desk in front of me are, as yet, unread. They begin in June of 1962, two months before my birth and just after the family's move to Winston-Salem, and they end in September of 1964, just before Mommy's death. Thirty-eight of them are written by Ruth. They are the largest collection of my mother's words I will ever see.

Ruth's letters are written primarily in blue ink with a ball-point pen. She sometimes used pale blue notepaper—paler now than thirty-three years ago—but usually wrote on white paper with her address printed in silver script at the top. The earlier letters have the address rubber-stamped in a stark sans-serif type—no time, yet, to order stationery. Occasional post-cards, Christmas cards, and even a telegram represent her side of the

Ruth and her father on her wedding day, 1955.

correspondence. Grandpa dated each of her letters in pencil. Ruth only
put the day of the week at the top before beginning, "Dear Daddy."

Before today, I had seen only snippets of Ruth's handwriting—a cap-
tion on the back of a photograph, the sparse entries in my baby book.
Now pages of her script lie before me. She writes in a neat, legible cursive—
yet not obsessively neat. Her lines are not quite straight, the letters not
always perfectly distinguishable.

Grandpa's side of the correspondence is typed, and represented in a
more uniform way than Ruth's—carbons on thin orange or yellow sheets
of $8^1/2$ by 11 inch paper. Each is dated in full and has Ruth's name (Mrs.
Robt. W. Lovett) and address typed in the bottom left corner. Nothing he
wrote by hand survives on these carbons, so I don't know if he signed his
letters "Howard," or "Dad," or "Father," or "Daddy." I wish I could see the
originals of his letters, the ones that Ruth held and read, but I count
myself lucky to have even copies.

The correspondence is voluminous, and though Ruth mentions phone
calls, many of these letters would not have been written in the 1990s with
low long-distance rates and e-mail. Yet despite their number, the letters
are surprisingly nonintimate.

My grandfather discusses weather at length, and rarely shows emotion on any topic. He closes his letters with "Devotedly" or "Affectionately." She occasionally goes as far as "Love." I can sense her excitement at the prospect of returning to Atlanta after a six-month absence ("I can hardly believe we'll be in Atlanta in two weeks") and his fear about the nature of her illness ("I suppose you know how worried and upset we have been"), but for the most part the correspondence remains on a surface level, not delving into emotional content even in its subtext. I am almost certain that Grandpa dictated his letters to a secretary.

Not until the onset of Ruth's illness do she and her father discuss anything that smacks of the unpleasant, and even that topic is couched in euphemism. The word "cancer" appears nowhere in the correspondence. Grandpa writes that he misses Ruth, but it's impossible to divine his true feelings about her moving permanently from Georgia—the only one of his children to do so. They tell each other of misfortunes—a stolen car, bad weather—but matters of real family pain, such as my grandparents' divorce, they do not even allude to.

Her letters give glimpses of her personality. Her sense of humor emerges, especially when she talks about her children. In one letter she writes with satirical self-mocking, "We have arrived! We are now the proud owners of a Mercedes! I hasten to add that it is far from new, a 1960 190 model with 40,000 miles on it. We are really tickled pink and can hardly believe that after admiring everyone else's Mercedes for so many years, we finally have one of our own for others to admire." My grandfather was a great lover of Mercedes, and he comes close to expressing pride in his response.

I am reminded of her upbringing—time, place, and social class—when I read letters in which Grandpa encourages her to get a maid as soon as possible. "You certainly can't do all that work yourself." She doesn't mention hiring a maid until more than a year after the move. "She comes by the hour whenever I need her. So far it's been about three days a week from 9:00 till 1:00. She is a college girl, goes to Winston-Salem State at night, and so is fairly intelligent." There was no need to explain this last remark to her father—that Winston-Salem State was the black college. A maid, Grandpa would certainly presume, is black.

My grandfather is straightforward and businesslike in his letters, though he varies the tone of each paragraph depending on the topic at hand. His paragraphs address points in previous letters sequentially, and nothing in the previous letter passes without comment. Ruth writes more casually, occasionally wandering toward her point. Phrases such as "which reminds me" pepper her prose.

She uses this casual style to her benefit, however. On several occasions she mentions items that would make good Christmas or birthday presents for her or my father, always couching the request carefully to make it polite and easily ignored. The requests are always met, as later thank-you notes attest. I sense that this straightforward manner of asking for presents is ubiquitous in the family, and the modest nature of her requests is what makes them so charming. The biggest gift she receives, a check for about $4,000 to pay off the mortgage on the house, is her father's idea. She drops a hint for a cookbook, and for a fifty-five dollar Coca-Cola light fixture.

My father has said Ruth only mentioned finances to him twice during their nine-year marriage, yet she corresponds with her father on all sorts of financial matters. Not only does he give her investment advice (once even recommending she sell stock in a company for which he served on the board of directors), but he carries out stock sales and purchases for her. She sends him a complete description of her portfolio and asks for information for her income tax returns that she prepares herself. During these transactions, Grandpa maintains a completely businesslike tone; some letters read as if written by a professional financial advisor. He encourages her to save for the future: "I would certainly recommend that you reinvest the money if you can spare it. The only way you will ever build up an estate is to reinvest profits as they are realized." His investment guidance is toward solid, conservative, blue-chip stocks.

Her father's practicality clearly rubbed off on her, and hers eclipses any concern she may have had for external appearances. The Mercedes was for my father. For herself she bought a red Volkswagen bus. "Bob says the more he looks at it the more ridiculous it looks, but I love it. It has heaps of space in it and that's what we need for trips to Atlanta." Like me, my mother didn't care if something looked ridiculous as long as it got the job done.

Other glimmers of my character show up in hers. My passion for the theatre is foreshadowed by her description of the fun she had working the sound board for the Junior League Children's Theatre. She writes in great detail about plans to visit Atlanta for Opera Week, the week each spring when the Met came to Atlanta.

In her letter anticipating Opera Week, 1963, I see her acceptance of her father's new wife, who went by the nickname "Pete," and who had joined the family less than two years earlier. "Pete, I have an extra ticket to *Otello*, *Fledermaus*, and *Tosca*. You are welcome, indeed invited, to go with me. Daddy, I'll give you my ticket to *Fledermaus* if you'll get all spruced up and escort your wife." Her letters are filled with affection for Pete, and the file includes a telegram of congratulations on Grandpa and Pete's second anniversary in December of 1963.

She writes about my father, Bob, and the things they did together. They visited the mountains often, which does not surprise me. My father and Mim bought a house in the North Carolina mountains where I spent my summers growing up. The mountains are such a part of my life and my identity that to see Ruth writing about them strengthens the bond I am already beginning to feel with her.

I am surprised how often she and Bob went camping in those mountains, once for five days. I can't envision my English-professor father spending the night in a cold damp tent on lumpy ground. As far as I know he never went again after her death. Whether he avoided camping to avoid the memories or he only did it in the first place to please her I don't know.

If I see in her aspects of my own character I also see weaknesses in myself that she apparently avoided. She doesn't seem to have any problem organizing a large house and three children yet leaving time for correspondence. I'm lucky if I remember to call my parents once a week. Most of the rest of my family rarely hears from me. She makes friends in a new town with remarkable ease, writing within weeks of their arrival that they are getting to know couples in the English department and less than a year later of joining an expedition of some fourteen people to the first annual steeplechase. Even though I grew up in Winston-Salem, when I moved back in the mid-1980s it took me years to establish a small circle of friends.

I wonder if her negative character traits would have any chance to be revealed in a correspondence such as this. I know those traits must have been there, but of course, just as no one speaks ill of the dead, no one writes about arguments with one's husband or problems dealing with children to one's proper Southern father.

I begin to see her as a homemaker.

Eight months pregnant with me she writes with pride of converting a basement room into a study for my father, who was juggling teaching duties with his Ph.D. work. "I laid most of the flooring myself . . . and I made some curtains." Grandpa writes back with humor and gentle concern: "It is just about time for the baby to come. . . . When you wrote about laying all the flooring yourself, I was wondering if you were trying to hasten that blessed event. Seriously, you must take care of yourself and not overdo things."

Later she and Bob redecorate their bedroom. "It has taken us one week, working from 7:00 A.M. till 11:00 P.M. every day, to get the darned walls scraped of all wallpaper and painted a decent color."

"My beautiful roses were in bloom when I got home," she writes one May. "There were a few bugs on them, but a couple of good dustings took care of that."

These ordinary actions of making a house into a home and a yard into a place of beauty bring her closer to humanity than anything else in her letters. The removed perfection of the angel photograph dissolves into a real person, a normal person.

I begin to see her as a mother.

She writes of my birth, the most tangible link between the two of us. While the decorum of the time and her relationship with her father prohibited details of that event, she writes with enthusiasm of my arrival.

"Well, you have a fine, big, husky namesake! He has lots of hair and dark blue eyes. For awhile, we thought about putting the 'Howard' in too, but decided that three first names is sort of a burden, so his official title is Charles Candler Lovett." So I was named after my grandfather, but not quite, and in retrospect that seems to reflect my relationship with my Atlanta family. I am a member of the Candler clan, but also not quite a member, the move to Winston-Salem and the death of Ruth having loosened the bond.

Ruth's concern for her children and the care she takes of us is evident everywhere. She writes details of various fevers and bugs I developed as an infant. Even after two other babies, she rushes to call the doctor when my temperature rises over 100 degrees. "Charles has been quite ill with a viral infection the last few days . . . He is so limp and weak. Just wants to be held and walked when he's not asleep."

But her concern is not limited to the baby or to illness. "Bob has taken the older children to see *20,000 Leagues Under the Sea* this evening. I hope Elizabeth didn't get scared of the octopus or anything. But she was warned and still wanted to go!"

And her mothering is not limited to concern. "Charles cut two teeth over the holidays! There are three other babies in the English department up here—all older than Charles—and none have any teeth yet! We aren't *very* proud!" There is joy—"The children love the snow of course. Even Charles was bundled up to his nose and put on the sled for a ride. I just pulled him around, but he *loved* it." Nor was she completely immune to the frustrations of dealing with three of us at once. "After two days of *no school*, I am now wishing for a *quick* melt."

The correspondence is revealing for what it does not contain. I find only one mention of current events. My father's younger brother, Chip, had been stationed on a ship in the Caribbean during the Cuban missile crisis. When Ruth mentions to her father that Chip is on his way home, Grandpa writes, "Of course if we ever do get into a real scrap with Russia and they start firing those long-range missiles, I guess it will be just as dangerous anywhere in the country as it will be right on the front. I pray that day will never come." Grandpa's breaking his silence on current events and writing with such obvious introspection is a testament to the incredible impact of that crisis.

Grandpa was on the board of directors of several corporations, and so a fairly powerful man in the business world, but in his letters to Ruth he wrote at much greater length about fishing and the weather than about business or events of the world. That was the nature of both the man and of his relationship with his daughter.

So many things she took for granted as mundane leap out at me as flashes of reality, tiny surprises. After visiting Atlanta for Christmas in 1962, she returned home with her three children, me as an infant, on the train. I adore train travel—the relaxed pace, the constantly changing views, the rhythm of the rumble beneath me—but I had no idea my association with the rails dated so far back to a shared journey with Ruth.

Figures of speech that I associate with my Atlanta family, which I never thought to connect with Ruth, creep into her prose. She heard that a football game was a real "lulu." The steaks that Grandpa brought them were "mighty good."

And all that red meat! The farm her father bought in 1955 was ostensibly for raising beef, and descriptions of roasts and steaks, which form such a tiny part of my diet today, suffuse her letters. "Last night we got out the rib roast from the farm beef and put it on the spit over charcoal for about an hour. It was fabulous! Perfectly done (rare) and tender and just great." Like me, though, she uses the words "perfect" and "rare" synonymously.

One of the letters is from my father, written while Ruth was in the hospital recovering from her breast operation. "Charles talks to his mother on the telephone, saying 'Mommy, Hi, bye-bye.' Ruth gets a kick out of it." It has been so easy for me to believe that I never really knew Ruth until I am confronted with this sentence. Something about the simplicity and sincerity of the act touches me deeply. I *spoke* with her, not just in person, but even on the phone. Much of my relationship with Lucy takes place over the telephone. I know what it's like for a parent to pick up a phone and hear the innocent and loving voice of a two-year-old.

Certain passages stand out. On Ruth's twenty-eighth birthday, Grandpa writes, "I hope you have a very happy day and many, many more in years to come." She would have one more. When I am fourteen months old she writes, "he still hates for mother to leave and screams at the top of his lungs if I so much as leave the room, but he always gets over it just about the time I get out of sight."

I discover she was born on June 5, 1935.

Two letters in particular tear at me. Reading them, I begin to see that hindsight can be the most painful kind of vision, that the reader who knows the end of the story starts to suffer sooner than the characters who move through its pages ignorant of their fate. The first is dated February 5, 1964.

Dear Daddy,

I have just come from the doctor's office and have some news which I thought you would want to know about. I have a sizable lump in my breast which must be removed. Dr. Cordell believes that it is benign and that there is nothing to worry about, but especially because of the family history of this sort of thing, he says it ought to be taken out just to be sure. I am on call to go to the hospital as soon as a bed is available, probably in two to three weeks. I will let you know when I go.

I guess I gave you all our other news yesterday.

Again hello to Pete.

> Devotedly,
> Ruth

The second, dated August 10, 1964, reads, in part:

We are planning a tentative outing without the children in September, after they go back to school. We will probably go to Ocracoke, then up the outer banks, spend a couple of days with Chip in Williamsburg, then go to Washington for a day, where Bob has a few hours' work to do in the Library of Congress and thereabouts. I do hope it works out.

Two weeks after writing that letter, on my second birthday, Ruth would be diagnosed as terminal. The only trip she would take in September would be in a coffin, returning to Atlanta for the last time.

Some months after I read this correspondence, my father loaned me a box of family papers, newspaper clippings, and other materials. In the back of the file marked "Correspondence—C. H. Candler, Jr.," a file fat with three decades of letters from my grandfather to his son-in-law, were the originals of Grandpa's letters to Ruth. The thicker white letterhead, the crisper type of an original rather than a copy, and the signature "Daddy," handwritten with a fountain pen at the bottom of each letter made these sheets come alive in a way the copies had not. The stationery was that of "Asa G. Candler, Inc.," a corporation set up by Grandpa's grandfather. The address was the seventeenth floor of the Candler Building—one of

Atlanta's first skyscrapers, completed in 1906 under the supervision of Grandpa's father and grandfather. My wife, Janice, used to work there.

I eagerly sifted through the pile looking for anything unfamiliar. I found three new letters. Two were quite ordinary. The third is the one handwritten letter in the file. Writing on hotel stationery from the St. Regis in New York in October 1962, Grandpa writes, "I will be proud and honored to be Charles' godfather. . . . I appreciate so much you and Bob asking me and I will be looking forward to the happy occasion." Even away from his office, his secretary, and his letterhead, he maintains his businesslike tone—"so stiff and cordial," a friend commented when I showed him these letters—but on this occasion I can sense the emotion just beneath the surface of his words.

Although my search for Ruth is just beginning, I am unlikely to find any other source that comes as close to her as these letters. I stare at them spread out before me—words written over thirty years ago—and wonder what else they can tell me. I have tried to look at them from every angle. I can think of only one other way to examine them, so I look in the phone book under "Handwriting Analysis" and call Bobbie Randall. For seventy-five dollars, she tells me, she can give me a complete analysis of Ruth's handwriting, if I send her a few letters to work from. Why not?

The report she sends me two weeks later runs four double-spaced pages and carries this caveat: "The science of Graphology, like medical science, is subject to error. The above information is offered in my professional opinion." Perhaps everything in the report is true, perhaps not, but it is presented in a dry fashion that makes it hard for me to relate it to Ruth—so different from the personal recollections I long for.

"The writer was adroit in dealing with people. She was tactful, even tempered, and well mannered. She was unusually perceptive of the feelings and attitudes of others." Other positive traits are listed—fair-mindedness, tolerance, geniality, loyalty, sincerity, forthrightness, frankness, sympathy. By the end of the first page I start to wonder if I will ever uncover any negative traits. Is there any chance I will ever see the full picture of Ruth, or will I only ever see her best qualities?

The report does write of a sort of reserve. "Her emotional responsiveness was mostly poised. . . . She tried to avoid criticism by adopting an attitude of diplomacy . . . She escaped the pain of criticism through self-deceit and clannishness. . . . She desired to reject ideas, memories, feelings, or impulses that were painful or disagreeable to her." Where I am most likely to believe this report, I find, is where it overlaps with my own personality. I am poised in my emotional responses. My fear of confrontation leads me to reject painful memories.

In the positive traits, too, I think I see a bit of myself. "Her sense of humor had lightening influence. . . . Creativity and literary ability were present in her writing. . . . She had an aptitude for initiating ideas into action."

"Rhythm was in her writing, which means that her creativity was probably in music, art, or writing," says Bobbie. I know that Ruth was musical—played the piano I believe—so perhaps there is some validity to Graphology.

But everything I read in this report seems unrooted. I want to cry out at those black words—give me an example! Tell me a story! Show me how these traits of her character affected her life, her family, her community. The words tell me nothing more. I continue the search.

III

If any one faculty of our nature may be called more won-
derful than the rest, I do think it is memory. There seems
something more speakingly incomprehensible in the pow-
ers, the failings, the inequalities of memory, than in any
other of our intelligences. The memory is sometimes so
retentive, so serviceable, so obedient—at others, so bewil-
dered and so weak—and at others again, so tyrannic, so
beyond control!—We are to be sure a miracle in every
way—but our powers of recollecting and of forgetting do
seem peculiarly past finding out.

—Jane Austen

A few days after sifting through Ruth's letters, I called my father. While I tried to think of a way to ease my project into the conversation, he asked how my writing was going. Before I knew it I had asked him if we could talk, sometime, about Ruth. He said he would be happy to, that he had always told us, meaning her three children, we could ask anything we wanted. I tried to remember being told this, but could not. Not that I doubt it—I'm sure he has probably said something of the sort. But still, even with an invitation, *what* do I ask? Where do the questions come from, and how do I ask the real question—who was my mother?

We had talked some. The one occasion I could remember clearly was part of the reason the talks I had with my father were so difficult. One night in the mountain house, when I was nine or ten, Daddy and his three older children sat around the fire and he told us the story of Ruth's death. I remember very little of the telling—I felt no more involved in the story personally than I would have in "Little Red Riding Hood." I remem- ber his emotion. I had never seen my father cry before; now he was overcome by tears just from telling the story. I found the situation painful and embarrassing.

Now, in that same room, with tape recorder in hand and only this one evening to talk face to face in the next few months, I prepare to ask my questions. I know I will find my role as interrogator awkward, that I won't be able to ask all my questions, that there will still be so much I don't know. Still, it will be a start.

Mim and Daddy bought Bear Knob—a white clapboard house and seventeen acres on a North Carolina mountaintop—when I was six and I spent the next twelve summers there. I've been back for at least a few days every year since.

Ruth and Bob visited those mountains on their honeymoon. Part of the attraction of Winston-Salem was its proximity to the mountains. During her two years in North Carolina Ruth wrote to her father about day trips to see the fall colors ("We went to the mountains on a picnic Sunday and already the coloring is beginning to get pretty"), camping trips in the summer ("We are going camping next week, leaving Charles here with a friend of ours"), and an excursion to the Scottish Highland Games at Grandfather Mountain.

The Games are held every year and accompany a Gathering of the Clans that Ruth was especially enthusiastic about, because the Candlers are related to Clan Gregor. "Jamie [their Scottish Terrier] stole the whole show! He was the only Scottie there and was posed for one movie, two stills, had several candid shots taken of him, and was offered two Scotches! . . . We went to the Games in conjunction with a five-day camping trip which was marvelous. Susan [Bob's younger sister] stayed with the children. It was the first time we had been without them in 2 years and it was almost like a second honeymoon."

I am rarely happier than when I am in the mountains—whether the Rockies, the Green Mountains of Vermont, the Scottish Highlands, or my own home Blue Ridge. I'm glad to know I inherited that love of mountains not just from my father, but also from Ruth.

The evening I pick to speak with my father, as Jordan reads in the armchair by the west window and Lucy sleeps upstairs, ends one of those perfect early August mountain days. Rain the night before has bathed the ridge in cool clear air; we can see every tree on Grandfather Mountain sixty miles away. The breeze whistles in the needles of the white pines, and gold-finches flit across the front meadow. By nine o'clock the pink and purple light will fade from the sky and the whippoorwills will start singing. We might see a deer wander across the meadow before then.

My father sits in the rocking chair near the stone fireplace—setting his empty beer cans on the hearth as the evening progresses. I sit at the end of a sofa he and I unloaded from the back of his station wagon fifteen years ago. A list of questions lies on the coffee table in front of me. Next to me sits Janice, whose presence makes my father repeat some stories he has told me years ago and that I have forgotten. I have sat in this room hundreds of times talking to my father—he told me about sex here; I announced my first and second marriages here. Now, I pick up my list of questions about Ruth and begin.

Ruth's correspondence is still fresh in my mind, so I start with simple questions raised by those letters, questions about Grandpa as well as his daughter. I learn the details of Grandpa's purchasing his farm in Georgia in 1955. I hear about the cars he drove—always a favorite topic for Daddy. The story of her father interests me, but I have come to discuss Ruth, and gradually I turn the conversation to that virgin ground.

I want to know about the VW bus (Daddy denies thinking it was ridiculous but he did sell it after she died). I ask about Opera Week and find out just how big a deal it was—the Metropolitan performing a different opera every night at the fabulous Fox Theatre.

"We went every night," Daddy says. "We didn't go to a lot of the post-opera parties. We weren't fashionable enough." Cleaning out the house recently, he found a program for one such party that Ruth and her Aunt Lou had attended. "Ruth was crazy about Aunt Lou," he says. "They got together and after a couple of scotches they decided the thing to do was to go out and get some autographs." Daddy tells me who signed the program, but I am unfamiliar with 1950s opera stars and don't recognize a single name. I do, however, as I will many times that night, form a new image of my mother—an image of her seeking out the performers she admired. Not long ago, Janice and I spent half-an-hour standing at a stage door waiting for Carol Burnett, so things have not changed so much in a generation.

"Her grandmother always gave her these gift certificates to Leon's where you could only buy party dresses and furs," says Daddy. "The only place she had to wear dresses that fancy was the opera. One of the reasons she had so many furs was because her credit kept building up. She loved the opera, though. It wasn't a question of going because it was a fashionable thing. We took *Opera News* and she listened to the Saturday afternoon broadcast from the Met." Ruth's grandfather had been instrumental in bringing the Met to Atlanta. "He used to keep all the programs and take them once a year to Emory, but after he died Ruth did that."

Ruth's modest participation in the theatre interests me more than her membership in a glitzy opera audience.

"She was very interested in drama," says Daddy. "The Junior League in Atlanta did a play each year and toured in the public schools. They did one performance for families and friends. She played the Tin Woodsman in *The Wizard of Oz* one year and scared the bejesus out of David. He was so upset I had to take him outside." I think about all the qualities it takes to turn yourself into a Tin Woodsman—not just some ability as an actor but a certain degree of self-confidence and, in this case, a desire to serve, to risk looking foolish in order to entertain underprivileged children. I suspect it was this quality most of all that drove Ruth to perform as an adult. "She did a lot of backstage work," says Daddy. "She liked acting, but she didn't think she had much talent." Modesty or low self-esteem? No way to know now.

We settle into a strange pattern as we talk. Daddy tells a story and I add things I have learned from reading Ruth's letters. Then a silence falls, Daddy takes a sip of beer and says, "Okay, next question," and I scan my sheet, looking for something to ask. It feels as if I have to start the conversation anew every ten minutes.

I ask about the house in Atlanta where he and Ruth lived before the move to Winston-Salem. I have a few snapshots of David and Elizabeth as toddlers that show the house in the background, but in all my visits to Atlanta, I have never driven by it.

"I went by there with one of Mim's friends last spring," says Daddy. "They've taken the roof off the house and put another story on it and it is the most hideous thing you've ever seen in your life. They've really screwed it up. It bears no resemblance to our house. It didn't look like any other houses in the neighborhood. All the rest were ranches and it was a modern house."

From the snapshots, I have judged that it was never that attractive to begin with. What surprises me, and even hurts a bit until I give the matter consideration, is that my father has driven a near stranger by this house where I was probably conceived, yet has never taken me there. Is it easier to view the relics of a lost past when we're not with those with whom we share the loss? Then I think about all my years of visiting grandparents in Atlanta and realize that my father was rarely there. Since my early teenage years I probably haven't spent a day in Atlanta with him except the day of my grandfather's funeral. I wonder if that is coincidence or an extension of his putting his past behind him, behind us.

At ten o'clock Janice and I take Jordan upstairs to bed. She's eight, but she's a night owl like the rest of her family. After I kiss her goodnight, I sit on the edge of Lucy's bed for a few minutes, listening to the crickets punctuate the rhythm of her breathing. She's three, but I find her life and her breath no less miraculous than when she was a newborn. It took a lullaby from Janice to put her to sleep tonight—Lucy was excited about being with us again—but now she sleeps without stirring. I kiss her cheek and she doesn't flinch and I go downstairs to keep talking with her grandfather.

Many of my questions are not questions but topics, and my father's answers are stories. Any one of these stories might expand into an entire evening's reminiscence, and I hope some day many of them will do just that, but tonight my time is short and so are the stories.

Topic: Cumberland Island, Georgia, where Ruth's family had a rustic retreat.

Story: "Just off the north end there's a small island, about four or five acres, that's essentially a marsh island—you could go over there with boots on at low tide, but you'd get wet at high tide. It was called Hushamouth Island. One of the nice times I had with Grandpa early on was when he and Ruth and I hiked over to Hushamouth. At that time there was some talk about where grandchildren might want to build houses and Ruth and I favored Hushamouth Island."

I try to reconcile in my mind two images—one of my mother in a fancy dress and expensive furs sitting in the audience of *Aida*, the other of her in mud-encrusted boots standing on an isolated islet and imagining having a cabin there, a cabin with no electricity or running water. I start to wonder—what was her attitude toward the wealth she was born into? It certainly gave her advantages, such as the chance to stand on a marsh island and dream of a house with no toilet. But how did it shape who she was? So I introduce the topic, and get this story.

"I went to college with two brothers who lived behind Georgia Tech in sort of a semi-slum. Their father was a part time Pinkerton guard. Their sister weighed over three hundred pounds and was very bright. She was Ruth's closest friend at Emory.

"When I had my appendix out, my roommate in the hospital was a bus driver. Ruth and I used to go over there and see him after that.

"She was absolutely indifferent to whether people had money or position. She was comfortable if they did; it didn't bother her if they didn't. She didn't pick friends on that basis."

And what about the money itself?

"We just never discussed money," Daddy says. "Next question."

And so the night slips away. Janice goes to bed and still we talk. I hear the story of how Bob and Ruth met and eventually fell in love. I hear the story of Ruth's parents' marriage and its long disintegration into divorce. I hear the story of her illness and death. And I hear the story of the silence that followed.

"In all the years after her estate was settled," says Daddy, "Grandpa only mentioned Ruth twice in my presence." Why haven't I spent more time in Atlanta with my father? Because, he explains, he felt his presence in the Atlanta family brought up painful memories. And I felt that way too, not about my presence, but about the topic of my mother, the possibility of conversation about her. In the next few months, I will have to conquer that feeling. If my asking about Ruth brings up painful memories, so be it. Painful memories are better than no memories at all.

One story Daddy tells me I have heard many times before. As a toddler, I sat with my family at a lunch counter and ordered my meal—a hot dog and fries. Ten minutes passed, then twenty, and everyone grew restless. The adults, being polite, said nothing. I was young enough for honesty and finally began banging my silverware on the table and shouting "I want my nunch!" Within minutes we were served. A typical family anecdote and always told to me in these terms—with no names other than my own. But tonight is different. Tonight my father talks about the last time Ruth visited Atlanta, just three months before her death.

"When we came back up from Atlanta it was just you, me, Ruth, and

Jamie [the dog]. David and Elizabeth stayed in Atlanta with grandparents. And that was the famous time when we stopped in Charlotte and you yelled 'I want my nunch!'"

Mommy was there. I have heard this story so many times that it has become a part of my identity in a way that Ruth, so rarely discussed, has not. But here she is, smack in the middle of this standard story, as if she had always been lurking in the shadows and only now chose to step into the light.

I do not learn everything I want to learn from my father that night, but I do learn I can talk to him about Ruth, that such a conversation does not have to be painful or even uncomfortable, that while he still shows signs of emotion, especially when talking about Ruth's death, thirty years is enough time to put most of that grief to rest. And so, the door opens between me and my father. In the months that follow we speak about Ruth almost casually, yet never without some trepidation on my part. I call him up with specific questions and he tells me more stories. True, there are some questions I never ask, and never will ask—but aren't these the questions that, essential as they are, we rarely ask of anyone and would be hard-pressed to answer ourselves? What did you talk about at night after the kids were asleep and the lights were out? What did she share with you that she didn't share with anyone else? What was your love like? They are questions that might be answered in the introspective smile on my father's face, or a quietness that creeps into his voice, or the angle of his shoulders as he leans back in the rocking chair. But perhaps even these signs are messages about memories and not about reality. Perhaps the true dynamic of their marriage was buried thirty years ago. Then again, perhaps it lives on somewhere within their son.

As I climb into bed, the midnight moon high and bright over the back yard, I see Ruth inwardly smiling as her almost two-year-old boy screams for his "nunch." And I smile back.

IV

This was the Candler family, the heirs of Coca-Cola, and whenever my grandmother spoke of them it was as though she were describing a collegial association of some scrupulous peerage. According to my grandmother, the Candlers were the nearest thing Atlanta had to a royal family, and she would not allow us to desecrate their walled baronage.

—PAT CONROY

In searching for her I am searching for myself and my own history. I assemble my evidence: A biography of Ruth's great-grandfather, Asa Griggs Candler, written by her grandfather, Charles Howard Candler. A file of obituaries of Ruth's paternal grandparents. Copies of magazine articles about her father's wartime service. And the notes from that long conversation with my father. The file folders that contain much of this material are labeled in neat printing in the same hand as Ruth's letters. Would she have kept such material, so carefully clipped and organized, if she did not feel a strong connection to her family background?

My brother, David, has traced Ruth's roots back dozens of generations in genealogical charts, and even the book about her great-grandfather begins in 1650. I am bored, though, by biographies that spend fifty pages on the ancestors of the book's subject. Still, one of Ruth's ancestors did have a tremendous effect on her life, her family, her city, and the world.

Asa Griggs Candler, so the biography written by his loving son tells me, was born on December 30, 1851. As a child, he watched the Civil War consume much of what his family had built. In 1873, he traveled from the small Georgia town of Villa Rica to Atlanta. He obtained a job in a pharmacy and in the late 1880s purchased the rights to an elixir that, at the time, was one of thousands of patent medicines on the market. The

elixir was called Coca-Cola, and
over the next thirty years Asa
built The Coca-Cola Company
into the most successful business in the South, and an in-
ternational enterprise.

I look at Asa's stern eyes
peering out from the frontis-
piece of his biography and wonder what he would think of me.
I could enjoy a life of idleness
because of his industry a century ago. I choose to use my
time not building industry or
leading a community, but
writing books and stories.
Despite knowing the facts of
his life, I have little sense of
how I might interact with this man.

Asa Griggs Candler, 1851–1929.

He did not just build a great corporation. When the real estate market
in Atlanta threatened to collapse in 1907, he bought over a million dollars
worth of homes to stabilize prices. In 1914, when a sudden drop in cotton
prices threatened the economy of the South, he built a vast warehouse
and bought bales at a higher price to store until the market went back up.
In 1916, he served a term as mayor of Atlanta, refusing to accept pay for
the job. And he provided the money, land, and leadership for the estab-
lishment of Emory University in Atlanta. When he died in 1929, Atlanta
mourned the passing of its "first citizen," and his family was left with a
fortune in real estate holdings and Coca-Cola stock. Ruth was born six
years after his death, but the money he made had a huge impact on her
life, as did his philanthropy. Not only was he responsible for the building
of the hospital in which she was born, the neighborhood in which she
grew up, and the university she attended, but the pattern of generosity he
established would be carried on by subsequent generations of his family.

Ruth knew her grandfather, Charles Howard Candler, Asa's oldest son.
During the twenty-two years of her life that he was alive, she never lived
more than a few of miles from his home, a magnificent Tudor mansion

called Callanwolde. He was known to his friends as Howard, to most of the world as Mr. Candler, and to his family as Popee. He spent much of his life following in the footsteps of his father—serving as president of The Coca-Cola Company, making huge donations of money and time to Emory University, and taking great joy in his own family. "One of Mr. Candler's outstanding characteristics was his love of and pride in his family," read his 1957 obituary in *The Emory Alumnus* magazine. "No 'joiner' or 'socializer,' he preferred—unless there was some Emory occasion calling—to remain at home in the evenings in company with his beloved wife, his children, and his grandchildren and great-grandchildren." His daughter, Catherine Candler Warren, my great-aunt Kit, raised her family at Callanwolde after her marriage, and the rest of the extended family visited there often.

Reading over the accomplishments of Ruth's grandfather and great-grandfather, I cannot help feeling proud, even from my great distance. How much more proud must she have felt seeing every day the results of her grandfather's generosity. He certainly could have afforded a Gatsby life-style and all the accouterments of vast wealth in the 1920s, but he preferred to continue the building of the university his father had started, he preferred the company of his own family to elite social gatherings, and he preferred work, whether paid or not, to leisure.

How do I feel about Coca-Cola? Of course I feel proud. Who wouldn't? I drink Coke and assiduously avoid that competitor not just on principle but because, quite honestly, I don't like the stuff. I have a pair of restored vintage Coke machines in my basement. People feel good about Coke. People come from all over the world to the Coca-Cola museum in Atlanta and first gaze on the face of my great-great-grandfather, and then take in the images, advertisements, sounds, and tastes that make them nostalgic for a past they never had. Naturally I'm glad to have had the good luck to be born into a family with some wealth. But of all the things family wealth might be built on, I'm especially glad it's Coke. I grew up in a town built on tobacco money and it was not without mixed feelings that I enjoyed the theatres, galleries, libraries, and schools made possible through the sale of cigarettes. But I have no mixed feelings about Coke. I will always hold stock in the company, but my investment in Coke is more than financial, it is emotional as well. Everywhere in the world there are

Coca-Cola signs—I have seen them from Times Square to Piccadilly Circus to the canals of Thailand. Every time I turn on the television I am likely to see a Coca-Cola commercial. Every time I take I drive, I might pass a Coca-Cola truck. The Coke logo is the most recognized trademark in the world. And every time I see that logo, I feel pride, and I see a tribute to my ancestors.

I placed a classified advertisement in *The Atlanta Constitution.* "Do you remember Ruth Candler Lovett (1935–1964)? If so please contact her son . . ." It ran for a month. I received one call.

"Mr. Lovett?"

"Yes."

"I saw your ad in the Atlanta paper." My breath catches and I wave my arm wildly indicating to Janice to turn down the volume on the television. "My mother knew a Ruth Lovett. Who did your Mom get married to?" I rifle through the papers on the table in search of a pen and something to write on, and say with forced calm, "Bob Lovett. She married Bob Lovett."

"Oh," followed by what seems a minute of silence but cannot be more than a second or two. "No, this woman's maiden name was Lovett." My hand stops its searching, comes to a rest on the edge of the table. "But I see your middle name is Candler, just like mine. I grew up in Villa Rica." What relation, if any, I am to this man who grew up in the same town as my great-great-grandfather I do not discover.

"Who was your grandfather?" he asks.

"Charles Howard Candler," I say, and then think to add "Junior."

"Then Charles Howard Candler was your, what, great-grandfather?"

"That's right."

"So," he says, "you're straight line Charles Howard Candler."

"That's right," I say.

"Well," he says, "You come from mighty good people."

Popee's eldest son, Charles Howard Candler, Jr., known to the family as Howard, was Ruth's father. As a young boy, Howard rode with his grandfather in a buggy to inspect the new roads and grand houses of the Druid Hills development that Asa had implemented. When he was sixteen, his family moved into Callanwolde, the center of family activity from 1920 until 1959.

Four generations of Charles Howard Candlers in the mid-1950s. From left to right: "Buddy" (III), "Chick" (IV), Howard (Jr.), and Popee (Sr.).

There's no doubt that Popee instilled in my grandfather a head for business, a frank way of dealing with people, and a conservative nature that, in old age, might at times degenerate into crotchetiness. His mother, Flora Glenn Candler, whom the family called Danny, gave him his kind, gentle nature, his easy way with children, and his ability to simply love his grandchildren when no one was looking. "Danny was the flamboyant one," my Aunt Betsy told me. Popee's kindness and gentleness were there too, according to Betsy and others, but, like his father before him and his son after him, he kept them more private.

Like my daughter, Ruth came from a home broken by divorce. Although, according to my father, Ruth never spoke of her parents' divorce, I begin to sense that it was a central event in her life. After all, Bobbie Randall had written, "She desired to reject ideas, memories, feelings, or impulses that were painful or disagreeable to her."

One side of my grandfather's character—the formal, clipped business-man evident in many of his letters—has always seemed to me incompatible with my grandmother. When I try my best to remember the purest mo-ments of his other side, his affection and quiet self-sacrificing gentleness that

I saw most often on his farm, I am able to imagine my grandparents married.

They wed on December 3, 1928, when he was twenty-four and she was twenty-two—Howard Candler and Ruth Ozburn. Their marriage day was his father's birthday and his parents' silver anniversary. I would never know them as a married couple, and would always call them Grandpa and Màmà—she signed her name with accent marks, but pronounced the A's as in "cat." He was a Methodist; she was an Episcopalian on her way to becoming a Theosophist. He would one day spend part of his time as a beef farmer; she was a confirmed vegetarian. They were childhood sweethearts.

In Màmà's basement not long ago I found two Emory yearbooks from my grandfather's student years. They appear to be hers, not his, for the inscriptions on the autograph pages are all to her. In 1923, in a yearbook dedicated to his own grandfather, he wrote "words can't express my thoughts!" In 1924, "to the girl of my dreams come true."

By the time I knew him, my grandfather referred to Màmà, when necessary, only as Mrs. Stillman.

Their first three children were born in rapid succession, Charles Howard Candler, Jr. ("Buddy") in 1930, Samuel Ozburn Candler ("Bo") in 1932, and my mother, Ruth Candler, in 1935. Six years later, when they had their last child, Flora Glenn Candler (Glenn), some described it as an attempt to hold the marriage together. According to my father, a trip to South America in the late thirties was another such attempt.

When the war broke out, Grandpa, who was too old to be drafted, organized some yacht-owning friends into what he later jokingly called the Georgia Navy. Because of the Candler family's

Three little Candlers (Bo, Ruth, and Buddy) in August 1937.

2,000-acre retreat on Cumberland Island, Grandpa and his boat captain Olie Olsen were familiar with the waterways along the Georgia coast. With outposts being established on the barrier islands, including Cumberland, but no boats available to supply them, Grandpa formed the Georgia State Guard Coastal Patrol in June 1942. A commendation issued to him by Brigadier General Eric Fisher Wood of Fort Benning reads, "you volunteered for this work, taking yourself away from your home and your regular civilian occupations. You contributed your two large cabin cruisers for the nominal rental of one dollar per year each. You contributed your personal services, at no expense to the Federal Government. Although having no military status, other than that of holding a certificate as a Major of the Georgia State Guard, you submitted yourself voluntarily to military discipline and procedure, and at all times gave an outstanding example of military obedience and good behavior."

When his unit was dissolved after a year of operation, Grandpa joined the Civil Air Patrol, first flying over coastal waters and later flying border

The family in the music room of Callanwolde, Christmas 1946. Left to right: Màmà, Buddy, Howard, Glenn, Bo, Ruth.

patrol out of El Paso, Texas. His country had not exactly called, but he had done what he saw as his duty. He had also stayed out of the house for most of three years. With the current state of his marriage, taking himself away from home and family, according to my father, was equal parts relief and hardship. I wonder if my mother had many memories of her father before the war, or if she had any memories of happy times in the marriage of her parents.

Ruth was eleven when Grandpa returned. He bought the family a new and larger house. More room for the children, but also more room for the parents to stay away from each other.

In 1955, a few months after my parents married, Grandpa bought Rolling Meadows Farm about an hour's drive south of Atlanta. He would spend many of the happiest days of the rest of his life there. Màmà rarely set foot on the place, except to visit her younger son, Bo, who built a house there and raised his family in the country. One reason Grandpa bought the farm was that he knew Bo and his family wanted to live on such a place.

Still the marriage lumbered on, but by May of 1961 the charade could be played out no longer, and Grandpa called a family meeting. Spouses were excluded so my father cannot tell me precisely what happened in that meeting. I know that Grandpa said he had hoped to delay the divorce until all the children were married, at which point Glenn, the youngest, announced her engagement. The marriage was kept legal long enough for Mr. and Mrs. Charles Howard Candler, Jr. to announce the marriage of their daughter Flora Glenn on September 6; later that month the divorce was finalized. Grandpa, who was fifty-six, said to my father, "If I'm going to start a new life, I'd better get on with it." On December 12, he married Inez Lee Edwards, whom the family would know as Pete.

When the announcement of Grandpa's impending remarriage was made, Ruth, who had been tired and run down, both physically and emotionally, became sick for several days. Still, as her letters indicate, no one in the family was more accepting of Pete than Ruth. Once her father remarried, she approached the situation realistically and pragmatically. Her parents were divorced, and those events were past. Her father was finally having some happiness in his life, and Ruth wanted to share in that.

That is the story of her parents' marriage, but it did not come from her or from anyone in her family. It was told to my father by Olie Olsen, the boat captain who worked for the family on Cumberland Island. In Daddy's words, "Ruth never talked about any of that."

I wonder if the model of marriage Ruth wanted to emulate was that of her grandparents, Popee and Danny. They were married fifty-four years, and their home was the center of family activity during Ruth's childhood. From her grandparents she inherited her passion for the opera—both were active in the Atlanta music scene and visiting performers frequently stayed at their home. While Danny shared Popee's interest in and support of Emory University, she was not merely an assistant in her husband's shadow. Danny made her own mark in the community, and even received an honorary degree in nursing from Emory for all she had done to help that program. She endowed the Emory concert series, which still bears her name, and was an enthusiastic supporter of the Emory Glee Club, in which Ruth's father had sung in the 1920s. For all their joint and separate interests, Popee and Danny valued family above all. Their home was as much a clubhouse for their extended family as it was their private residence.

A lot of people in the South have an old family home. The Candlers had many houses in Atlanta, but for four decades, one was *the* family home. The house was built by Popee, who could sit in his office in the Candler Building in downtown Atlanta and watch the construction progress several miles away. He moved his family there in 1920, and lived there the rest of his life. In 1959, Danny, then widowed two years, finally moved out and, like many old family houses, ours passed out of the family—too big to be practical. Danny donated it, with much of the furniture, to Emory University. Today the house is an arts center. Rooms where my mother played as a child are offices. The courtyard between the house's two main wings has been transformed into a dance studio. The dining room where the entire family gathered every Sunday night is rented out for wedding receptions and anniversary parties. It is not so different from many old family homes that have become art museums, conference centers, or historical societies. Most people who aren't from Atlanta have never heard of it.

Unless they read books or go to the movies. In a strange twist of Southern Literature, my old family home became a symbol. In a stranger twist of

Hollywood editing, its name became a catchphrase for evil. My father always referred to it by the address: 980 Briarcliff Road. But the house had a name: Callanwolde.

The name has been translated "Candler's Woods," and it harkens back to a castle and property in Callan, Ireland, which was granted to one of Popee's ancestors by Oliver Cromwell in 1653.

In his 1986 novel, *The Prince of Tides*, Pat Conroy writes of my family's home. It is walled off from the Wingo family, symbolizing the wealth and status that they cannot possess. When the Wingo children venture into the confines of the Candler estate against their mother's will, evil is visited upon their home in the person of a seven-foot rapist whom they nickname "Callanwolde." Conroy writes of watching the Candlers at dinner.

> Servants were wheeling in food on elaborate dollies. The Candlers, erect and pallid, ate their meal as if they were attending a church service, such was their seriousness, their unruffled ecclesiastical mien. . . . There was no laughter or conversation from the royal family, and the rich, we assumed, were silent as fish.

At the time of this imagined scene, my mother was fifteen and a frequent

Ruth's photograph of Callanwolde, taken in the mid-1950s.

visitor in her grandfather's home. A little over a year later she would start inviting my father to the Callanwolde Sunday-night dinners, a symbol of the seriousness she placed on their relationship. But who were those silent, pallid people Conroy described? Certainly not Ruth or her siblings or her mother. Certainly not her grandmother or her aunt's family. Only her father and her grandfather might possibly fit the description, but only at their most reserved, and their reserve melted away in the bosom of family.

When he adapted *The Prince of Tides* as a screenplay, Conroy eliminated the Callanwolde scene, but apparently couldn't resist the euphony of the name. Callanwolde. My stately family home. What a wonderful name for a rapist. With the mansion left out of the movie, Barbra Streisand asks Nick Nolte why they called the escaped convict Callanwolde.

"It was the name of the prison he escaped from," he replies. It is one thing to have my family home—the home in which my father became accepted into the Candler clan, in which my mother spent so many happy times in her youth—turned into a symbol of the dichotomy between classes in the South and the dangers of trying to cross from the lowest class to the highest; it is quite another to have Callanwolde turned into a state prison.

But if I object, it is to protect something long gone—a memory of a memory. For if the Candlers were once, as Conroy says, "the nearest thing Atlanta had to a royal family," if Callanwolde was their castle, it is no more. There are no more Sunday-night dinners, no more tight-knit clan pulling several generations together once a week. When my grandmother dies, the last of the Candler homes that might properly be called a mansion will probably pass out of the family. We are scattered now, and though some remain in Atlanta, we no longer inhabit grand houses or rule grand corporations. And the first of her generation to break from the traditions of Callanwolde, the first to make a permanent move away from Atlanta, the first to pursue with all her might the path of the ordinary, was Ruth.

About the same time the fictional Wingo children lay in the darkness, awed by the display of Candlers at dinner, my father became an occasional guest at Callanwolde. He and Ruth were friends, part of the same group of high school students that enjoyed what 1950s Atlanta had to offer. Ruth was dating someone else, an older member of the group. Pool parties were common at Callanwolde, and Bob was also invited to the Christmas party. Unlike the Wingos and some of Ruth's other friends, Bob was not intimidated by Callanwolde.

My father was born in 1934 in New York City and spent his early childhood in Flushing, Long Island. In the summers, his father, Heyward, worked as director of the Lake Delaware Boys' Camp on Aknusti, the estate of Robert Gerry near Delhi, New York. When Heyward was offered the position of general superintendent of the estate in 1940, the family moved upstate, living on the Gerry property in a beautiful stone house down the road from the main mansion. From an early age my father learned to live in proximity to and in harmony with vast wealth.

Family members on the grounds of Callanwolde. Popee and Danny are second and third from the right.

Mrs. Wingo had compared the Candlers to royalty, and at first that comparison might seem apt in light of a saying at the time—"there are three kinds of people in Atlanta: ordinary people, high society, and Candlers." But if the Candlers were so differentiated it was not because they set themselves above the rest of society, but rather because they set themselves aside from it. Instead of strutting their stuff at the Piedmont Driving Club on Sunday nights, they dined with their own at home. Instead of vacationing at posh resorts with Vanderbilts and Rockefellers, they spent their summers in rustic houses on a practically deserted island off the Georgia coast. Callanwolde, with its twenty-seven acres of grounds, gave the family a place where they could enjoy their privacy without leaving Atlanta.

An article in *The Emory Alumnus* of October 1959 reads, "Callanwolde throughout its life has been one of Atlanta's most 'showable' places, but it has never been, in any sense of the word, a show place. The unostentatious Candler family loved it and was proud of it, but they had no interest in putting their home place on public display. It was for the use and enjoyment of the family and their friends." The article tells of parties the Candlers threw for Emory fraternities and private concerts given by the Glee Club. "But most of all—and for most of the time, exclusively—Callanwolde was a *family* place."

No member of the extended family in Atlanta would dare dine anywhere else on a Sunday night. In-laws were invited; casual dates were not. Ruth's grandparents had three children. Louisa moved to Florida when she was married in the 1930s, but Kit, her husband, and their three children lived at Callanwolde. Ruth's family lived a few blocks away before and during the war, a few miles away after they moved in 1947. With the grandchildren's spouses and eventually great-grandchildren added to the mix, Sunday dinners at Callanwolde could easily number fifteen or twenty people. The dinners were not strictly limited to family. Potential family could be included as well. When Ruth said to Bob, "Would you like to come to Sunday dinner at Danny's?" the invitation was something short of a marriage proposal, but not far short.

Growing up on the estate in New York, Bob had become comfortable in that awkward position of being neither servant nor family, something more than an ordinary guest but something less than a relative. At Callanwolde, he fit right in. Years later he speculated that his ease at Callanwolde, his lack of the awe that so many of Ruth's young friends displayed, may have been one thing that attracted her to him.

"Would anyone like a drink," Danny asks at about five o'clock on Sunday evening, as if this thought has never occurred to her before, as if she is not surrounded by a family who worships the sanctity of cocktail hour. "Of course," everyone agrees, "Danny has had a splendid idea." "Why," their tones of voice imply, "didn't any of us think of that?" And then Bob's preordained role in the weekly stage play begins.

"Bob," says Danny, "would you get the wherewithal?" Bob takes drink orders, as if he does not know that everyone always has the same thing, starting with Popee's scotch. And my father becomes a part of the spontaneous ritual of Sunday nights at Callanwolde—a ritual far less stiff and formal than what Pat Conroy imagined, but, perhaps, no less scripted.

The first time I visited the Callanwolde Fine Arts Center I was twenty-nine, the same age as Ruth when she died. No activities were being held and the grounds and house were nearly deserted. I wandered through the empty rooms downstairs, trying to gain some sense of what the house had been like as a home. My footsteps echoed off the stone arches in the entry hall and across the expanse of hardwood floor. This could have been the house of any wealthy family. In the billiard room I felt a connection. High on one wall is a small stained-glass window of the Candler family crest and coat of arms—the familiar armorial bearings that hang in my hall at home. On a banner of glass below the coat of arms is the family motto: *Ad mortem fidelis*—faithful until death.

The Candler coat of arms in stained glass in the Callanwolde billiard room.

I climbed the wide double staircase to the open hall upstairs that must be twenty feet wide and three or four times that in length. This was the central room of casual family activity. Danny sat here watching television, escaping from the formality of the downstairs. On every side, doors were shut to me, rooms that contained part of my family history closed off like so many memories.

The door to one side hall stood open, and I ventured in. On one wall was a row of bulletin boards tacked full of notices of art competitions and events; on the opposite wall hung a dozen or so black and white photographs of the home as it had been—fully furnished with chairs and tables and chests and rugs, many of which I recognized. This chest had been

given to Ruth and my father and still stood in the living room. That rug
must be the same one in my grandmother's dining room.

"Excuse me," said a voice, "but are you some kin to the Candlers?"

Who else, I thought, would have such interest in these old photos. I
turned to explain myself, and then it happened. It has never happened
before or since.

"Why you must be Ruth's son," said the woman who stood in front of
me. I stood in shock for a second before responding.

"Yes, I'm Charles Lovett."

"You have her curly blonde hair," she said.

I hadn't thought of my hair as blonde for some years, but then I didn't
think of Ruth's as blonde either, judging from her pictures. But so much
of life is a question of perception. If this smiling woman who was taking
me by the hand into a large office to meet the director was wrong in her
perception of my hair, the conclusion that perception led her to was hauntingly accurate. As I exchanged pleasantries with the director, Sonja stood
in the doorway shaking her head.

"You sound just like your grandfather," she told me. I had never thought
that, either.

Sonja Olsen Kinard is the daughter of Olie Olsen, the Candler's boat
captain who had told my father so much about the family. Olie had been
one of my grandfather's closest friends, and the best man at his second
wedding. He had spent his summers taking Candler children fishing and
swimming and generally entertaining them on the island. Sonja later told
me that her family always said that Olie raised the Candler kids, but not
his own.

Now, decades later, Sonja was working in the house the Candler family had built in Atlanta. She had known Ruth only in passing, but she
recognized me as Ruth's son. The presence of my mother was with me all
along—I only needed someone to point it out.

When I began sending out letters to anyone who might have known Ruth
asking for memories of her, the first response I received was from Sonja
Kinard. She wrote of the one time she was together with Ruth, a summer
afternoon when her father allowed her to ride the boat over to Cumberland
with Ruth and some of her friends. "Being the employee's daughter," she
wrote, "and not knowing Ruth very well, I felt very awkward being with

her even though she was nice to me. She was also with her friends, and they had their own conversation going."

The image of Ruth and her friends riding out to the island, and Sonja, two years older than Ruth, going along for the ride but feeling somewhat left out of the clique, is cinematically real to me. I can close my eyes and feel the engines of the boat and the warm salt air and see the laughing faces of teenage girls on their way to a weekend at the beach and see the sun that must have turned Ruth's hair blonde every summer.

The other memory Sonja wrote of in her letter summoned up no such images, but it did suggest more intrigue. When she and Ruth were in college, both were dating pre-theology students. My father was majoring in philosophy with an eye toward the priesthood in the Episcopal church. Sonja's fiancé was on his way to becoming a Lutheran minister. Sonja's parents disapproved of the match, and Sonja also heard conversations her mother and father had suggesting Ruth's parents were concerned about her potential husband too.

How can this be? Didn't Ruth's parents treat Bob like a son long before he and Ruth were married? At Grandpa's funeral, didn't his second wife, Pete, tell my father that, in some ways, Bob was closer to Grandpa than his own sons were? Wasn't every indication given that the family as a whole was not only pleased with but enthusiastic about Ruth and Bob's marriage? Certainly there was no open opposition to the match.

On the other hand, didn't Ruth's parents send her away to Sweet Briar College in Virginia for a year in the middle of the courtship? Might there have been some concern about the difference in social class or with the possibility of her marrying so young?

But, Ruth's friend and sister-in-law Betsy Denny told me Ruth followed her to Sweet Briar—perhaps sharing Betsy's desire for a year away before settling down. Besides, when had the Candlers ever shown any allegiance to social standing in picking spouses? And what was so wrong with marrying young? Could Sonja have misunderstood or misremembered an overheard conversation? Could her father have exaggerated a concern of his employer in order to solidify his own case against Sonja's fiancé?

Three paragraphs of unanswered and unanswerable questions introduce me to the hazards of human memory. But, if there was some small objection to Ruth's match with my father, the family's deep and loving relationship with Bob in the past five decades has wiped out all memory

of it. The only person who might recall such an objection would be someone outside the family, someone whose father was my grandfather's closest confidant, someone like Sonja.

How *did* Mommy and Daddy get together? The story was fuzzy to me—
tidbits floated back from near forgotten conversations, but no clear picture would assemble.

The night Daddy and I sat up late talking, I skirted the subject. The
evening had begun, when I was upstairs getting Lucy ready for bed, with
his telling Janice how he and Mim got together. Much later, after Janice
had gone to bed, a half dozen beer cans stood empty on the hearth.

"Janice asked about how I met Mim, but you didn't ask about how
Ruth and I ended up together," he said.

"Well, I've heard some of that story," I said, "but I don't know if I've
ever heard it beginning to end." And so he told me.

My father moved to Atlanta in 1948 at the age of thirteen. His family
moved into a large house far out on Peachtree Road several miles north of
the Buckhead neighborhood where Ruth lived. The following year, Barclay
Coggan, a school friend of Bob's, invited him to come to his church, St.
Luke's Episcopal in downtown Atlanta, which had an active young people's
group. There Bob met many of the people who would be his closest friends
for the next several years, including Ruth.

Before long, there was a definable clique who socialized together
and eventually dated one another—Barclay Coggan, Paul O'Shields,
Bill Emmonds, and Bob Lovett on the boys' side of the table; Ruth
Candler, Betsy Denny, Patsy Cathcart, Sheron Hallum, and Ruthe
Yeargan on the girls' side.

"We used to double-date and go out all together. I dated all of them at
one time or another. Ruthe and I had a thing going a little bit one time. I
would have to say that Ruth and I were very good friends, I mean just
really *very* good friends, close, close friends at that point. Ruth had been
dating Paul and when he went off to Tulane, he said, 'Take care of Ruth.'
When he came back for spring holiday he said, 'Well, I'm concerned she's
not getting any companionship.' Well we were doing *H.M.S. Pinafore* at
Marist, my high school, and we were down to the dress rehearsal and so I
thought well maybe she'd like to come to the dress rehearsal. So she went
to the dress rehearsal. Then I said 'do you want to come to the

performance?' So she came to the last performance and we went to the cast party and that was pretty well it. We had a young people's hay ride about a week after so we went to that and that pretty well cinched the whole thing right there."

I don't know what they said to each other or how, exactly, the deal was cinched, but I know that the best of friends can fall in love quickly, and in the spring of 1952, Ruth and Bob did. Shortly thereafter, Ruth issued the dinner invitation.

There was still one matter to attend to. Poor Paul was still at Tulane worrying that his sweetheart was feeling lonesome. Bob picked up Ruth at her house late on a spring Sunday afternoon and pointed the car toward his future.

"I need to stop by a mailbox somewhere between here and Danny's," said Ruth. And she didn't need to say anything else. She didn't need to say that with her posting of a Dear John letter to Paul, this evening would be doubly symbolic in solidifying Bob's place as *the* beau. She mailed the letter, and a few minutes later they were on their way up the drive to Callanwolde, where warm lights in the windows welcomed their arrival.

One person at dinner that evening was Ruth's cousin Billy Warren. If, as Sonja Kinard suggested, there were any reservations on the part of the family about a match between Ruth and Bob, Billy certainly doesn't remember them.

"I do recall her dating a boy here," he wrote, "I think his name was Paul O'Shields, who some of us, at our young ages, thought was not Ruth's style and when she started dating your father, we were more than a little relieved."

I showed this letter to my father and he shook his head and laughed. He'd had no idea that he was considered by anyone a superior match to Paul. But perhaps that's part of what made Ruth love him.

What of myself do I see in this story?

I still remember going to see our Junior High production of *H.M.S. Pinafore* when I was in the first grade and singing, "I am the Captain of the Pinafore" on the school bus for months afterwards. Two decades later I would design and build the set for a production of *Pinafore* at the same school. I've always loved that show. For no particular reason.

I never could get enthusiastic about the youth group at church. Even before I went off to boarding school I felt like an outsider.

I see in my own story episodes that are hauntingly similar to experiences of Ruth and Bob, yet I also see places where my life is the opposite—not by rebellion or design, but through the quirks of my own individuality. Like everyone, I am made up of my parents, but I am essentially myself. And, in some small way, I, too, am a child of Callanwolde.

V

Funny things happen to you when you really start to re-
search something like this. I made a couple of serendipi-
tous discoveries. One was that . . . well, my mother kept
a trunk. I knew that. All good Southern ladies kept a
trunk that they carried with them through life, and my
mother was no exception.

—RUSSELL BAKER

There is always a trunk in the attic. In stories of people who delve into their family's past, the best secrets hide in the trunk in the attic. It is nearly so predictable as to be a cliché, but there *was* a trunk in our attic— a trunk that held what little remained of my mother's life after thirty years.

Once, after I was grown and married, I hauled it from the dust and spent an evening looking through it. I spread the yellowing newspaper clippings, high school yearbook, wedding pictures, and college diploma out on the floor. I read the contents of the envelope marked "Letters, Notes, etc. on the Death of Ruth Candler Lovett." I stole a picture of my mother and her sister Glenn at the Stork Club in New York with their parents in 1954—the only picture I had ever seen in which both my grand-parents appear and both appear happy. Then I loaded everything back in the trunk and shoved it back into the dark.

It is late August, a month and a half after I set out on this journey. This month my father and Mim moved to a new house, marking the end of thirty-three years he had lived in the home he bought with Ruth and several months of emptying closets, drawers, basements, and garages. They gave the trunk to my sister, Elizabeth. Now, she has loaned me the con-tents, and I sit among the scattered remnants of Ruth's past, frozen mo-ments of her life.

*At the Stork Club, New York City, in January 1954—Howard, Màmà,
Ruth, and Glenn.*

My favorite item is her high school senior yearbook. When I think of
my mother, I picture a twenty-nine-year-old woman with three children.
But here I see the life of a teenager—pictures of her in the Glee Club and
the school play, gossipy inscriptions. She was more than halfway through
her life when these girls wished her good luck. I realize as I turn its slick
pages that the majority of her life was spent in childhood and adolescence. The 1953 edition of *Facts and Fancies*, the yearbook of Washington Seminary, is a glimpse into Ruth before adulthood, Ruth as she was
for most of her life.

I knew Washington Seminary was a small private school for girls, but
Facts and Fancies lets me know just how small and private. Ruth's graduating class of forty-five represented almost a third of the 136 enrolled at
the high school level. In the first through the eighth grades were another
120 or so. The school did not operate as a corporation, but was owned by
one person. It was founded by two sisters in 1878, sold twice, and handed
down by the third owner to her nieces, one of whom still owned it in
1953, the year of its diamond anniversary. The cover of *Facts and Fancies*
for that year bears the dates, "1878–1953," like a tombstone. The summer
after Ruth's graduation, Washington Seminary ceased to exist. It was bought
by The Westminster School, a larger private school that still flourishes in
Atlanta. In 1955, the twenty-six columns of its neoclassical main building,

along with the rest of the campus were pulled down by a bulldozer to make way for a motel. I still visit Woodberry Forest, my high school, on occasion. Every year I send a check to the alumni fund. It gives me a sense of the solidity of my past to know it's still there. But my mother's high school, like Ruth herself, exists only as a memory, only in the dark recesses of unopened file drawers, only in the yearbook that lies open on my desk.

Facts and Fancies is weighted toward facts: "Ruth Candler—Entered '47; College Preparatory; Class Vice-President '49–'50; Class Treasurer '52 and '53; French Club '49–'53; Science Club '53; Current Events Club '51–'53; Rabun Gap-Nacoochee '49–'53; Tallulah Falls '51–'53; Junior Carnival Skit '51; Missemma Staff '53; Facts and Fancies Staff '53; Red Cross Staff Aide '51–'52; Quill and Scroll '53."

She won a State of Georgia medal in a French contest her sophomore year and won a medal for the Southeastern region her junior year. (What, I wonder, happened senior year?) The *Missemma* was the student newspaper, named for Miss Emma Scott, the owner and head of the school. *Quill and Scroll* was an honor society for journalists, though I marveled at this honor when I finally obtained a copy of the *Missemma* and discovered Ruth had apparently been no more than a copy editor. Then again, perhaps she wrote articles for issues I will never see—how I would love to see pieces she wrote, to judge how her formal use of language connects with my own. The cryptically named Tallulah Falls and Rabun Gap-Nacoochee were charity fund-raising groups.

The Current Events Club sounded drab until I read that the girls traveled to Washington to see Eisenhower inaugurated in January of 1953. The "News for Women" column of *The Atlanta Constitution* printed a story about the impending trip along with a picture of Ruth, my future aunt Betsy, who was already dating Ruth's brother, Bo, and their friend Patsy Cathcart. The girls are posed with suitcases, Ruth draping a scarf over her hair. At first glance I don't notice the design of the confederate battle flag on the scarf—a reminder of how Southern she was and of how much things have changed in the chasm between her world and mine.

"Washington will welcome these Atlanta Belles among the thousands of visitors attending the inauguration of President-elect Dwight Eisenhower. The girls will have special seats at the inauguration ceremony and will visit many points of interest in and near Washington." I'm no huge fan of Ike, but the thought of attending *any* presidential inauguration thrills me. Yet the trip was described in such a cursory manner. I longed for more.

The archivist for The Westminster Schools came to my rescue. She found two issues of the *Missemma* from Ruth's senior year, one of which proclaimed, "Operation Washington a Glorious Success. . . . Those happily married seniors, Ruthe, Patsy, Betsy, and Ruth, waved tearful goodbyes to their loved ones," the article teased, "who were sure the girls would die before the Seminary Special made its way back to Atlanta." The girls arrived in Washington by train on Saturday morning and headed for the

The main building of Washington Seminary, torn down in 1955.

Capitol on their own bus. "Doris immediately hooked the guide, who told her all. Next was the White House. Jane Lee got in a fight with a Democrat who wanted to know if there were any Republicans in Georgia." The afternoon included a visit to the "magnificent National Cathedral." Less than a dozen years later, Ruth's name would be inscribed in the Cathedral's book of remembrance when Paul O'Shields, the boy she threw over for Bob, endowed a building stone in her memory.

Sunday in Annapolis, if the article is to be believed, the girls spent their time ogling midshipmen. The sightseeing schedule on Monday was the most impressive—Bureau of Printing and Engraving, Supreme Court, Pan-American Union Building, Lincoln, Jefferson, and Washington Monuments, historic Alexandria, Arlington Cemetery and the Tomb of the Unknown Soldier, and finally, Mount Vernon. When I imagine covering that much territory in the short January daylight, I realize that one thing lacking from our 1953 capital was traffic!

Then came the big day. "In our seats by 12:00, we saw Ike and Truman [she saw Harry Truman!] ride down Pennsylvania Avenue for the inauguration ceremonies. Then on loudspeaker systems, the oaths of office were heard. About 2:00, the parade began with Ike, who stood up and waved at us, in a beautiful cream 'Caddie' with Mamie. Then came floats from all the states, high government officials, and most important, the Kaydets from West Point, Middies from Annapolis, the Marine Cadets, V.M.I. Cadets, and Coast Guard Cadets. Everybody was glad to have her knee socks after sitting in that grandstand for six hours." I've seen three presidents in my life. Ruth saw three, if you count Nixon, in one day.

"On our last morning, we visited the famous Smithsonian Institute," which of course lacked the Museum of American History, the Air and Space Museum, and most of the other buildings that now make up the institution on the Mall. "By the time we were ready to leave we could have left our bones with those already there as exhibits of 'What Happens to a Georgia Peach When She Gets Too Far North'."

Their return train from Washington arrived at the tiny, unheated Emory station early on the morning of the twenty-third. Ruth's father and Bob met the train. Nearly three decades later I would park in the freshman lot behind that old depot and walk to the Emory Summer Theatre where I had a job building sets and where I would meet Janice twelve years before she became my wife.

Ruth's visit to Washington was much like my ninth-grade class trip. We, too, visited the Capitol, Supreme Court, an enlarged Smithsonian, and other historic sights. Two of the sights I always stop by now, if only for a moment, every time I'm in Washington—the Vietnam War Memorial and John Kennedy's grave site—were unimaginable when she walked the Mall and visited Arlington in 1953. With me nearby in my playpen, she would watch the news from Dallas; most of the news from Saigon she would never hear.

I had thought of my mother primarily in terms of her relationship with her family and friends, but looking at the picture of her preparing to witness the inauguration of an American president brings her relationship to world events into focus. From the earliest days of her childhood, the world was under the threat of war; before she turned four that war became reality. Did Atlanta, for a time, remain an innocent place for a child of wealth?

The biggest social event in the history of the city took place when she was four and a half. Clark Gable, Vivien Leigh, Olivia de Havilland, and David O. Selznick arrived from Hollywood for the world premiere of *Gone with the Wind*. The night before the premiere, the Junior League gave an elaborate charity ball. Ruth's mother helped with the planning, and her father took snapshots of the stars. Less than two years later, bombs would fall on Pearl Harbor, and Ruth's father would be only a part-time presence for the next three and a half years.

She was ten when the bombs fell on Hiroshima and Nagasaki, the same age I was when peace talks in Paris finally brought Americans home from another, much more confusing war. Did her parents try to shield her from the horrors of the war news or the worse horrors of the news from the Nazi camps after the war?

How did she feel at ten when the only president she had ever known died less than a hundred miles from Atlanta and his body passed through town on the train, bound for Washington and Hyde Park? Did thirteen-year-old Ruth stay up listening to returns on the radio when Truman upset Dewey in 1948? Did she guess that in four years she would be a guest at the inauguration of General Eisenhower?

Her rise to adulthood took place in the era of McCarthyism, the Korean War, and civil defense drills. Can it be any surprise that she was attracted to the idea of normality, of a peaceful existence as a housewife and mother? And in that desire was she not only looking to escape the failures of her parents' marriage and the troubles of the world, but to emulate the models given by television and popular culture? Is it so surprising that she sought out that simple existence when her entire life before her marriage had been lived in a world either at war, on the brink of war, or desperately trying to recover from war?

She has been described to me as generous and loving. I know, though, that she grew up in a time and place where black citizens were often servants of the household and were denied many of the rights of whites.

How did she respond to Martin Luther King's speech in August of 1963? Her father, I imagine, ignored it. Her children, retrospectively, applauded it. Her generation of educated Southerner was left somewhere in the middle.

She watched the rise of the Berlin Wall, never dreaming that her children would watch it fall. Like everyone else in the nation, she prayed through the Cuban missile crisis. On November 22, 1963, like millions of American housewives, she called her husband at work and told him to get to a television.

Did she watch the Beatles on Ed Sullivan in February 1964 while she waited for an appointment to open up for her breast surgery, or MacArthur's funeral in April while she recovered? Did she give any thought to the Gulf of Tonkin in August as her back pain became worse and worse? Did she look back, during September, when she knew that death was near, on the world she had lived in and the way it shaped her life?

In the notes written in her yearbook by classmates I begin to see Ruth at eighteen, and just how serious she and Bob were about their future together. But I should not have read these inscriptions after teaching a class on the use of concrete detail in fiction. Most of them are so vague as to be nearly meaningless.

"This has been a really great year." "You are a great gal." "It was fun, wasn't it?" "We finally made it." "Will you ever forget the good times we've had?" "It's been wonderful knowing you." "I'm going to miss you a lot." "Good Luck!"

They might as well be inscriptions in my yearbook, or anyone's. The few flashes of specificity are tantalizing, though. Some make comments about her character beyond "good" and "sweet," but not far beyond. "You are one of the finest, truest friends anyone could have." "I'll always remember your gracious manner and winning smile." Of course, if she had classmates who thought she was annoying, snotty, or stand-offish, she probably didn't ask them to sign her yearbook. Some compliment the job she did as class treasurer over the past two years. "I'll never forget your speeches about paying for May Day flowers." "I'm sorry I didn't bring my money sooner." Others allude to events I can only guess about.

"I'm going to miss our little sextet next year." "Please don't make another 100 in Chemistry so Mrs. Sessions will think the exam was too

Ruth as a sophomore at Washington Seminary in 1949, about the time she met my father.

easy." "Thanks for all the help in math." "Tinsley and I never would have passed Chemistry if it hadn't been for you and Betsy." "Do you remember our drama lessons with Miss Russell—your pogo stick?" "We've had a great time, especially the singing orgies at recess."

The women whose faces appear in that yearbook had a basis of knowledge I can never share, a language of nicknames and references impossible for me to deci-pher. I dream of finding a member of her class with a wonderful memory—a Ros-etta stone who can lead me through the inside jokes only a group of girls schooled to-gether year after year can de-velop.

At the very least, I hope I can find someone who can explain about the seat.

"Dear Ruth, You have a good seat, even if you do lock your patients up at night." "Dear de Ruth, I think you has a very good seat . . ." "You really have a good seat, so don't break your neck." "You have such a good seat." "Wonder who will get our famous seats next year?"

She wonders? I wonder what in the world these people are talking about. And who is Stew Pot? And why is my mother nicknamed Cat Woman? And what are the zombies?

But if they know things I do not, the reverse is also true. I can see into the future of these frozen images, and see their past from a different angle. Three girls mention a trip with Ruth to Cumberland Island, and I wonder if they are the same three whom Sonja Olsen watched chatting while her father piloted the boat. Several mention Ruth's future with Bob, and their wishes bear a distinct mood of finality—like blessings to a couple already married.

"Be good to Bob and I hope you two will be very happy." "Loads of luck to you and Bob." "Take good care of Bob." "Loads of love to a great minister's wife."

Their assumption that Ruth and Bob were destined not only for marriage, but also for happiness was correct. But in this secret sorority I have invaded, only I know Bob will abandon his plan to become a priest in the Episcopal church and will instead become an English professor. Only I know the details of their happiness, the number of their children, the names of their friends ten years after these inscriptions are made. And only I know that eleven years after these girlish notes are written, Ruth will be dead.

I'm embarrassed to say this, and afraid I'm rushing to judgment with only a scintilla of evidence, but, outside of her senior formal—an earlier version of the angel picture—Ruth looks, in this yearbook's pictures, a little goofy. I had always imagined her courtship with Bob as one between the perfect woman in the angel picture and the square-looking guy in old snapshots of my father—skinny as a rail, ears sticking straight out. While the power of her smile is clear even in group pictures of the newspaper staff and the Current Events Club, she is not the glamorous beauty I imagined. She reminds me of myself as a teenager—distinctly goofy. In the picture of science class, she sits with arms folded and legs crossed on the end of a row, and I see again her lack of a chin. In the series of posed pictures of the class play, she lurks in the background, looking stiff and uncomfortable, her gaze directed to the camera, not the other actors. Elsewhere I sense her discomfort any time she does not use her weapon—that remarkable smile. I don't believe she bequeathed me the smile, but, like her, I've never felt natural in front of a camera. I thought I had inherited that tendency only from my father, who still looks a little awkward in most photographs even in his later, distinguished years.

I hate to say my mother was not beautiful—I think she was, and I'll probably go on thinking that no matter how many goofy-looking pictures of her I see. Her children may not win any beauty contests, but, like Ruth I'm sure, we have incurred jealousy over that Candler curly hair.

The power of Ruth's smile and the power of the angel picture will always work on me. Besides, which of us looked our most handsome at seventeen? I only hope future generations won't judge me by the pictures in my high school yearbook. But Ruth has left me so little that I must give at least some weight to these frozen instants. Of the millions of moments that made up her high school days, I have perhaps a dozen, robbed of their color, their smell, sound, and emotional underpinnings, preserved for me. Studying them is like viewing a sliver of landscape through the turret window of a castle—I can try to deduce what the rest of her experience was like, but though my view tells me infinitely more than darkness, it tells me only an infinitesimal part of the truth.

On the back row of the photograph of the sixth graders is my aunt Glenn. Ruth was born in 1935 and Glenn in 1941 and both these dates seem so distant to me that I had thought of these two women only as members of the same generation—as bound together by age not separated by it. But here is Glenn near the back of the book as a girl, while her sister at the front, for all her teenage looks, is a young woman who has chosen her husband and the path that will guide the rest of her life. How much, I wonder, will Glenn be able to contribute to the search for her sister?

The inscription in her yearbook that is most poignant in both its knowledge and ignorance of the future stands alone on the front page.

"*Dearest Ruth—To the past and all the wonderful times we've had. To the present, and all the love we share. To the future, most of all, for we will spend it together. Love, Bob.*"

It is the closest thing to a love letter between my parents I will ever see.

The *Missemma* for February 1953 tells me that as a member of the Science Club, Ruth heard a talk on tuberculosis and as a member of the Current Events Club a lecture on Peru. A short article on the front page notes that only a handful of sophomores and seniors achieved an "A" average for the first semester. Among the five seniors was Ruth Candler. On the same page an article previews the production of *The Curious Savage* in which Ruth will play the role of Miss Wilhelmina. It's time to find a copy of this play.

Set in a home for patients who have lost touch with reality, the play examines the notion of sanity by showing that many of the patients are more sane than some outsiders. Miss Willie, the role played by Ruth, is on the staff of The Cloisters and helps deal with the patients. I realize the girl who wrote in Ruth's yearbook "even if you do lock up your patients at night," was referring to Miss Willie. She is perhaps the most bland of the characters—everyone else has some eccentricity or obsession, but Miss Willie seems boringly normal.

Only in the final scene do we realize Miss Willie is something more than a stock character—the helpful nurse. For Miss Willie saves the day—contrives to get rid of the wealthy Mrs. Savage's annoying family and to save her ten million dollars in bonds. She is, we discover, not a regular staff member, but the wife of a patient, Jeff, who constantly complains that her attentions to him could be misconstrued. Earlier in the play, Miss Willie insists on kissing Jeff's cheek and fixing his coffee for him, in spite of his complaints that his wife might find out. "She'd explode," Jeff says, to which Miss Willie replies, "She would if I know her."

A dated play, but not as dated as many drawing room pieces of the forties and fifties. I have to remind myself that it was running on Broadway, with Lillian Gish as Mrs. Savage, less than three years before Ruth played in it. There are few things I enjoy more than being in a play. As I write this, I'm in rehearsals for *Twelfth Night*, playing the role of Feste. My wife, too, loves stage work like nothing else. So, even if Ruth did not venture onto the stage as much as I have, I feel a connection to her work having followed Miss Willie over the pages of this script. Even though Miss Willie is a woman's part, I think about how I would play certain scenes. And I feel a closeness to Ruth through this script, too, because on these pages is the only sizable collection of words (with the exception, I suppose, of the 1928 *Book of Common Prayer*) that I know, beyond any doubt, issued from her lips.

The heart and soul of the trunk in the attic, the place where grief still pulses palpably, and the impact of Ruth's life and of her death converge, is the packet of condolence letters sent to my father after her death. There are twenty-one of these letters. Had a tragedy befallen me at thirty, I would have felt lucky to receive half that number. They speak of things I rarely speak of—not merely Ruth's death and the pain of her absence, but also of faith. Bob, the once future priest, the man who befriended his future wife by giving her rides to church and courted her at Youth Group activities, would have his faith tested like never before or again. Many of the friendships he had in 1964 had been forged in those early years, and those friends now came forward to offer themselves in whatever way they could and to remind him of the power of that faith.

"We have thought often of you and of Ruth and the time spent in contemplation has helped me, at least, to accept her absence and to renew my faith in things eternal. In the quietness and the sunlight of the mornings and even in the sobriety of the night I am happy in my understanding of resurrected life. I know that this faith comforts you now. Be assured that we all, even as we suffer for you, are satisfied that Ruth's life is forever free from pain now and forever happy." Emily Wilson, who wrote this beautiful letter, later published several books of poetry. Her sentiments are taken up by many others who are not poets, but who still speak with eloquence, and their faith in Bob's faith is clear.

"Of all my friends, you probably are the one who least needs to be reminded of the reassurances that Christianity affords."

"I know you well enough to know that I do not need to give you Christian counsel at this time."

The letters are more about my father than about Ruth. They are a testament not only to the sincerity of his faith, but also to the deep friendships he and Ruth formed. Though I envy no man the loss of his wife, I am, on some level, intensely jealous of my father for both his faith and his friends.

"We have so many happy memories of the time spent with you in Atlanta and count you among our dearest friends."

"I am sure you realize, Bob, how much you two meant to me. You became dearer and dearer in the last few years when we talked over so much."

"You must know that you were the first Atlantan I could call 'friend'; and it was Ruth's kindness and hospitality that first made me feel at home here."

"A year or so ago, the subject of friends was under discussion at work and one of my men asked how many firm and true friends I had. 'Friends' being interpreted in the strictest sense, I told him that there were five who I would do anything for without question and for whom I would drop everything. Now there are only four."

The letters speak of both the shock with which people met the news of Ruth's death, and the helplessness they felt. Despite the best intentions of those around him, despite the outpouring of love and support from friends and family, my father had, ultimately, to meet his tragedy in isolation. Whatever comfort those around him may have offered during the day, each night he had to close the door, and slide into a cold bed, alone with his God.

Many of the names on these letters are familiar to me. Some are family, some remain friends; as for others, I can remember the days the phone rang, bringing news of their death. Others are mysteries, proof that our lives do change, that even the closest of friends pass in and out. Most of those who wrote were not from Winston-Salem. Though he was transplanted in North Carolina, Bob's roots remained in Atlanta. He was still working on his Ph.D. at Emory. Thirty years later, the Atlanta friends are mostly fond memories, and now my father's home truly is in Winston-Salem. But in 1964, he stood on a cusp—still making a place for himself in a new community, but removed from his long-time friends. When news of Ruth's death spread, he found out just how strong those old friendships still were, and just how good a job he and Ruth had done of finding new relationships in their new life.

One other thing strikes me about these letters, the refrain heard again and again—the children.

"Betsy and Nell said you are holding up so well and I know you are a great comfort to your children right now when I am sure they need you so badly."

"You have your wonderful children that will be of some comfort to you in these sad days."

"I am sure that David and Elizabeth will remember her all their lives . . . Parental prompting helps a child's mind to hold these memories so that they are retained in the mind during adulthood."

"She did leave a wonderful legacy, though—those darling, bright, life-loving children. And she instilled in them an unusual capacity for appreciating beauty and a desire to learn. Her influence on them was so strong that I'm sure it will always remain in them."

For the most part, the writers of these letters, like me, did not want to bring painful memories into Bob's mind. With his wife dead only a few days, they knew his healing must begin by looking forward, by treasuring his children and his work. Not that they encouraged him to forget Ruth, but their silence on the details of her life implied he should not dwell on her or their past. To me, though, the few passages that do speak directly of Ruth and of their marriage are the most powerful. Although in places they smack of the generic, they still provide tiny strands I can grasp in an attempt to pull her life back from the realm of the forgotten.

"She was a lovely girl. Bob and I were both most impressed with her personality and poise."

"You and Ruth were a rare team—intellectual—artistic—and home-makers—all in one!"

"In my mind Ruth will always symbolize grace. Her kindness, gentility, gentleness, and joyfulness are only small parts of what caused us to love her as we did and still do in our memory."

"She was a person of surpassing beauty. There are so few people like her in the world. It is hard to face the loss of even one. To those of us who knew you and Ruth, you present an exemplar of what a home, both in the relation of a man and wife and in the relation of parents and children, can be. If it is not presumptuous of me to say it, Ruth knew the love and devotion of a truly good husband and the joys of children attractive in character as well as body. Longevity is not always a blessing, but love is."

In these letters from the trunk in the attic I see not only what my parents' friends thought of them, but I hear the voice of my own fantasies, my own dreams of how I hope one day to be seen. Ruth was twenty-nine, my father had just turned thirty. At thirty-three, I still entertain hopes of being described as artistic and intellectual, of attracting the admiration of friends, of having people envy my contentment and admire my faith. Can it be coincidence that the qualities I strive for are the qualities so many people recognized in Ruth? Is it possible that she passed on, even to a two-year-old, her desires and passions? And if so, why do I feel I've yet to realize those desires when she seems to have reached contentment so young? Why do the same talents she employed in the service of normality, the service of living a contented life as housewife and mother, beckon to me because of my belief they will raise me out of normality? She earned respect through striving toward a life that most would call ordinary. I yearn for respect through achieving the extraordinary. Which of us, really, is most likely to achieve immortality?

VI

*I am profoundly impressed that what our country needs
is not more secularized education, but more of the education that is fundamentally and intentionally religious.
To this end . . . I offer . . . the sum of One Million Dollars, for the endowment of such an institution, the plans
and methods of which are to be definitely directed to the
advancement of sound learning and pure religion.*
                              —ASA G. CANDLER, JULY 16, 1914

It is early September and I have finished sifting through the contents of
the trunk. Today I received in the mail Ruth's transcript from the year she
attended Sweet Briar College in Virginia. I wrote and asked for it and it
showed up in my mail box. At first glance it seems completely impersonal.
Just her name followed by a list of courses and grades, along with a list of
units she accumulated in high school. In one corner is a rubber-stamped
notice saying that this information "may not be released to any other party
in any form without the written consent of the student." I realize this is an
intimate document. I have never seen my father's grade transcripts or my
wife's. I'm not sure I could remember what *I* took my freshman year in
college without doing a little research. Yet all I had to do was ask, and this
fragment of her, this intimate photocopy, is handed over to me without
question. All I had to do was ask, but it never occurred to me before *to*
ask.

   She attended Sweet Briar from 1953 to 1954, her freshman year, returning home a few days before her nineteenth birthday. She was, at the
time, deeply in love with my father—this, I gather, was part of the reason
for her being sent away and most of the reason for her returning. Her
brother, Bo, had fallen in love too. He had gone so far as to get engaged to
Ruth's friend, Betsy Denny, and Betsy, too, was packed off to Sweet Briar

Part of the Sweet Briar campus in 1954.

for a year. Betsy was married a month after she got home from the rolling hills of piedmont Virginia.

I attended Woodberry Forest School, another two hours north of Sweet Briar, from 1977 to 1980. My first wife's parents lived in central Virginia and we visited them often. So, at least two or three times a year for about fifteen years, I passed by the end of a long wooded drive marked by a sign that said "Sweet Briar." Almost every time, I said to myself, "Someday, when we're not in such a hurry, I'd like to stop and look around." I never did. Now I live a thousand miles away and I'm staring at her transcript.

To become a college English professor, my father must have taken his studies seriously and been good at them, and I imagine he picked a girlfriend who would do the same. I have always assumed that Ruth was a dedicated and successful college student, but I had never seen the slightest concrete evidence that this was the case.

Ruth got all A's and B's except for a C+ in "Modern History." She took a French course called "Survey of French Literature." I assume the texts were studied in French, making it essentially the same course I took as a sophomore in high school. She took physics (junior year in high school for me), religion (Old and New Testament), and English. The future wife of an English professor got an A in Freshman English the first semester. Second semester it slipped to a B. She made freshman honor role first semester. In the spring she fell just short of the mark. Perhaps she was homesick, or missing her boyfriend. It was the only time in her life she would spend more than a few weeks away from family.

The list of her high school units, each representing a year of study, includes two of Latin, three of French, one of chemistry, and three of history. One of the history courses is called "History of the Theatre." Again, I took the same course, but not until my senior year as a theatre major in college. I would have loved taking this course in high school. I would have hated taking Latin.

There is little else. Her maiden name. Daddy had told me she had no middle name, but had never seen that terse entry: Candler, Ruth.

What impresses me most about this transcript is not its content, but its existence. Thirty-one years after her death, there are still tiny pieces of her life buried in files at places where no one has heard of her. I know this should not surprise me, but it does, and already I am calculating where else I might find such fragments. Dying at twenty-nine, I thought, would not give her much opportunity to leave a mark. But I did not realize how subtle and lightly sketched the marks we leave can be. Even when I am gone, her transcript will sit in a drawer in the middle of Virginia, waiting for someone else to ask.

This single sheet of paper declares in words simple and clear: she existed. More than airbrushed pictures or yellowed snapshots or even her letters, certainly more than family stories and anecdotes, this official-looking document attests to her reality. It is something I never doubted intellectually, but often lost sight of emotionally. My mother's life was real, and here, in stark black and white, is the proof—evidence that comes not from family, but from an independent source.

She existed. She walked the earth and left her footprints. Some have not yet faded.

When I wrote to Sweet Briar asking if they could send me a copy of Ruth's picture from the 1954 yearbook, they sent me a copy of the book itself. This generosity touched me and encouraged me not to be so shy in asking people about Ruth. The responses have been remarkable.

The book did not tell me much. Ruth's picture appeared with her class, but she was not listed in any campus organizations. From the photos of the campus, I gathered that life at Sweet Briar must have had something in common with life at Woodberry Forest—the red brick buildings, the rolling green hills, and the mountains in the distance all reminded me of my own days in Virginia. But the book speaks nothing of Ruth's particular experience, and I have to wonder if she saw her year at Sweet Briar as merely biding her time until she could return home.

A week later, my sister sent me Ruth's own copy of the 1954 *Briar Patch*, a treasure from the trunk that she had overlooked in the first shipment. Like her Washington Seminary annual, it is signed by friends, though not as many. The inscriptions give me only a glimpse of her year at Sweet Briar.

"Dear Ruth, It's too trite to say I'm glad to have known you (but it's true) so I'll say it was delightful to play bridge with you instead!"

"Dear Ruth, Well, gal, this year is finally over. I'll never forget it—from the train ride up here to that last Physics exam. Take good care of Emory and Bob and write me. I've loved knowing you this year and don't be surprised when your doorbell rings. I just may come to Atlanta some day."

"We all wish you were coming back next year, but since you're not, best say good-bye now. Till we meet again . . ."

They knew her for nine months. They knew her much better than I ever will.

I knew that eventually I would have a chance to talk to my Aunt Betsy about the year at Sweet Briar, but in the meantime I wrote a letter to Jane Pinckney Hanahan—Ruth's roommate. Jane remembered little, but was still kind enough to write me. Hers was one of many letters I would read over the ensuing months that began with a disclaimer ("I don't have any memories of your mother") and then, in its wanderings, stumbled upon recollections I found illuminating.

"She seemed to be totally in love with your father and wasn't interested in dating in Virginia. . . . I think Ruth was involved with the campus YWCA organization. We had nondenominational services at Sweet Briar with excellent visiting ministers. . . . It seems to me that Ruth was in constant contact with your father, either by letter or phone or both. I think she liked Sweet Briar all right, but she wanted to be with your father. I don't remember her being homesick. I don't think we had heart-to-heart talk. . . . One memory I have is of Betsy singing the Pepsi-Cola jingle to tease your mother."

Jane told me of the sheltered life Ruth lived at Sweet Briar—at least as sheltered as what I had experienced at Woodberry. "We had to sign out every time we left campus and were limited in the number of nights we could spend away from college. We could stay only in approved places in Lexington and Charlottesville. If we wore shorts they had to be covered by a raincoat, and on and on."

I undertook my schooling in Virginia because I wanted to go to boarding school, to strike out on my own, and to get the kind of education that I couldn't get in Winston-Salem beyond the junior high level. I went to Woodberry for three years, worked hard, and felt proud of what I accomplished. I have no doubt that Ruth worked hard and had reason to be proud, but it seems she never thought of Sweet Briar as anything other than a temporary arrangement. "I don't think she considered returning a second year," wrote Jane.

Nothing could be more appropriate, in terms of family history, than Ruth's enrollment in Emory University as a sophomore on September 21, 1954. Her great-grandfather, Asa, had provided the money and the land to open a Methodist university in Atlanta; Asa's brother had been the first president of Emory University; Ruth's grandfather served as chairman of the board at the time of her enrollment. Many members of the family had attended both the university and its precursor, Emory College in Oxford, Georgia. My father's family, too, had some generations of Emory graduates, and he would earn his Ph.D. there. Years later I would meet my future wife, Janice, on the Emory campus on the day of her graduation, so even in the present generation the connection remains.

Like Sweet Briar, Emory sent me a copy of Ruth's transcript. This one was longer, more formal looking, and bore at the bottom the words "Deceased Sept. 25, 1964."

My first thought on opening her transcript was to compare her college performance with my own. I earned a 3.5 cumulative GPA at Davidson College, good enough for me to make *cum laude* by the skin of my teeth. Her GPA was 3.13 for the three years she spent at Emory. Mostly A's and B's as I expected. My eye was drawn to the C's, though. Where did she have trouble? The first, ironically, was in Sociology 213—"The Family." By all accounts I have heard, and from all I can deduce, she was marvelously skilled at running a family. Studying it as a sociological phenomenon was something else. But this told me more about the futility of studying sociology than it did about Ruth. The catalog described the course as covering "problems of mate selection and marital adjustment." Ruth took the course three months before she got married. Mate selection was not something she needed to be taught.

Other C's came in all three terms of philosophy's "History of Western Thought." I wonder if I could do much better faced with the grim prospect of an entire year of philosophy. The one C that really surprised me was in "Shakespeare." After all, we were an English-department family. As I recall, though, despite my passion for the bard, I barely earned my B in "Shakespeare," so perhaps we are not so far from one another.

She majored in humanities, an interdisciplinary study that gave her the opportunity to take fine arts courses that were, perhaps, comparable to those I took for my theatre major. In "Introduction to Music," "Introduction to Architecture and Sculpture," and "History of Opera," she made A's.

She took only one course in the Spring of 1957—the colloquium in her major. With just that course to worry about, she still only made a C. Staring at the date, I realized why her college experience was completely incomparable to mine. In the spring of her sophomore year, when she got two B's and a C, she was planning a wedding. She and my father were married on August 23, 1955, just before she started her junior year. For her, college and the struggles of early married life were simultaneous. They moved into their first apartment a few blocks from campus and she continued to go to school full time. On March 20, 1957, in the middle of spring break, she gave birth to my brother, David. She spent her entire senior year pregnant, took a course while dealing with a newborn, and still managed a C. Her GPA seemed an insignificant measure of her abilities.

I was struck by her choice of major—humanities. A woman with visions of a career outside the household, even in 1957, would not choose to major in something so nonspecific. It is the major of someone with a genuine interest in her own education, but of someone who sees that education as an end in itself, not a means to an end. It is the major of a woman whose most earnest wish is to be normal, raise her children, be active in her community and church, and be stimulated intellectually by her friends and her husband. It is a major that seems perfectly in keeping with all I know of Ruth.

Bob, David, and Ruth in December 1957, just a few months after Ruth graduated from Emory.

The librarian at Emory sent me two photocopied pages from yearbooks. In her sophomore year, "Ruth Candler" looks much as she did as a senior at Washington Seminary. Two years later, "Ruth C. Lovett" has her hair pulled back tightly, and suddenly looks much more like her daughter, Elizabeth. Plenty of the seniors pictured on the same page with Ruth have their middle names spelled out. I wonder if she or someone else made the decision to shorten Candler to an initial.

I did not expect to find any of the twenty or so professors who taught Ruth forty years ago still active at Emory, but I hoped I might find some alive who remembered her. Several of my letters were returned marked "Address Unknown." Three were returned marked "Deceased," including the one to her advisor, Professor Joe Conant. Some of my letters arrived just a little too late.

"My husband of 56 years died in 1993," wrote the widow of one professor. "I wish you luck in your search—to have such a devoted son speaks well of her."

"My father died in March 1994. As a still-grieving son I wish you well as you search for information about your mother."

But I did find a few of Ruth's professors. Some had no memory of her, one had moved in 1992 and only then thrown out his old grade books, but some did remember, or at least still had those grade books from four decades ago.

In "American Social History," Ruth wrote book reviews on Fitzgerald's *This Side of Paradise* and Elson's *History of American Music*. Her term paper was titled "Church Architecture." Insignificant details? Perhaps, but details nonetheless. Specific and concrete, not the vague recollections of those who knew her. I long to see her term paper. I studied British Ecclesiastical architecture during a term abroad in high school and I've had a fascination with cathedrals ever since. Could she have shared that interest?

And how much more do I long to see the paper she wrote for her course in "The Romantic Poets." She only received a C+, Professor Ward Pafford told me, on her "introductory autobiographical essay," but how I would love to see what she wrote about herself at age twenty-two. "Your mother was a diligent and sound student," wrote Professor Pafford.

Another professor wrote that "she was knowledgeable but rather quiet. On written work she excelled. She got the only A in the class on the hour test and one of the three A's on the final exam. In short, she was an excellent student."

Floyd Watkins, who recently retired from the English department, was the one professor I reached who remembered both Bob and Ruth well. Floyd called me to chat about Ruth and told me how glad he was that someone had asked his help on something—anything. After helping students for over forty years, it sounded as if he felt useless in retirement. Another professor had written me, "I am pleased to be remembered somehow (or indeed anyhow) after all the long years since the summer of 1957." I had not expected my inquiries to make others feel wanted, but any journey has its happy by-products. Floyd told me that Ruth was an "extraordinarily sweet and kind person," and that her B in his "American Novel" class was "a damn good grade." Later, he sent me the reading list: *The Scarlet Letter, Moby Dick, The Americans, Look Homeward Angel,* and *All The King's Men*. Others he could not recall, but the total was around nine novels.

"I remember her as good, kindly, hard-working, pleasant," said Floyd. "My vague recollection is that she was very attractive, no picture-beauty queen, a little plump, solid as a person."

Ruth was graduated from Emory on August 17, 1957. According to *The Emory Alumnus*, the ceremony was moved from the Glenn Memorial Amphitheater into the Glenn Auditorium because of steady rain. Both spaces were named for the family of Ruth's grandmother, Danny. The magazine shows a picture of Ruth, diploma in hand, being kissed on the

Ruth embraces Popee after receiving her Emory diploma.

cheek by her grandfather, the chairman of the board. Popee had the pleasure of watching several of his grandchildren graduate from Emory. Ruth would be the last. The issue of *The Emory Alumnus* that contains the article about her graduation is dated October, 1957. The November issue has her grandfather on the cover, with the dates of his life: 1878–1957. The article about his life recalls the graduation of his granddaughter just six weeks before his death on October 1.

"Mrs. Lovett was a source of unusual pride to her grandfather, for she not only worked her way in part through the University but as an undergraduate she got married and had a baby son. Furthermore, she was the first Candler girl to receive an Emory degree, for the University became fully coeducational only in 1953. Coeducation, incidentally, was a step which Chairman Candler opposed, but the graduation of his granddaughter might belatedly have changed his mind."

In Popee's pride of Ruth's accomplishments I see the precursor to my own pride—pride that my mother loved learning and was willing to work hard to uphold that love. And I feel gratitude that she passed those values on to me.

VII

There are more things in heaven and earth, Horatio
Than are dreamt of in your philosophy.
—William Shakespeare

It is mid-September, two months into the quest. I am in Santa Fe, New Mexico, a different city from the Santa Fe that Ruth and Bob visited in 1956. But the surrounding country—the mesas and mountains, gorges and cliffs—is unchanged in centuries of human habitation. It is the same dramatic country that Ruth saw nearly forty years ago. I park my rental car outside the home of Rand Lee, who calls himself an empathic clairvoyant. In a few minutes I will cross his unkempt front yard and step across flecks of peeled paint on the shabby front porch and into his house and a world I have never entered. My palms sweat, my heart beats faster, my stomach flutters. I feel like I'm waiting for a job interview. I am not nervous because of any fear of confrontation with Ruth's spirit. Rather, I cannot squelch my sense of being an intruder. I'm curious and open minded, but still the feeling nags at me that I do not belong in the world of Santa Fe psychics.

If one person in Ruth's family might belong in such a world, it would be her mother. Màmà has a deep interest in spirituality. I regret I never talked with her about this side of her being. Now, she talks so little of anything it is unlikely I will ever fully understand her beliefs. Like her second husband, Carl, she believes in reincarnation and much of what is taught in Hinduism. The particular branch of thought she has followed for much of her life is Theosophy, but she also takes things such as astrology quite seriously. Theosophy was always something of a dirty word in our family, referring to the odd side of Màmà—the side she did not share with the rest of her family, but did share with Carl. I assumed that because Carl, too, was a devotee of the philosophy, that it must be, like so many other things

he believed in, unconventional and, to me, unacceptable. But years before
Carl joined the family, Ruth took at least two trips with her mother, one
to Chicago and one to New England, that involved meetings of the Theosophical Society. Until she was fifteen or sixteen, Ruth was a vegetarian
like her mother—a diet closely linked to Màmà's religious beliefs. Even
though by her teenage years Ruth's religious practices and beliefs were
more closely linked to Bob than to her own family, she grew up in a household where one parent pursued the path of Theosophy.

Through the Internet I obtained some pamphlets about Theosophy,
and my research surprised me. Some of what the Theosophical Society's
publications say reflects my own beliefs. It is a movement that seeks to
combine religion and science and to look within all religions and to find
common truths. It emphasizes study and discourages proselytizing.

But, Theosophists also believe in karma, a "law of recurring cycles in
nature," that ensures that we reap what we sow. They believe in reincarnation as the way in which we evolve from lower life forms to higher and
higher levels of consciousness, meeting the same "Egos" in each life. Between incarnations, Egos go into a state called "Devachan." I believe there
may be lessons to be learned from studying these ideas, but I will never
accept them as my own. I wonder, though, if Ruth, as she lay on her death
bed, gave any thought to her mother's beliefs or entertained fantasies of
another incarnation.

In spite of a mother who was a Theosophist and a father who was a Methodist, Ruth, like me, was a confirmed Episcopalian (her mother actually
considered herself an Episcopalian *and* a Theosophist). In the Episcopal
church, the sacraments are referred to as "outward and visible signs of
inward and spiritual grace." I have always felt much the same way about
the Episcopal liturgy—that the service enables people to come together as
a group yet still express their innermost feelings privately. For me, a shyer
and more inward person than many suspect, the structure of the Episcopal liturgy, framed by moments of quiet introspection before the service
and after the communion, caters to my own balance of the intellectual,
spiritual, and emotional. It is a superb service for someone who feels deeply
about God, thinks often about God, but is uncomfortable talking casually about God.

I suspect Ruth felt much the same. So many people—friends, family, and even college professors—have described her as a quiet person. Like me, she seems to have blossomed in the company of family and friends, but felt a streak of shyness among those she knew less well. And, like me, her deepest feelings about religion seem to have remained largely unspoken.

"I never heard her talk about God," wrote her sister Glenn, "but she and Bob loved the church and did a great deal for it."

In the General Thanksgiving, Episcopalians ask God that we "show forth thy praise, not only with our lips, but in our lives, by giving up ourselves to thy service. . . ." While Ruth may not have used her lips to express her feelings about God, she certainly used her life to do so.

Even her attitude toward her illness suggests the beliefs of someone of deep faith. The priest who conducted her funeral in Winston-Salem described her as "a good soldier who did all she could until the end." Her doctor called her "a sweet patient, and uncomplaining, even under the worst of circumstances." A friend said of Ruth during her final days that she seemed "not as afraid as I felt."

As much as I love the Episcopal service, as much as it caters to that balance of the outward and visible and the inward and spiritual, I still suspect that I have a long way to go before my faith approaches the strength of Ruth's.

Rand Lee is an impressively large man, an inch or two taller than me, but with a chest that begins swelling below the shoulders and blossoms into a rotund belly of remarkable girth. His handshake is firm and confident, yet comforting in its fleshiness. With a smile, he pulls me into his living room. The place is furnished dorm-room cheap. Two sagging sofas face each other over a yard-sale coffee table. Rand immediately apologizes for the candles on the table's edge. "I don't usually do this," he says. "I was just in a mood today." Everything about him—his tone of voice, ease of carriage, and relaxing banter—suggests that he doesn't take himself too seriously. This inclines me to take him more seriously than I might otherwise.

The previous night on the phone I told him about my quest. Now he takes some basic information down about Ruth (her name and hometown) and confesses that this is only the second time he has tried to glean psychic impressions of a dead person. This puts me further at ease. In some way, at least, the experience will be new for both of us. I have been in the room less than five minutes and my flutters have settled. Rand and I are beginning to feel like fellow travelers.

I came to Santa Fe for a conference on writing memoirs and personal essays. Here my relationship with my mother is turned inside out. Everywhere else I have been in life the fact that my mother died has remained hidden, at least for a while. It simply doesn't come up in casual conversation on the first day at boarding school or a new job. "Hello, I'm Charlie. My mother died."

But here the thirteen people in my workshop have read the opening pages of this book and dozens of others heard me read an excerpt on the first day of the conference. Now instead of being a secret, Ruth's death is my identity. I have become "the guy who is writing about his dead mother," a liberating identity to possess. I feel as if I have skipped over the first days or weeks or months of casual acquaintance and can speak to these people about deep emotions and buried family secrets. Here, for once, I can walk up to someone and say, "Hello, I'm Charlie; I'm the one whose mother died," and we can talk about it.

Still, it's odd to hear Rand Lee pronounce Ruth's name—a name that for so long has seemed like a password. He says it with reverence in the invocation that begins our session, asking that the divine parent "help us invite Ruth Candler Lovett into this space of love." Rand sits on one sofa, his eyes closed, hands resting palm upwards on his knees, his voice just above a murmur. Opposite him, I lean back in the depth of the couch, my hands lying limply on my thighs, my mind as open as I can make it.

"The first impression I've been getting is of music," says Rand, and I try not to look impressed. "Like piano, or . . . just music, a love of music." Rand asks me if that seems accurate, and I have to tell him that it does. Later he will tell me that Ruth's sense of connection to God came through music and since her death she has seen everyone in my life, from my father to my second wife, Janice, in terms of music. He will tell me that she had early dreams of being a concert pianist or working with music professionally. I will feel both faith and doubt in these remarks, but when Rand first mentions Ruth's connection to music, the skepticism I have been trying to suppress begins to melt away.

"Of course you know Ruth was musical and could play almost anything," wrote Aunt Betsy. "I remember her bringing things like a violin or accordion to school and some of us gathering in the parking lot to sing-a-long during free time. Her real instrument, however, was the piano and classical music, but she enjoyed playing jazzy tunes at get-togethers. I, who could only read music as written, was impressed that she could change the timing on a tune to make it a march, waltz, boogie, etc., which she would do but not ever in a show-offy way."

Ruth's musical exploits in high school sound like my own in college. I never had the patience to become a good music reader, but by junior high I was playing piano by ear and imitating the styles of Elton John and Billy Joel. In college, our parties would often end with hours of singing around the piano, my playing in the style of improvisation Betsy describes. Playing by ear, I often didn't understand how I was able to pick out a tune, but I'm sure Rand would say that Ruth was guiding my hands.

After moving to Winston-Salem, Ruth transferred to the local Junior League (she had been a member in Atlanta) and was assigned to work with the Radio-TV Council. This group produced short radio versions of children's books that were played for school children throughout the area. Marge Sosnik, who worked with Ruth on the council, wrote, "Some women adapted these stories from books. Others like me were the readers. Ruth was one of the accompanists. We all thought she was the best. It was up to her to insert introductory themes, bridges and closing themes for each story, as well as staccato exclamation points at just the right time. . . . My

Marge Sosnik and Ruth working on a radio program in 1962.

memories of her center on our delightful sessions together in your den. She would be at the piano and I would be sitting nearby working on the latest script. . . . You would be nearby too, having a terrific time in your playpen." Unfortunately, Marge told me, the tapes of those programs are long since lost.

In college, I played introductory and incidental music for a children's play, and hit more than a few "staccato exclamation points." I had related that experience more to the work of my father's mother, who played in an all-girl orchestra in the 1920s, before and during silent pictures. I imitated the old cliff-hanger chord progressions and chase scene minor melodies, never knowing that my mother was as much a precursor as my grandmother.

Now piano playing is a private affair for me, enjoyed when the house is empty and I can play and sing as loudly as I like, or on evenings when the chemistry is right and Janice and I sing together and make music for the pleasure of the moment. And I wonder, at those times, if Ruth and Bob ever sat down at the piano and sang each other love songs, or show tunes, or old standards that were not then so old, and if the music drifted up to me asleep in my crib, and rested in my heart.

My brother and sister are far more musically talented than I. David pursues music as a career, something he has done off and on since he took up the banjo as a teenager. His band plays in clubs and records in a studio he built in his basement. Elizabeth, like me, plays the piano, but her patience is greater than mine and her classical repertoire extends beyond the three or four pieces I can pick out by ear.

My great joy, however, is that Ruth's music does not stop with our generation. My daughter, Lucy is one of the most musical little children I have ever seen. Her inventory of songs sung in the car or while she plays seems endless. Not only could she carry a tune at age two, but she did so without the reinforcing power of the words—she hums tunes to herself, and even makes up her own words to songs she has learned. And she looks like her grandmother. Sonja Olsen Kinard's sister Virginia wrote of Ruth at an early age: "If you ever have a little blonde, curly-haired girl, you can feel assured that you have a little Ruth."

Before I read Betsy's letter, I had known that Ruth played the piano, but no details. The thought of her playing the violin or accordion was something else entirely, but why not? I envision something like a gypsy dance of her high school friends in the parking lot of Washington Seminary. How different from the image created by those soft formal fifties photos in her senior yearbook. I took violin lessons for two years with no success. Janice was an accomplished violinist in high school. We keep saying we need to get her violin fixed so she can take it up again. And, oh yes, she's been wanting to buy me an accordion!

For the first few minutes of our session, Rand gleans what he calls initial impressions of Ruth. The first of these is of her love of music, but he goes on to describe her as compassionate and intelligent. She enjoyed the rituals of Christmas, he says, and had a surprising physical sensuality. As a young girl she needed physical activity, yet at the same time she was self-absorbed in her inner world. All of these qualities I can easily relate to what I already know of her, and most of them I can see in some measure in myself—particularly the notion of having a strong inner life as a child.

But Rand also perceives some tension between Ruth and an older woman who may have disapproved of her match. He says she had strong psychic abilities, though she may not have known it. And she had writing ability—may have even started a book. These impressions balance my opinion of the session—not because I can disprove any of them, but because they seem less compatible with what I know of Ruth. Then Rand hands me a deck of tarot cards and tells me to pick ten.

The blue design on the back of the cards is worn around the edges and they feel soft in my hands. I try to lend some significance to each card I choose, to let some spiritual force, whether from within or without, guide my selecting, but I know I am only acting the part, pretending to make the process seem significant while I pick ten cards at random. I may believe what Rand says he sees in the cards, but I can't believe that my choosing them was anything other than luck.

I had my tarot cards read once before—by an amateur at a party. The tall blonde man who was supposed to change my life never showed up. Now Rand uses the tarot to look into the past rather than the future. The first two cards reveal Ruth's intense interest in the internal and her sense of spirituality. I can take it or leave it. As we progress further into the reading, though, Rand's comments become more concrete, and more Ruth-like.

"She was capable of considerable merriment. . . . She really did like having a good time. . . . She had a lot of sheer pleasure in people and living . . . that odd quality of deep silence and need for solitude and also sheer enjoyment of life." In my mind a vision of teenage girls putting on a play or traveling to Washington or singing along with Ruth merges with an image of the more adult Ruth throwing a dinner party, something my father told me she didn't do often, but enjoyed on occasion.

"And she sure did love your father." Of course anyone who hears the story—twenty-nine-year-old mother of three small children dies, leaving grieving widower—can guess this, but something about the change of tone in Rand's voice from speculation to certainty, sincerity, and respect, draws me into believing that he understands the depth of their love.

"She does seem to have had a head for money," Rand says, before I tell him about Ruth's wealthy family or that she excelled as class treasurer in high school. The middle cards are pushing me in the direction of belief, opening me up to receive the impact of what will follow.

"She was a very happy woman. . . . She had exactly what she wanted. She married the man she wanted. She had the baby she wanted. She had the freedom to be alone when she wanted. . . . Seven of Cups is 'your wish is granted.'" Hearing the story of the young woman's death would not incline the average listener to this conclusion, but I believe Rand is right. He reminds me of what Ruth's friend Marge Sosnik said in her condolence letter to Bob, a passage I have read so many times I can almost repeat it from memory:

"I was always impressed with her air of complete happiness. One day in a rare moment of serious talk between us, she remarked that she couldn't imagine being married to anyone but you and that she couldn't ask for a better life. . . . I envied her total contentment."

It is a remarkable achievement that, in the short span of her life, she reached a level of satisfaction that most of us strive toward for decades without reaching. Who would not envy her? Yet can she possibly have lived a full and complete life in only twenty-nine years? According to Rand and his cards, she could.

"It's always hard to tell someone, Charlie, that your mother finished what she came to do, but she did. This is the most complete spread of a life finished without loose ends I've ever seen." And now I am torn between an ego that would love to believe, as Rand says, that I was "the ultimate act of creativity of her life" (I haven't mentioned my brother and sister in this session), and a soul that longs for her presence to have extended longer. It was important for me to be born, Rand says, but also important that Bob and Mim have a relationship and that that be part of the shaping of my character. Whether phrased in terms of karma or Christianity, the sentiment is the same—everything is part of a plan. How can I believe that? How can I believe anything else?

"You know, they're not even any cards here of severe suffering, even though death from cancer is a terrible death," says Rand. "It's as if that's all a slightly uncomfortable dream. . . . It would probably be mawkish to say that she was happy until the end, but in a way, it's almost like it didn't touch her. She was so full."

Was she happy until the end? She was "endowed with an unusual amount of equanimity," wrote one of her doctors. Less than a month before her death, her sister-in-law Betsy visited her. "She was in bed and rather weak, but active in her attention to her children. I remember her calling out spelling words for David and making sure you all had everything you needed for school." Even the resolution passed by the Winston-Salem Junior League recording "with deepest sorrow" Ruth's death reads, in part, "In spite of a serious operation six months before her death, Ruth kept up her volunteer work and accepted any future jobs offered to her. She considered her duties a privilege and carried them out with interest, energy, and conscience." Certainly she experienced anguish over the imminent loss of her children and of her husband, and Rand mentions this as well, pointing out her deep concern for what would happen to Bob emotionally after her death. But so much seems to confirm Rand's assertion that Ruth was somehow above the tragedy of her own illness.

The image of Ruth I see when I think of those closing weeks of her life, the short month between the diagnosis of terminal liver cancer and her final, brief coma, is one that came to me a few days ago in a letter from Emily Wilson, the poet. Emily wrote, "I saw her once walking in Reynolda Gardens with your father . . . and I thought she was very pretty and natural." Intellectually, I know that Emily is probably thinking of another time, perhaps after Ruth's breast operation earlier in the year. I don't believe she ever left the house in those last weeks. Emotionally, though, I see the image in all its reality.

Ruth, with the full knowledge of her impending death, walks in a public garden with the man she loves. She takes in the smell of freshly cut grass and blooming roses and gives her attention, more than ever before, to the shapes of leaves and the sound of blue jays bickering overhead, knowing as each impression washes over her senses that it might do so for the last time. She holds her husband's hand a little tighter, and walks on into the sunlight. She is at peace.

After the tarot reading, Rand announces he will go into a full trance. "I don't drool or roll around on the floor," he says, "it's just an aspect of my subpersonality that can sometimes see other things." The "other things" Rand sees include green beans, which he cannot explain, and African-American children, whom he sees Ruth working with, had she lived. He speaks of her commitment to the role of wife and mother, and her interest in music, art, and writing. She was a homebody, more interested in raising her children full-time than in traveling.

Rand allows me to ask specific questions about Ruth's life while he is in his trance. I pull out a coupon from my hotel room on which I have scribbled some thoughts. I am curious to know about Ruth's reaction to her parents' divorce. Ruth never spoke about this issue, even to Bob. Perhaps Rand will.

"Her response to her parents' divorce was deep and angry and . . . the anger she felt she was not able to express easily. In fact, difficulty in expressing anger directly is a kind of trait you share with her." In all the letters I have read about her, in all the memories those who knew her have shared with me, the word anger is absent. Gentleness and grace are mentioned most often. Clearly Ruth was a woman who, if she felt anger, did not express it openly. I can freely admit to acting in exactly the same manner. The open display of emotions is difficult for me, and the open display of deeply felt negative emotions I have often found impossible. My father is the same. With two partners who disliked expressing anger, it is no wonder that Bob and Ruth's marriage was so peaceful.

Rand goes on to say that Ruth's suppression of her anger was a contributing cause of her cancer. Is this possible? After all, her reaction to the news of her father's decision to remarry was several days of sickness. But *was* Ruth angry about her parents' divorce? After living for so many years in a household where the marriage was dead, after leaving that household as soon as she could to start a life of her own, could she really have been

angry? Wouldn't the divorce, finally, turn her remaining anger into sadness and relief? Whatever emotions she felt—anger, remorse, distress, guilt—
she kept them to herself. I probably would have done the same.

Rand also speaks of Ruth in other lives, though he makes no attempt to
force his belief on me. He tells me that Ruth and I have lived many past
lives together, so many that we needed some separation in this life to give
us the opportunity for independent growth. Ruth, he says, has not yet left
the planning state, what the Theosophists call "Devachan." There is no
sense of time in this state, he says, so all of my life has been "like a day of
TV" to her, yet she blesses, guides, and encourages me.

Rand takes a moment to come out of his trance, relaxing his arms and
rolling his head as if to relieve a stiffness in his neck. I know the session is
over. I do my best to make small talk, but somehow that's much harder
than confessing the secrets of my soul. As I start for the door, Rand tells
me to wait.

"I want to give you something," he says. He takes a small wooden box
off a shelf and searches through it, and then brings me a small clear crystal that feels cool in my palm. "This is *so* Santa Fe," he says, "but still, I
just had this feeling you should have it." At home two days later, I will
discover that I left it in my room at the Budget Inn, and I will regret that
this talisman never had the chance to become important.

Do I believe the things Rand Lee told me about my mother? I don't know.
I believe there *are* more things in heaven and earth than are dreamt of in
my philosophy, and that many of those things have to do with the powers
of the human mind. I am no longer eight, so I do not accept notions such
as reincarnation and past life connections just because an adult authority
tells me to. I walk the edge of the ridge—a cynic with an open mind. My
visit with Rand was part of my journey toward Ruth, and if everything he
told me was an elaboration of things I had told him, or luck, or guess-
work, it helped me think about her life in a different light. Call him a
therapist or a psychic or a fraud, but I thanked him and meant it as I
stepped from the dimness of the candlelight back into the blazing sun of
Santa Fe noon.

VIII

When people spoke about my mother it was always in generalities—her wonderful qualities, her gift for making those around her happy, and so on—that didn't tell me anything I didn't know before. It was as if they couldn't see her clearly for what had happened to her. And to us.
—WILLIAM MAXWELL

During the first weeks of September, I sent out over one hundred letters to Ruth's teachers, friends, classmates, family—any name I could attach to both her life and a current address. When I returned from Santa Fe, the first replies waited for me and my trips to the mailbox became adventures back in time. Every day after hearing the idling of the mail truck outside my window, I ran downstairs and out to the curb to look. What I received back from a few letters of inquiry was priceless. For months responses trickled in, some leading to further inquiries. Still I approach the mailbox with hope. Some people I haven't heard from yet. When I began to write the letters, a part of me doubted I would receive anything in response. How could anyone remember after so long? Now I believe.

The first thing that impressed me about the letters was their universally stated praise for my endeavor. No one, not even members of the family that I had perceived as being so quiet, complained about my dredging up painful memories. On the contrary, nearly every letter opened or closed with some sort of validation of my search.

"What a wonderful idea! And what a wonderful mother to discover!" —Marge Sosnik, Winston-Salem

"I think it is wonderful of you to write a memoir about Ruth. She was very dear to so many of us." —Ruth's Aunt Kit, her father's sister

"Writing a memoir about Ruth will bring you many happy true stories about a wonderful person." —Beverly Holliday Cresse, Washington Seminary '53

"I think what you are doing is great, not only for yourself but for future generations." —Jane Lee Taylor Crockett, Washington Seminary '53

"What a wonderful tribute to your mother and how very happy she would be to have such a caring and industrious son." —Jane Young, Washington Seminary '53

The further I travel on this journey, the less dangerous it feels.

Some people wrote back to say that their memories of Ruth had slipped away—"I'm sorry that I cannot remember your mother Ruth that well—thirty years have a way of blurring memories, I'm afraid."

To some, I brought the first news of her death. That event is so central to my identity I had assumed everyone who knew Ruth also knew of her death. "I was saddened to learn Ruth had died so young," wrote one classmate. "I was terribly sorry to hear your mother had passed away, and at such a young age," wrote another. I had expected to be on the receiving end of information about Ruth, but I spread news as well.

Some remembered her death better than her life.

"I attended the funeral service of your Mother, although I must admit that I have no recollection of ever having seen her when she was a student." —Jake Ward, Dean of the College, Emory University

"In 1964, my husband and I went with a couple from here on a special football train to Atlanta to see Tech play University of Miami. When I called mother to say we were in town, she told me Ruth had died and I stayed up there for the funeral. It is so sad to think that the most vivid memory I have of your mother was attending her funeral." —Ruth's Aunt Lou, her father's sister

Of course, like the inscriptions in her yearbooks, the letters contained their share of generic praise.

"I remember your mother as a very pretty, pleasant, and very attractive young woman." —A. Robert Cordell, M.D., Winston-Salem

"Your mother was a lovely young lady who, obviously, got called Home way too soon." —Ruth's first cousin, Billy Warren

"She was probably the sweetest and kindest person I ever knew."
—Ruth's older brother, Buddy

The letters work like a Seurat painting—each dot carries little meaning, but together they begin to create a picture.
"Sally was in a car pool with your mother. She was quiet and retiring. She developed breast cancer and yet still did her part as best she could."
—Rev. E. Dudley Colhoun, Winston-Salem
"As best I remember, her complexion wasn't all that great. She was fair and had the usual problems with pimples as a teenager. . . . She was a natural as a mother—I never remember her getting angry or yelling at you (I suppose she did some time), but she always seemed to have such patience and to always know what to do. I believe you children were her life."
—Ruth's sister, Glenn
"She was a true rarity—a woman very happy with her life. As a matter of fact, she told me that she planned to have one more baby. I also dimly remember that she had a yearning to visit Scotland and maybe even live there for awhile." —Marge Sosnik
"I love to look at you, Elizabeth, and David because I see Ruth in each of you, and as her friend I cherish my memories of her. She was very young and very brave. I honor deeply her short life." —Emily Wilson

And each fleck of color reflects off of those already on the canvas and gives them depth. Her desire to live in Scotland, for instance. While I first see this as a reflection of my own plans to spend six months in England, I come to see it in the context of her life. I remember her enthusiastic letter to her father about the Highland Games and her Scottish Terrier. I recall a file in the box of papers I borrowed from my father that included her certificate of membership in the American Clan Gregor Society. A slide of her in full Scottish regalia flashes through my mind. And of course, I return to myself, equating her own interest in her Scottish heritage to my search for her.

Forty-four young women graduated with Ruth from Washington Seminary in 1953. Through the alumni department of Westminster, the school that subsumed the Seminary that summer, I obtained addresses for thirty-five of the survivors. Nearly half of those wrote to me with memories of

Ruth. The Washington Seminary Class of 1953 has proved the most faithful group of correspondents one could hope to discover. I only hope I have the chance to meet them all some day. In their letters, I have found the most crisp portrayal of Ruth yet. The provide not only general impressions, but details of specific events. They each remember something different, yet all their memories fit together like the pieces of a puzzle—none seems inconsistent with the others. Some knew her in her grade school days, when she attended Druid Hills Elementary School. Others met her when she transferred to the Seminary in the seventh grade. Some came to the Seminary only in their last two years of high school, but even they remembered Ruth.

Some of the questions raised by inscriptions in Ruth's yearbook were answered by her classmates, who brought me further into that secret circle that made up their class. Sandra Epstein explained to me about the "drama lessons with Miss Russell." Nannette Crowdus elaborated on the trip to Washington. Each new letter brought a fresh discovery. I began to feel that, because I was usurping their memories, I was becoming a part of the family that was their high school class—a class with strong ties even after over forty years. I wonder less about how Ruth might fit in had she lived than I do about how I might fit in if I crashed their reunion.

"My friendship with Ruth goes back even further than some, since we were together at Druid Hills Elementary School before we each transferred to Washington Seminary. My earliest memory and one I often think of is that my very first prom was in the seventh grade and guess where it was? At the Candler's house on Lullwater Road. Of course we weren't dating at that age, so all of our parents brought us and picked us up. We wore long dresses, danced, played games (probably Spin the Bottle!) and had refreshments. That was in the spring of 1947, and it was a wonderful party. Not everyone in the seventh grade was invited; I remember it not being too large, and clearly Ruth and I were pretty good friends." —Constance Wilson Treloar

"When we were in grammar school (age 7, 8?) I vaguely remember going to [Ruth's] home. We had a private [drama] instructor a Miss Edith Russell. We met on Saturday mornings and there were maybe seven of us, mostly girls. I don't remember one person in that group other than your mother.

Ruth had the courage to really act out the parts Miss Russell gave us. I believe I was too shy then to do much. Your mother always encouraged and was the first to say let so and so do that, I'll do something else. She was the hostess and knew how to share, even at an early age." —Sandra G. Epstein

"Indeed I remember Ruth Candler. We were, I think, good friends. I remember her as very smart, gracious, unassuming, attractive and always beautifully dressed and groomed in her cashmere sweaters with either a collar, pearls, or a scarf. Our mothers took us to a variety of concerts (our fathers declining that treat!), and we often rode together to the Auditorium for the performances." —Nannette McBurney Crowdus

"My fondest memories are of those who have made lasting impressions on my life. Your Mom was one of those. She walked with grace and carried kindness in her arms. I always remember her smiling no matter. If the rest of us were unhappy about anything—exams, the weather, bad date, no date—it just seems she coped, and coping is not what young girls do best!" —Sandra G. Epstein

"She wasn't cliquish as high-school girls tend to be. She seemed to be above all that. School seemed to be so easy for her. I believe once she showed me that she had a photographic mind, so learning was second nature for her. I remember she was a little shy, but took part in everything in our high school. Maybe she wasn't really shy, just not as loud and crazy as some of us. Being silly for Ruth was showing us how double jointed she was; bending her arms back until they looked broken. I also remember her always eating fresh fruit for dessert at lunch time, while most of us ate junk food." —Beverly Holliday Cresse

"I was the 'new girl.' I really was not in the 'in group,' but I always remember how nice your mother was to me. She did not make me feel unwelcome as some of the girls did. I never heard her gossip or use bad language. We sometimes went to the Varsity at lunch together." —Joanne Taber Young

"We did not move in the same financial circles as did many of my classmates at the Seminary. I well remember the slights and snubs of many of those cruel little girls. Not so with your mother. If financial position gives one the right to snobbery, then she probably had a better right than anyone at that school. She was unfailingly kind, pleasant and polite to all, not just her immediate circle. Her mother, whom I met one afternoon when Ruth invited me home after school, was the same way." —Elizabeth Millis Ormsby

"Your mother was a wonderful person who was most friendly and made me feel welcome when I arrived as a new student." —Bettye C. Maddox

"We had quite a trip to Eisenhower's inauguration! There we were in our heels and gloves and hats. I know, it's difficult to imagine getting all dressed up to sit up all night on a train. My mother and your grandmother decided that Ruth and I should have the opportunity to have a really nice meal. So we, along with our chaperone Mrs. Peacock, left the others and taxied off through the traffic to dine at the Mayflower Hotel. You can imagine how incredibly crowded it was, but we had a grand time trying to spot famous people." —Nannette McBurney Crowdus

"There was a period of time when she had a notebook. Every day she would write a new word out of the dictionary in it and that way learn a new word every day. How many sixteen-year-olds would do that?" —Jane Lee Taylor Crockett

"Ruth was a good close friend. She was one of the first to have me in her home to spend the night. I'll never forget that first visit. Early in the morning, Ruth placed an order for breakfast by calling the kitchen on her telephone, by punching a lot of buttons on her phone! This was in 1948. I had never seen buttons on a phone before. I was very impressed." —Ruthe Yeargan Proctor

"I do remember playing pool downstairs at Ruth's. I'd never seen a pool table except in the movies." —Jane Lee Taylor Crockett

"You have undoubtedly heard about the Seminary's May Day doings. Truly it was a spectacular achievement for a school of its size. Your mother and I had enjoyed ballet lessons growing up, although I stuck with it a lot longer than she. Nevertheless, she was always in the final ballet number, usually performed to Tchaikovsky." —Nannette McBurney Crowdus

"I know she spent her share of time meeting your father at the foot of the Seminary's driveway after school (being met by a guy after school was really something), eating at Rusty's and the Varsity, going to movies at the Fox, the Paramount, and the Rialto, attending high school sorority and fraternity dances on Friday nights, and fraternity parties at Emory and Georgia Tech. Looking back on the scene now, I have to believe we led charmed lives with few cares. Exquisite hoop-skirted ball gowns, cashmere sweaters, our own cars as soon as we hit sixteen, etc., etc. The Korean War intruded a bit—there were those we knew who went off to war—but somehow it didn't seem real at the time." —Nannette McBurney Crowdus

"Our friendship led to invitations to Cumberland. I have had a lifelong affair with the sound of the ocean and seashells. I believe it was because of Cumberland and Ruth. There was a time when your grandmother drove a group of us to Cumberland after school. We had a picnic in the car and Ruth taught us a new song to sing to a full moon. She played the ukulele and we sang." —Ruthe Yeargan Proctor

"We all went many places in her new car that Danny gave her for her birthday. Ruth and I went to the Varsity a lot. Sometimes we didn't have enough money on us to order anything, but Ruth, in her nicest voice and sweet smile would get a plate of dill pickles for us—free! We enjoyed having long serious talks about Theosophy and life while we ate our pickles! Ruth knows you and is very proud to be your mother (it's because of the long talks at the Varsity that I know this). She was an angel in disguise then and is now. I regard her as an instrument in my life that gave me deep faith in the Lord at such an early age." —Ruthe Yeargan Proctor

So many images, so many details, so much life. And so many places, again, where her life criss-crosses mine, so many images of my own, from meeting a friend in that same lobby of the Mayflower Hotel in Washington, to playing pool in the basement of my grandmother's house on that same pool table, to eating onion rings (the best on the planet) at the Varsity (the largest drive-in in the world, "No food over 24 hours old").

Another musical instrument is added to Ruth's personal orchestra, and I remember a stringless ukulele in a battered case resting under those same eaves that sheltered the trunk in the attic. Did she eat fruit instead of junk food for her health? Now they tell us such a diet helps us avoid cancer. Has there been a time since the 1940s when little girls and their friends were given private in-home drama instruction? And how I wish I could have been hidden in the back seat at one of those long talks over pickles at the Varsity—finally a report of Ruth's opening up about her faith and who knows what else.

I stand in awe of the depth of memory with which Ruth's classmates are blessed. Without the continuation of Ruth's presence in their lives to remind them of her qualities, they have retrieved these details from her past. Washington Seminary was torn down forty years ago, but it still lives.

The first response I received from the Washington Seminary Class of 1953 was a long phone message from Wight Crawford, the woman who had written about "singing orgies at recess" in Ruth's yearbook. "Ruth was one of my dearest friends at the Seminary," she said. "I want to tell you all about our trip to Cumberland and Ruth's mother scaring us to death with ghost stories. . . . We had a little singing trio, and oh, we thought we were the Andrews Sisters. . . . I miss her, I miss her terribly, but she lives on with a group of people who never forget and those were our golden years. The Seminary years were the best years of our lives and your mother just loved every minute." Wight's message wandered, but her memories seemed clear and I called her back as soon as I could.

She told me more about the trip to Cumberland she and some other girls took with Ruth the summer after eighth grade. She remembered expeditions to the old deserted Carnegie house at Dungeness. She spoke of afternoon swims at Callanwolde. "We thought nothing of it," she said. "Ruth's grandfather just happened to have a pool and almost no one else did."

Wight was a confessed member of the wilder group at the Seminary, and some of her references to "we did this," and "we did that," are probably memories of escapades that did not include Ruth. Still, it was refreshing to know that some of her friends, in the words of Wight, "just jammed." They smoked cigarettes behind the school building and drove around Buckhead without licenses when their parents were out. "It never occurred to us," said Wight, "that our parents could feel the hood of the car to find out what we'd been up to."

"We were always cooking up something," she said. "It was us against the parents." But Wight also described Ruth's mother as "just like one of us." "Mrs. Candler told wonderful stories, and she was always game for anything." That description held true a generation later. I can recall Màmà taking her grandchildren to rock concerts, amusement parks—whatever they were up for she was up for.

Wight said, "I never saw Ruth without a smile on her face. She was full of fun, joy, and life." Wight still had several editions of the Washington Seminary yearbook from before her senior year as well as snapshots taken at Cumberland during the summer of 1949. When she invited me to visit her during a trip to Atlanta, I eagerly accepted.

Wight lives in an apartment in Buckhead that's wildly eccentric. The interior decor looks like an antique shop, only more cluttered and eclectic than most. Her unit is on the third floor, and the decor begins on the flight of steps leading up to her door—concrete lions, an antique sofa, plastic greenery, a potpourri of statuary and indoor and outdoor furniture, an oriental rug, gilt sconces, a mirror with gold frame, a dead plant, a car seat, and some wet towels.

I ring the bell and am met by a southern accent on the other side of the door. In a moment, Wight is showing me into the apartment that, if anything, is furnished in an even more bizarre manner than the stairwell.

"Oh, you look just like your mother," she tells me. "I'm so glad you came to visit." Wight's hair is long and black—it's hard for me to tell if either condition is natural. Her voice, gait, and dress (a fur coat over jeans— she has just come from "the lake"), all speak of someone younger than what I know must be her sixty-plus years. During my brief visit I meet her boyfriend, who looks about my age, her daughter, who looks about my age, and her granddaughter, aged two. The room we chat in is lit by candles and a fire that trickles ashes onto the hearth to the concern of no one. I am at once charmed and appalled.

We take an hour or so to look over old yearbooks together, Wight remembering her friends, and in some cases how they died—one in a car accident not long after graduation, one from anorexia before anyone had heard of anorexia, one from nicotine poisoning because she smoked while wearing a nicotine patch. I show her Ruth's senior yearbook, and while she is not able to unravel all its secret lingo she does identify "Stew Pot" as Anne Stewart Morris. "Cat Woman" was a fictional being, the central character of an often repeated dirty rhyme that Wight claims Stewart and Ruth coined down at Cumberland. She shows me pictures of my grandmother in her bathing suit on the beach, and one of Ruth and Glenn in bathing caps playing in the ocean.

In a yearbook she finds the picture of the Science Club in which the rebellious faction all surreptitiously raised a middle finger to the photographer. I discover that my father was in a play at the Seminary during the 1951-1952 school year, playing George Biddle in *Room for One More*. Ruth served as stage manager. Over the years Ruth's picture appeared most consistently with the Glee Club and the French Club. Wight's earliest yearbook is from 1949, and Ruth's eighth-grade picture shows her with shoulder-length frizzy hair.

"She really looks like her daughter here," I say.

"Oh, I wish you had brought some pictures," says Wight, and I am saddened and embarrassed by the fact that, in my eagerness to make my own discoveries, I have neglected to consider what others might want to discover.

"Now let me see," says Wight, picking up the scrapbook. "Someplace I've got some more of her from that year."

The resemblance to Elizabeth is even more evident in snapshots that Wight pulls out of her scrapbook—pictures of Ruth and her friends cutting up behind the school, prancing in a chorus line and raising their skirts well above their knees to show a little leg.

In the front of the eighth-grade yearbook, Ruth has written to Wight "Shake! Ruth (Connors) Candler (I wish)." A new mystery—I haven't heard of a crush named Connors.

The yearbooks reveal other tidbits that anchor me in the times and the place—a picture of girls performing in black face at a carnival, a large model of the newfangled "television" used in the 1951 May Day celebration, the boisterous joy with which Ruth's sophomore class reportedly mounted the stairs for their first session in upperclass study hall.

Wight's mind flits from classmate to classmate, from one memory to another. "Your grandmother was a noted beauty," she says, "and her white hair—she was known for that. . . . Ruth was always playing the piano. . . .

Mademoiselle Groleau threw an eraser at Stewart Morris . . ." and so on. Frequently her memories have nothing to do with Ruth, but visiting with her is a delight nonetheless. With the dinner hour fast approaching, I finally excuse myself. I embrace this classmate of my mother's as if we have known each other for years, and as I make my way down her cluttered stairwell I recall what she said to me at the end of our phone conversation. "I'm so happy you're coming. I thought I would never get to see Ruth again in any form, but now I'll have that chance."

She may be eccentric, but no one would argue that Wight is full of life, and in that vivacity I see Ruth and how she might be had she lived. Wight may have gotten as much out of our visit as I did, and I realize that even now, Ruth can accomplish wonderful things—casting me into this situation where I helped someone relive the memories of a time gone but not forgotten, the happiest time of her life.

IX

Dear Ruth and Bob, I wish for both of you every happiness. I hope that as the years unfold there will come to your united lives a richness and depth that will surpass all of your dreams.

—J. MILTON RICHARDSON

October 1. Before today, I knew one fact about my parents' wedding—that it took place August 23, 1955. I knew this because the date is engraved on a plaque affixed to the lid of the chest holding their silver flatware. Growing up, every time I set the table for a dinner party or a holiday meal, I saw that date. I assumed they were married at St. Luke's, because they both attended that church and it played an important role in their courtship.

I learned the story of their wedding from two albums filled with pictures and mementos. My sister, not wanting to entrust them to the mail, waited until I was visiting in Winston-Salem to give them to me. September was winding down, and I came to return Lucy to her mother after a visit, picked up the wedding albums, and headed back to Kansas City on the next flight.

The next morning, after Jordan had gone to school and Janice had left for her student-teaching job, I sat alone for the first time in ten days, and Lucy's absence finally hit me. I feel a mixture of depression and exhaustion after a visit with Lucy—like the feeling I had at boarding school at the end of a dance weekend—after pouring so much emotion into such a short period, one feels empty. I miss Lucy always, but I miss her most when her voice still rings in my ears and I can still feel her little hands' embrace. In such a melancholy mood I approached the wedding albums, but I couldn't help but be caught up in the happiness the books revealed.

Like Ruth's high school yearbook, the wedding albums smelled of our attic in Winston-Salem, a mixture of mothballs and aging pine resin. But there was another smell here, too. A wedding album smell—some combination of old newspaper, fake leather, photographic chemicals, and love. It was the smell of the past. With that smell full in my head, I opened the "Bridal Memories" book and, like Lucy "reading" her picture books, began to recreate the story of the wedding using only the illustrations.

The Atlanta Journal & Constitution, May 1, 1955: "Ruth Candler's Troth To R. W. Lovett Told, Chapel Ceremony at St. Philip's to Unite Popular Members of Atlanta's Young Set." My only assumption about their wedding—that it took place at St. Luke's—is proved wrong on the first page. Aunt Betsy will tell me that Ruth and Bob decided against getting married at St. Luke's because of the large size of the nave and also because St. Philip's was just a few blocks from Ruth's parents' house on West Wesley Road.

The newspaper article announces that the wedding will take place in late summer, not naming the specific date and time of Tuesday, August

The family at Callanwolde, Christmas Eve, 1954. From left to right: Betsy, Ruth, Bo, Màmà, Chick (Buddy's eldest), Buddy, Howard, Claire (Buddy's wife), and Glenn.

25, at 10:30 in the morning. The fact that Ruth and Bob are both full-time college students may explain why they choose that date, for how else can they hope to allow themselves time to deal with the tasks even a small wedding presents to the bride and groom. This is the public beginning of the engagement, but I wonder when, exactly, my father popped the question.

I know he is in class this morning, so I send him a fax. Late in the afternoon the answer to "When did you and Ruth get engaged?" comes back: "Ring given December 24, 1954." Among the pictures that various family members have sent me are two of the family posed on the staircase of Callanwolde on Christmas Eve, 1954. Ruth's left hand is not quite visible, but she does seem to be fidgeting with her fingers and there's an excitement to her smile. Perhaps it is my imagination, or perhaps I am naturally inclined to look at her and no one else, but Ruth glows in these photos.

There is a third album that Elizabeth gave me—Ruth's book of pictures and announcements from other people's weddings. Here I see weddings were nothing new to Ruth. At sixteen she first played the role of bridesmaid. She served as one of twelve bridal attendants in her cousin's wedding and one of seven in her brother Buddy's ceremony. Three years later, she stood as maid of honor at the marriage of her brother Bo to her friend Betsy. The final pictures in this album show grown and married Ruth, the mother of two, as matron of honor for her sister Glenn in 1961. Ruth looks consistently radiant—from an excited sixteen-year-old being included in adult celebrations to the knowing older sister.

Three pages of Ruth's own wedding album display the invitations to parties in honor of the bride and groom. Connie Wilson, a friend from Washington Seminary, hosted a luncheon at the Peachtree Golf Club on August 10th. On the 19th, Aunt Kit gave a lunch at the Piedmont Driving Club and later that same day another friend threw a kitchen shower where Ruth received a garbage can from her mother and a garlic press from her future mother-in-law. The next evening, Saturday, Danny and Popee held a reception at Callanwolde, and on Monday night Bob's parents, Helen and Heyward, hosted the rehearsal dinner at Hart's restaurant. A whirlwind week before the wedding, but not nearly what it might have been.

With the wealth and standing of the Candler family, Ruth and Bob could easily have chosen to have the wedding in the nave of the Episcopal cathedral on Peachtree Road rather than in a small side chapel. They could have had parties all summer instead of just a few the week before the ceremony. But "neither one of them was very showy," said Wilson Sneed, one of the priests who officiated at the marriage. Ruth, according to Aunt Betsy, who would serve as her matron of honor, had no interest in a big fancy wedding.

"She really copied my wedding from the year before," said Betsy. "Same dress, same location, even the bridesmaids' dresses were similar."

In the weeks before the service, the presents poured in, and Ruth kept a log of them—151 in all. In the far column of the list, Ruth placed a check mark on every line, indicating a thank-you note written. One hundred and fifty-one thank-you notes, not counting those for kitchen shower gifts or those to the hosts and hostesses of parties. Doubtless much of Ruth's summer vacation was taken up with the careful penning of, "So many thanks for the paperweight. . . ."

The list of gifts is both impressive and shockingly dated. My father dabbled with a pipe for a time, but neither he nor Ruth smoked at the time of their wedding. Still, they received thirteen ashtrays, two cigarette boxes, and a table lighter. Now, such gifts seem in extraordinarily bad taste. Of course, they received heaps of silver, china, and crystal. I recognize several names on the list as members of Ruth's class at Washington Seminary, and a few as friends of Ruth and Bob from St. Luke's, but many are unknown to me, doubtless friends of the Candler family who have long since moved on to other friendships, other towns, or other lives. I also recognize many of the gifts themselves—the furnishings of my childhood kitchen and dining room.

Exactly seven years before the day of my birth, The *Atlanta Constitution* reported, "Tuesday morning in a quiet ceremony in the presence of their families, Miss Ruth Candler became the bride of Robert William Lovett. The ceremony took place at 10:30 A.M. in the Mikell Memorial Chapel at the Cathedral of St. Philip, with the Rev. Wilson Sneed and the Rev. Alonzo Wood officiating." Rev. Sneed was a priest at St. Luke's who had known Ruth and Bob during the Youth Group days. Rev. Wood was Bob's uncle, and had officiated at the wedding of Bob's parents twenty-two years earlier.

Glenn, at fourteen, served as her sister's maid of honor, and Betsy was matron of honor. Bob's younger brother Chip served as best man.

"I remember when they announced their marriage," Bob's sister Susan wrote to me. "Chip immediately said he wanted to be best man, and I said I wanted to be flower girl. Well, he was best man, but they didn't have a flower girl. I got to keep the bride's book which was fine, and I did catch the bride's bouquet!" Susan was ten.

If everyone at the wedding signed the guest book, forty-six people attended the ceremony, including the bride and groom and the two officiants. The service was short and simple—the rite laid out in the 1928 *Book of Common Prayer*. After the vows had been exchanged and the pronunciation of marriage proclaimed, one of the officiants offered my parents this blessing:

> God the Father, God the Son, God the Holy Ghost, bless, preserve, and keep you; the Lord mercifully with his favour look upon you, and fill you with all spiritual benediction and grace; that ye may so live together in this life, that in the world to come ye may have life everlasting. Amen.

St. Philip's is an impressive gothic cathedral that stands on a wedge of land formed by the intersection of Andrews Drive and Peachtree Road in Buckhead. To me, St. Philip's has always meant Easter—we often visited Atlanta for Easter during the glories of Southern spring and attended services at the cathedral. There trumpets blared and choirs sang and the organ rang out and all was pomp and ceremony as we asserted that "The Lord is risen indeed!"

Late in the afternoon of a wet day in Atlanta, as the clouds are finally starting to break and the rain is tapering off, I will stop by Mikell Chapel. Compared to the vast formality of the Cathedral's nave, it is a simple space—dim, quiet, and peaceful. Only ten short pews line each side of the aisle. Down the left wall is a row of small stained-glass windows, and a multifoil window above the altar incorporates the words "Greater Love hath no man than this—That man lay down his life for his friends." The

Mr. & Mrs. Robert W. Lovett, August 23, 1955.

floor is polished flagstone. The walls are paneled below shoulder level in rich dark wood, and the ceiling is a simplified hammer-beam. As I usually do on those rare occasions when I find myself alone in a place of worship, I will slip into a pew and kneel to pray. I will pray that being in this place might bring me closer to Ruth and to an understanding of the marriage that began here. I will pray for guidance in seeking out her life. And I will pray for peace for the soul of my departed mother. Then I will stand, walk down the aisle where Mr. and Mrs. Robert W. Lovett took their first few steps as a married couple, and emerge into the late afternoon sunlight finally breaking the grip of gray that holds Atlanta on that day.

Following the wedding, according to the newspaper account, "the bride's parents entertained at a breakfast at their home on West Wesley Road." Many of the pictures in the wedding album are of the party that followed the service. The bride and groom, with and without the rest of the wedding party, pose in the formal living room; the guests crowd into the front hallway or watch as the couple drives away. Ruth's captivating smile is at its best. Bob, in spite of his dislike of picture taking, makes a real effort. If his smile seems either forced or absent in many shots, I, at least, know this has more to do with his feelings toward cameras than toward his new wife.

I see the bride and groom sharing a champagne toast—Bob with one hand in his pocket. The feeding of wedding cake is here too, Ruth and Bob helping each other through the first slice of a double ring cake large enough to feed many times the number of guests.

Two pictures in particular strike me—one for its familiarity, one for its unfamiliarity. In the first, on a white table cloth spread across the pool table in the basement, the wedding presents are arranged for display. I see that chest of silver marked with the date as well as dozens of other pieces of silver, china, crystal, and cookware that filled the cabinets, shelves, and sideboards of my childhood home. The silver tea service from the corner table in the living room, the candlesticks from the dining room table, the "old" china from the house in the mountains, the Revere ware that hung in the pantry, and the silver bread basket that emerged from the corner cabinet on Thanksgiving and Christmas—all these are together, untarnished, unchipped, and unfaded—as new as the marriage they celebrate.

The other picture is of the two fathers, my two grandfathers, shaking

Charles Howard Candler, Jr. and Heyward Meriwether Lovett, my two grandfathers.

hands. Ruth's father, Howard, I knew well. Bob's father, Heyward, was struck by a car and killed in 1958. I know even less about him than I did about Ruth. In the pictures of family at the wedding, his is the one unfamiliar face, discernible only twice—once in the background of the crowded front hall, and once where he shakes hands with Ruth's father, the two men holding up their champagne glasses. Like their children, Howard smiles broadly showing white teeth and Heyward seems to force a small grin through tightly pressed lips. Heyward is a handsome, rugged-looking man—taller than Howard by an inch or two. His high forehead gives way to carefully slicked-back wavy dark hair and he wears a thin mustache. I tried for a long time to figure out who he reminded me of, and my wife finally pointed it out—Walt Disney. Heyward's thick neck and deeply set eyes give him a strong and intense look—a startling contrast to his pencil-thin bespectacled son. I have often thought that my father seemed to fit better in Ruth's family than his own, and this photograph of a grandfather whom I knew so well, and who was such a friend to my father, shaking hands with a grandfather who is a complete stranger to me, does little to shake me from that conception.

The final pictures in the album show Ruth in her going-away outfit—a polka-dot blouse and a simple suit, a corsage on her right lapel, and white gloves. Friends and family throw rice as she and Bob come out the front door, and wave and take pictures as they drive away. It is a wedding like any other.

Cards, notes, and telegrams arrived congratulating Ruth and Bob. "They are both very fine young people and deserve the very best life can give them," wrote one friend to Ruth's mother. "I hope that as the years unfold there will come to your united lives a richness and a depth that will surpass all of your dreams," wrote Rev. Milton Richardson, who had served as their rector at St. Luke's. If any of these well-wishers peeked into Ruth and Bob's lives eight years later, they would see all these wishes coming true. If they stopped by nine years later, they would arrive twenty-four hours short of Ruth's terminal diagnosis.

After the wedding came the wedding trip. Ruth was now Mrs. Lovett, so the accommodations may not have been what she was used to from trips to Mexico City or New York with her parents. They drove to the mountains of North Carolina, visiting Biltmore House in Asheville, which I have toured several times, most recently with Lucy, Janice, and Jordan. They stayed at a resort village next to Fontana Dam in the Great Smokies. According to the brochure that Ruth saved in the wedding album, their cottage had been part of the Dam's construction village. Ruth took pictures of the dam, the mountains, Biltmore House, and the white clapboard cottage where they stayed, carefully numbering the slides and making a log that described each view. Ruth applied her organizational skills to the honeymoon just as she had to the wedding book and the thank-yous. The trip was anything but glamorous, and I doubt either Ruth or Bob had ever been as happy. As for the more traditional activities of the honeymoon—I would know nothing of such things if Ruth were alive, and I don't think the fact of her death makes them any more my business.

Ruth's wedding is the most documented event in her life. In these two albums that I now carefully replace in their deteriorating boxes, are pictures, autographs, newspaper clippings, letters, matchbooks, and a 1943 sixpence that has left the permanent impression of George VI on the scotch tape that holds it into place. Here, Ruth set out to recreate the story of her wedding, and shortly after what would have been her fortieth anniversary, I see that she succeeded. Her illustrations have let me tell the story.

But the story is external. Nowhere does Ruth write what she was feeling. Like the sacrament of marriage itself, the albums are only the outward and visible sign of an inward grace I will never see. But the outward sign is there, and I have no doubt about the depth of the inner happiness it signifies.

X

*And Ruth said, Intreat me not to leave thee, or to return
from following after thee: for whither thou goest, I will
go; and where thou lodgest, I will lodge: thy people shall
be my people, and thy God my God: Where thou diest,
will I die, and there will I be buried: the Lord do so to
me, and more also, if aught but death part thee and me.*
                                    —THE BOOK OF RUTH

The Book of Ruth is one of the shortest in the Bible. It tells of a woman
who chose to leave the homeland of her parents because of her devotion
to her husband and his family. It also tells of someone who loses a spouse
through death, yet finds a way to go on and live a full life.

Talking on the phone one afternoon, my father uncovers another memory.
    Shortly after the wedding, Ruth and Bob sit in a restaurant in Atlanta.
An acquaintance stops by the table and introduces his companion.
    "This is Mr. and Mrs. Candler," the man says, and Ruth does not
correct him because she knows he does not see her as a person, but only as
a name, a name meaningless in most of the country, but one that blinds
people to her humanity in her hometown—Candler.

It is late October and I have come to Winston-Salem to pick up Lucy for a
visit. This morning she's at preschool, so I have borrowed the key to my
childhood house at 1943 Robinhood Road from my father. He and Mim
moved out of this house two months ago, and it is still on the market.
Today I will have a chance to see it as Ruth first saw it—empty.

"Ruth said early on that she wanted to leave," Daddy told me during our
long conversation at Bear Knob. "She thought you couldn't have any kind

of normal life in Atlanta being a Candler." She didn't want to spend the rest of her life being gawked at, and she didn't want her children raised where people would treat them a certain way because of their mother's maiden name. Ruth had social status, recognition, a wealthy family—the things that many people believe they want. But those things didn't interest her. I believe what she wanted more than anything else was to be normal, to be just like all the other mothers on her block, to raise her children in a place where they would be treated like all the other children.

I push open the familiar front door and am met with an unfamiliar hollow sound—the echo of a door opening into an empty house. Without their furnishings, the rooms seem smaller. The paneling in the den looks more elegant without being covered by Ruth's piano, and a cluttering of furniture, prints, and paintings. The hardwood floors need refinishing, but I can see how they would have looked thirty-two years ago when Ruth first saw them. Only at the edges of the room where no rugs covered them are they scratched to a duller color by three decades of dog paws. The downstairs rooms—kitchen, dining room, living room, den, and porch—are arranged in a circle we used to race around. Even stripped bare they call forth a flood of memories, none of which contain Ruth.

In the Spring of 1962, when Ruth was pregnant with me, my father was offered a job as an English instructor at Wake Forest College. The college had recently moved to Winston-Salem from a small town in eastern North Carolina, and he had no idea when he joined the faculty in 1962 he would eventually be teaching at one of the leading universities in the South.

Upstairs at Robinhood Road are four bedrooms, including two that were mine at various times. At thirteen, I moved to the attic to make room for my youngest brother John. Now I climb those steps one last time, my feet sliding on threadbare carpet. The attic was the retreat of three adolescent boys over the years. In the closet under the eaves was an old slide projector and a box of slides taken by Ruth. I can remember laughing at the pictures she took of this house just after they moved in—hideous wallpaper in the hall, dining room, and master bedroom, and a paucity of furniture. I remember Robinhood Road as a cluttered house. Not only did Ruth and

Bob accumulate more in the next two years, including a wonderful chest from Callanwolde, but when Mim, an orphan, moved in, she brought all her parents' furniture. Looking at pictures of the house with a few 1950s-style chairs and tables, ugly wallpaper, and nothing hanging on the walls amused me, but now, as I walk back down two flights of stairs to the kitchen, I realize that the funny house in the slides, and not the cluttered cozy home I remember, was Ruth's house.

My parents traveled to Winston-Salem to go house shopping.

"Ruth spent some of the time resting at her friend Bungy Valk's house," said Daddy. Bungy's husband, Henry, was the doctor who would prescribe the pain medication during the last weeks of Ruth's life and who would sign her death certificate. Bungy would sit with me and David and Elizabeth on the floor of the den in the house my father was out shopping for, and play blocks while the rest of the family attended Ruth's funeral.

They arrived at their new home in June, Ruth accomplishing the move while seven months pregnant.

Standing in the kitchen, completely remodeled in the early 1970s, I make a mental note of all the changes in the house since Ruth knew it. Not only have rooms changed color, wallpaper, carpeting, and furnishings several times each, but structural changes have taken place, too—a deck added to the back, the screen porch turned into a sun room. A big house with lots of bedrooms is good for raising a family, but did Ruth know just how well this house would adapt to meet our needs? I look out the back window at a yard that has seen dozens of dogs since the days of Jamie, her Scottie, and that has undergone at least a half-dozen major landscaping renovations. Beyond is an open field, owned by a neighbor, but used as a play area for Ruth's children and their friends. Certainly she saw the potential there. I feel an inevitable sadness knowing I will never stand in this house again. This house, and the home Ruth made here, continued to shape my life long after she was gone. Now it will pass out of the family, and one of my last tangible links to Ruth will be gone.

"Grandpa understood the move to Winston-Salem," said Daddy. After all, he had bought his farm south of Atlanta in 1955. He missed Ruth and her family, certainly ("I sure do miss Bob and the children and I am looking forward to seeing you again soon"), but, judging from Daddy's recollections, he sympathized with her decision to move out of the family nest, to step away from Callanwolde Sunday nights and Cumberland summers toward an independent life.

Ruth's Aunt Lou, her father's sister, who had lived in Callanwolde since she was eight, left Atlanta for Florida after her marriage in the early 1930s.

"Ruth had tremendous admiration for Aunt Lou," my father said.

As for the rest of the family—"They saw the move as a little adventure," said Daddy. The Lovetts off for a jaunt from which they would return with tales to tell around the dinner table. "When are you coming back?" they would ask. "How long do you think you'll stay?" For them Atlanta was, and always would be, home. The roots grew too deep to pull up and they could not imagine Ruth and her family would not return after their little experiment.

Taking care not to trip on the dimly lit stairs, I descend into the basement, the part of the house that has changed least since 1962. There is not much here—a washer and dryer, a storage room, a furnace and water heater, the pockmarked wall where I used to play darts. In the back corner is a small separate room that was once my father's study. Here Ruth laid tile on the floor while eight months pregnant. That tile is still there. The cheap metal shelving that held my father's books still stands. Daddy didn't use this room much after he finished his Ph.D. in 1969, but I did my homework here sometimes—swiveling in his old fashioned desk chair and typing essays on his Smith Corona. The shelves are empty now. I stand on tiptoe and run my hand across the unseen dusty top of one of the cases looking for . . .

My fingers touch a worn old school textbook—the type that as a book dealer I would have dismissed as worthless. The words "Standard French Grammar" are barely legible on the spine. I open the cover and can't resist a smile at the irony of this book's being the only personal object left in the house. "Ruth Candler, Washington Seminary" is written on the endpaper in blue ink. Below that, Ruth's address and, best of all, two huge, red lipstick blots. The permanent print of my mother's lips, unseen for thirty years. All the years I lived in this house, all the hours I spent in this room, this book sat here. On blank pages Ruth has written Paul O'Shields' name, initials, fraternity, and college in fancy script. I imagine no one has touched this book since Ruth, unpacking a box of things from Atlanta, tossed it up on top of this bookcase. Walking out of the house for the last time, I carry this relic of her school days under my arm and marvel that it has waited for me all this time.

The Atlanta family may have thought that the Lovetts would come back, but we didn't. Winston-Salem will always be my home town and I will always feel like a visitor in Atlanta. My mother was raised as a Candler, but she saw the value in raising me as a Lovett. I did benefit from the wealth of her family—I went to superb private schools, I spent my summers at a home in the mountains—but I also benefited from her escape from Atlanta, the seat of that wealth. I like to think she would have loved Bear Knob, our home in the mountains, because, while it was a second home that provided us with escape from the city, it was not a luxurious mansion overlooking a golf course. We spent our summers putting up hay and gardening, not playing bridge and tennis. My life has been a remarkable combination of the opportunities afforded by wealth and simple values symbolized by that courageous move Ruth insisted on making.

I lost something in that move, though. I see my Atlanta family seldom, and when I do visit, I feel like a guest in someone else's club. My cousins, aunts, and uncles are always kind and gracious, but I do not feel like a real part of that family. David and Elizabeth lived in Atlanta, if only for a short time. I have always felt, if not always consciously thought, that because of that, they must be closer to the cousins, better understood by the grandparents, more a part of the family than I am.

I'm sure Ruth knew that by moving us to North Carolina she would diminish the place of her children in the Candler family, that we would never experience that sense of unity that came with daily or at least weekly interaction. She didn't know that her death would ultimately compound our distance from the family, but she understood the consequences of the move. As much as I would like to know my family better, as much as I would like to feel a part of that club my cousins seem to belong to, as much as I long to fit into their world, I'm still glad she took that leap. Even though I didn't get to grow up with my mother, her values shaped me, and gave me the wonderful worlds of Winston-Salem and the North Carolina mountains.

I look to her love of places such as those mountains to affirm my love for travel. In my first twenty-nine years I traveled to Europe half-a-dozen times, as well as throughout the United States. Since that time my travels in the States have become more extensive, and I have ventured to the Far East for the first time. But in her twenty-nine years, Ruth's travels were more modest—a family vacation in Mexico City in 1946; a trip out West by car with her mother, Glenn, and a friend in 1949; a vacation in the Canadian Rockies, a favorite spot of her father, that was cut short because of the death of her maternal grandmother in 1950; twice to New York; the journey to Washington to see the inauguration in 1953; a quick trip to Chicago with her mother for a meeting of the Theosophical Society and a trip to New England for another such meeting; and a long driving trip out West with my father's family in 1956. She left the country only twice, to Canada and Mexico, never went to Europe, never even had a passport. Other than the grand trip out West in 1956, her travels after marriage were limited to the Southeast—Cumberland, the mountains, a trip to historic sights in Virginia.

Before I began this book, I knew only about the 1956 Western trip. The others I discovered in letters to her father, the memories of her sister Glenn and her brother Bo, her high school yearbook, and my father's recollections.

I asked Daddy if Ruth had told him about the Mexico City trip. "They flew to Brownsville, Texas," he told me as we sat on the sun porch of his new house, "and spent a few hours in a hotel with no air-conditioning resting for the trip into Mexico." While they visited a pyramid, the floating gardens, and other tourist sights, what Ruth remembered best, Daddy said, was a bus ride across town.

"The driver had a newspaper taped to the wheel," Daddy said, "because the traffic was so slow he could read and drive at the same time." In all of Mexico City, that driver made the biggest impression on eleven-year-old Ruth Candler. I think of my own journeys, though, and how I often remember little things. The monuments and scenic views are often no different from the postcards, but a cab ride, a hot dog, a parking lot, a sidewalk, all might provide the memory that lasts beyond the snapshots.

In the box of slides in the attic closet at Robinhood Road was a large collection of pictures that Ruth took during the 1956 Western trip. "Ruth took all the slides," wrote Bob's sister Susan. "She arranged them in order, labeled them, and typed a list to refer to when showing them. She did a great job." As a teenager I set up the slide screen in the attic late at night and gazed at places unlike any I had ever seen, dreaming of following in the footsteps of that trip—of seeing mountains tall enough to be topped with snow in the summer and trees big enough to drive a car through. Since then I have seen many of these places. Others still beckon to me. Even though she took this trip eight years before her death it stands for me, because of those slides, as *the* trip that defines her as a traveler and provides me with the opportunity to link my own travels to hers.

"We left Atlanta about nine o'clock the night I graduated from college," said Daddy. Ruth and Bob had been given the task of driving a Studebaker that belonged to a client of Bob's father as far as Denver, where it would be delivered to its owner and my parents would meet up with the rest of Bob's family—his parents Heyward and Helen, Chip, his younger brother by three years, and Susan, who was twelve. Ruth and Bob had been married less than a year.

Their initial destination was St. Joseph, Missouri, and they drove straight through for twenty-seven hours to get there. Ike may have been president, but the interstate highway system was still in the future. Daddy drove all night long and Ruth took over after they crossed the Mississippi into Hannibal. Bob spent some of the rest of the drive on the floor of the car laughing hysterically he was so tired. It sounds exhausting, suicidal, crazy, and fun.

Eventually they delivered the Studebaker, and then spent some time in Denver, the city Bob's mother had grown up in—until she ran off to New York to join that all-girl orchestra.

"Your mother and I rented a boat and rowed out on a lake in some city park one night," Daddy recalled. They listened to the music of a concert in the bandstand drifting across the water. In so much of what my father says about their courtship I see friendship and in so much of what I have learned about them as parents I see love, but it is nice to have this one scene preserved in my mind, after marriage and before family, in which I can see romance.

With the family united in Denver, they headed for the mountains, and Ruth began taking pictures. Now, Lucy and I are back in Kansas, and with the chill of ending October keeping us inside, we play in the basement. She rearranges the plastic furniture of a plastic doll house; I project forty-year-old slides on the wall. Ruth must have been amazed, as I always am, by snow-capped peaks in summertime—slide after slide of snowy Rockies flashes across my wall. She loved the art of man as well as the art of nature—shots of sculptures at the Huntington and other galleries are interspersed with pictures of scenery. Holy places—churches and graveyards—also seem to have fascinated her.

They took the road to the top of Mount Evans that I would drive up with my first wife and a college friend thirty years later. They visited Central City where Ruth bought slides of the Opera House and the Teller House—named for ancestors of my wife, Janice, whose maiden name was Teller. In Salt Lake City, Ruth shot close-ups of the top of the Mormon Temple just as I did at fifteen. The only other time I visited Salt Lake I was asleep on a train bound for San Francisco, her next destination.

Heyward had business meetings on the West Coast, ostensibly the reason for the trip. They drove to San Francisco where Ruth took pictures of the Japanese Gardens, Golden Gate Bridge, and Coit Tower that look just like mine taken decades later. But in 1956, prisoners still lived in Alcatraz and, judging from the image on my basement wall, Fisherman's Wharf still had more fishermen than boutiques. In Yosemite Ruth took stunning pictures, like Ansel Adams in color.

"What are you doing, Daddy?" Lucy asks me, looking at the picture of El Capitan on the wall.

"I'm looking at some old pictures from a trip Granddaddy took a long time ago," I say, and even as Lucy returns to her play I realize what I have said; I have denied Ruth's existence as I did for so long. I know the time is coming to tell Lucy about her grandmother and to bring my daughter along with me on this journey.

In Los Angeles Ruth and Bob took a day away from the rest of the family and walked the galleries and gardens of the Huntington. After Rodin's "The Thinker," the next slide on my wall is of Main Street U.S.A. I cannot believe my father, who loathes tourist traps, actually went to Disneyland, but a quick phone call confirms it. Susan was the right age to enjoy the park, but in 1956 the whole idea of a place like Disneyland was new—the park had opened only the year before. People of any age might enjoy the novelty. I've been there twice, not realizing I was walking in my mother's footsteps.

From Los Angeles they drove through San Diego, across the desert to the Grand Canyon, Carlesbad Caverns, and Santa Fe, where I sat in Rand Lee's living room a few weeks ago.

After Santa Fe they returned to Denver and then home via Wichita and Memphis. The trip had taken a month. Ruth was twenty-one. She would never leave the Southeast again.

Those deserts nag at me. "Nuclear testing" they tell me. Wasn't there nuclear testing here in the 1950s? Duck and cover? It was the bomb that gave her cancer.

Ruth awoke early one morning and took a walk around the motor lodge, watching the sun inch its way above the desert horizon and seeing another light, a flash in the east just where the sun was starting to show, as if that star were exploding into a brilliance that would consume the planets. And that is how she got cancer.

Or maybe Santa Fe—an hour's drive from Los Alamos. Who knows what secret radiation was lurking in the air? Or what about those plants down along the Savannah River, where they made the radioactive ingredients for the H-bomb? How far were those from Cumberland Island, where she spent so many summers? What sort of spills did the government never tell us about? And what about all that red meat?

This is the way my mind works. Searching for a reason, searching for someone to blame, unable to accept the fact that she just got it. She just got cancer. People do. People die.

XI

The mystery in how little we know of other people is no greater than the mystery of how much. . . . The least anybody can do for him is remember right.

—EUDORA WELTY

Early November. For four months I have researched Ruth from afar. I have a binder full of letters, documents, clippings, and notes of telephone conversations, and a gradually growing pile of photographs, but I have not visited the places that were important to her. With the door to Ruth's life finally open to me, I feel ready for a trip to Atlanta—a trip not only to visit her homes, her church, and her grave, but also to talk to some of her family, and to mention her name in their presence for the first time. Ruth's sister Glenn has an apartment in Roswell, in the northern suburbs. Her brother Bo and his wife, Betsy, who was so close to Ruth in high school, live about an hour's drive south of town. Her aunt Kit has lived in the same house in Buckhead since she moved out of Callanwolde in the 1950s. All these people are eager to visit with me and share memories, scrapbooks, and photographs. Sonja Olsen Kinard has even promised me a private tour of Callanwolde.

Lucy has enjoyed her visit to Kansas. Janice made her a feathered cap to go with her "different colored bird" costume for Halloween, and I had the joy of canvassing the neighborhood with her and Jordan—listening to Lucy tweet and Jordan, as the Queen of Hearts, order decapitations. Three days later, Lucy and I board a flight from Kansas City to Atlanta and she joins my quest for Ruth.

My wife's college roommate, Lisa, and her husband, Ron, are kind enough to let me and Lucy stay at their house in Decatur—a suburb on the Emory side of town. Lucy can gnaw on cheese-covered bagels and watch "Sesame Street" when she hits her exhaustion point in the late afternoon, and I have room to spread out my notes and maps and plan my days. Best, though, is the friendship. Lisa and Ron patiently listen to my account of each day's discoveries. For me, the process of discussing Ruth with others who never knew her makes her that much more real.

On our first full day in Atlanta Lucy and I eat breakfast at Evans' Fine Foods, which, according to its menu, has been serving food in the Emory area since 1949, so I feel sure my parents must have eaten there forty years or so ago. Lucy orders pancakes, and I ask her about death.

Once a child starts having friends, visiting relatives, and going to playschool, a parent is never quite sure what that child does and does not know. This uncertainty is compounded for a parent who sees his daughter only a few times each year. I have no idea to what extent the concept of death has been introduced into Lucy's world view. I heard her say once that she hoped to get a cat, "after my dog, Tillie, dies." Presumably death is not entirely foreign, but how does one discuss it with a three-year-old distracted by syrup and orange juice?

"Do you know what it means when somebody dies, Lucy?" I ask.

"What?" She answers questions with questions.

"It means that person goes away and you never get to see them again." Silence.

"Do you think Tillie will die sometime?" I say.

"I think so."

"And will you ever be able to see Tillie after she dies?"

"No. And then I can have a cat." We seem to be making progress. Losing a grandmother twenty-eight years before you are born is not the same as losing a mother, but I'm determined that Lucy not end up afraid to discuss that loss. I feel sure that no one has ever mentioned Ruth to her, and I hope, by the time I take her back to her mother in a few days, she will feel comfortable asking about the grandmother she never knew. But how to begin?

"Do you know how you have a Mommy and she loves you very much and plays with you and does things for you? Well, do you think Daddy had a Mommy, too?"

"Of course, you silly. Everybody has a Mommy."

"That's right. But did you know that Daddy's Mommy died when he was just a little kid, even littler than Lucy?"

"She did?" There is real curiosity in her voice. A discovery like this seems worth putting her next bite of breakfast back into the pool of syrup and listening.

"That's right, my Mommy died when I was just two years old. Do you remember when you were two years old?"

"I think that was before my last birthday."

"So I never got to see my Mommy again after I was two, isn't that sad?"

"Yes."

"But you know what? My Daddy is your Granddaddy Bob and he got married to Granny Mim, so I got a new Mommy."

"You mean you have two mommies?"

"That's right. Only my first Mommy died, so I don't ever get to see her again."

"Where do people go when they die?"

I was afraid she would ask this one. Again, I don't know the extent of her religious training, but I imagine she has at least heard of heaven. "They go up to heaven. But you can't see them when they go there." She seems satisfied with the answer, and we finish our breakfast.

Our first stop is the home of Aunt Kit, Ruth's father's sister. Kit and her family lived in Callanwolde until after Popee's death when Danny finally moved out. Since then, they have lived in a lovely house—not a mansion, but certainly spacious—in Buckhead. At eighty-nine, Kit still lives there with one of her sons. Any of us can attribute our existence to a number of people, and Ruth could attribute hers, in part, to Aunt Kit, who introduced my mother's parents and arranged their first date.

Kit is still in fairly good health, and looks after herself with some help from her son. She has a back problem but a sense of humor to go with it, calling herself "an old hunchback." As my younger brother John put it, "Aunt Kit never has to wonder whether her shoes are tied."

It is mid-morning, the air cool and sharp and the sun shining through bare branches when we ring the bell and she opens the tall front door to us. Lucy has never met Aunt Kit before, but with pancakes in her stomach and the energy of morning driving her, she offers a happy hello. She sticks close to me, but curiosity is as strong in her as shyness. When Aunt Kit shows her the cabinet of toys reserved for the visits of grandchildren and great-grandchildren, Lucy deserts me. For the next hour she plays on one side of the room while Kit and I talk on the other.

Aunt Kit's sitting room is just as I remember it—though I haven't visited here in at least fifteen years. Built-in bookcases line the wall on either side of the doors to the marbled entrance hall. On one side, shelves are filled with Coca-Cola bottles from around the world. I remember a dozen or so bottles with strange scripts sitting on these shelves when I was a child; now there must be fifty. Above where Lucy plays hangs a portrait of Asa Candler, Kit's grandfather and founder of The Coca-Cola Company. I distract her from her toys long enough to point it out to her.

"Do you know who that is?" I ask.

"Who?"

"It's your . . ." I have to count "greats" in my head. "Great-great-great-grandfather." But Lucy is more interested in toys than ancestors. The next day when we see another picture of Asa at the Coca-Cola museum and I tell Lucy that he is the same man whose painting was hanging at Aunt Kit's, she will say, "Oh. When do we get to taste the Coke?"

Before our visit, Aunt Kit has written me, "I remember in 1935 my brother telephoning me to say Ruth and he had a baby girl just born." Now she talks a bit about the younger Ruth, remembering particularly her talent as a musician. Most of what Kit tells me I have heard before, but when she pulls out a stack of photographs she has assembled for me, a new door is opened. Here, for the first time, is a substantial collection of photographs of Ruth as a child—and many are not glossy snapshots, either, but oversized black-and-white images printed on thick art paper with deckled edges and a soft finish.

Five of the pictures are portraits of Ruth alone, dated on the back from 1940 through 1944. In the earliest ones, five-year-old Ruth is missing front teeth. By the time she is nine, the new teeth are in and I wonder if she later wore braces. Like me before orthodontics, she has big upper teeth sticking out in an overbite. She wears her hair up with a bow in the front, and a locket hangs around her neck. At this age, she looks like my sister's elder daughter, Catherine, who was named for Aunt Kit.

"Lucy, come look at these pictures of my Mommy," I say.

"The one that died?"

"That's right." Lucy sets down a fire truck and walks across to the coffee table. "See," I say, "here she is."

Ruth the day before her ninth birthday in 1944.

"She's just a kid. She doesn't look like a Mommy." Aunt Kit smiles.

"These are pictures of Ruth when she was just a little kid. Don't you think she looks like your cousin Catherine?" I ask.

"I don't think so."

"Do you think she looks pretty?"

"Sort of pretty," says Lucy, and turns back to her toys.

My favorite picture from Aunt Kit is undated, but in it Ruth looks about three. She is sitting with her brothers, Buddy and Bo, in the prow of a small boat on the water, I assume near Cumberland Island. The land is visible in the background and the three children are laughing, Ruth's head tossed back slightly, her curls caught in the wind. It is a moment of lovely innocence. The difficulties of life, from war to divorce, lie ahead of her, yet Ruth's smile in pictures through all those later years retains the sparkle it has here. I believe, as Rand Lee said, that she was a happy woman and she had much to be happy about, but I also believe she learned the art of happiness early in life, and those times of joy and innocence at Cumberland laid the foundation for the happiness she carried through her life.

When we finish looking through the pictures, Aunt Kit takes me to the back hallway outside her bedroom where the wall is covered with framed photographs. Lucy follows us, pulling a wooden dog on a string.

"Why don't you take that one, too," Kit says, pointing to a picture of Ruth in her wedding dress on her father's arm.

"I don't want to take things off your wall," I say.

"I'm not going to be around that much longer," she says, "and who's going to want them after I am gone?" With guilt and glee I add two framed photos to my growing collection.

Lucy is still playing happily as Aunt Kit pulls out a scrapbook and turns to a page devoted to the surprise party given for Danny's eightieth birthday. Ruth, she tells me, did most of the planning for the party, which was held at the Piedmont Driving Club. She even made the place cards. Aunt Kit's son, Billy, has sent me his place card, which he saved all these years. Now Kit pulls out the scrapbook page and hands it to me—it includes a clipping from the newspaper, three snapshots, and her place card.

Danny was born in 1881, so her eightieth birthday fell in 1961. Ruth realized that both of these dates could be turned upside down and still read the same, so she designed a topsy-turvy place card. In the upper left corner was the date 1881 and in the lower right 1961. Each person's name was printed twice across the middle, once upside-down and once right-side up, the initial letters touching each other to form a central motif. All

Bo, Ruth, and Buddy on a boat off the coast of Georgia about 1938.

The place card Ruth designed for Danny's 80th birthday party.

this was accomplished by hand in gold ink, and made enough of an impression that at least two of the guests saved the cards for thirty-five years. "A simple card," wrote Billy, "but would you have thought of it?"

The snapshots show Danny entering the room, escorted by Ruth's parents. Her reaction makes it clear the surprise succeeded. Another shot shows the dinner—my father is the only person I recognize. What I can see of this party is somewhat like what I know of myself. While I cannot see Ruth, there is much evidence of her hands at work, and the result is a joyful thing.

I thank Kit repeatedly for the photographs. Lucy replaces the toys in the cabinet and hugs Kit good-bye. I marvel at how quickly she gives her affection. As I am stacking the pictures onto the back seat of our rental car, Lucy proclaims that she wants to collect some leaves, so I give her a minute or two to peruse the bursts of yellow and red and oak and maple that carpet the driveway. With four or five of these treasures in hand, she climbs into her car seat and we pull away, Aunt Kit waving gently at us from her front portico, Lucy smiling and waving back with her leaves.

November in the South brings crisp air, changing leaves, and occasional days of rain—the kind of rain that fluctuates from drizzling to pouring all gray day long, but never completely stops. Our second day in Atlanta is one of such drabness, and after another round of pancakes, Lucy and I set out from Decatur to visit my Aunt Glenn in Roswell. The drive takes forty-five minutes or so, plenty of time for Lucy and me to practice our catechism. I am trying to teach her about Ruth, about her own history. I ask her questions to reinforce what I've told her. Each time we have this conversation, I add a little more.

"Do you remember my Mommy's name?"

"Hmm."

"I'll bet you remember what her middle name was? Is it the same as yours?"

"Uh-huh."

"What's that?"

"I don't really remember."

"You don't remember your own name?"

"I don't remember her whole name."

"Do you remember her middle name?"

"Candler."

"Do you remember what her last name was? Same as yours . . ."

"Lovett."

"Right."

"What's her whole name?"

"Her whole name was Ruth Candler Lovett."

"Ruth Candler Lovett. That's a funny name."

"And what happened to her?"

"She died."

"And how old was Daddy?"

"Two."

"If somebody dies, can you ever see them again?"

"No."

On the doorstep of Glenn's apartment, I hold my coat over Lucy's head in a vain attempt to keep her dry. The door opens and Glenn smiles at us. She has tried to call, she says, to tell me she has a cold. Do I really want to bring Lucy in? But this is my only chance to visit her. Lucy and I are both just recovering from colds, I explain. Not much chance we will catch another one so soon.

Glenn is now a grandmother, and like Aunt Kit, she keeps a box of toys for her grandchildren. But Lucy is feeling tired this morning, and prefers to sit by the window with a few of her own books. As Glenn and I talk, Lucy recites from memory various *Curious George* stories, turning pages at precisely the right moment.

Glenn was born in 1941. The memories she has of Ruth are of a big sister, far enough removed in age that she shared little with Glenn in terms of friends or activities. But Glenn experienced the same family traditions Ruth grew up with, and because those traditions remained unchanged for so long, Glenn's view of them cannot be all that different from Ruth's.

Of course genetically Glenn is the closest person to Ruth on the planet—her only sister. I can't help wondering, as I settle into a chair, how closely Ruth and Glenn might resemble each other had Ruth lived. Would she have Glenn's lovely silver hair? Her relaxed attitude? Aunt Kit gave me several pictures that included Ruth and Glenn as children, but they show no great resemblance.

Glenn's voice has the musical lilt of a true Southern accent—the accent close to being extinguished by the grating twang to which so many Southerners have devolved. "Ruth's voice sounded very much like mine," Glenn says. "It used to scare Bob sometimes, we sounded so much alike on the phone. Even now, when I listen to my voice recorded, it sounds like Ruth's."

Like me, Glenn divorced two years ago, though she has not remarried. I have not seen her in several years, and never spent more than a few hours with her in my life. There are gaps in our conversation. Her boyfriend calls from the West Coast and she tells him she will call back after I leave. In spite of all this, being with Glenn feels natural. Her memories of Ruth and of her childhood days are few, but enlightening. For the first time, I am talking with someone who grew up in the same house with her, attended the same school, and rode in the same car to all those years of Sunday dinners at Callanwolde.

I talk to Glenn about those dinners and about Pat Conroy's portrayal of the Candlers. She admits that the china, crystal, and furniture were formal, "but we were just people."

Glenn remembers that a vast buffet would be laid out on the countertop of the butler's pantry—a long narrow room just off the dining room that the "History of Callanwolde" pamphlet calls the "Buffet Kitchen." Glenn describes an array of salads and other dishes and marvels at how they were all prepared. "I suppose they must have had a cook," she says, "but at the time, I only saw the finished result."

Aunt Kit gave me a picture of a Callanwolde dinner from May 1940, before Glenn was born. The men wear coats and ties. Candlesticks, silver, and an arrangement of daisies decorate the table. Glasses of milk alternate with crystal goblets as children are welcome at the table. Ruth sits in

Dinner at Callanwolde, May 30, 1940. Danny is turned towards the camera in the foreground; Ruth sits in a high chair.

a high chair while Aunt Kit's youngest sits on her lap. The picture was taken on a Thursday night, with a mere thirteen people at dinner, but the Candlers surrounding that table don't look like royalty; they look like "just people."

"After dinner we used to watch Ed Sullivan on Danny's television," Glenn says. Ruth was grown and married by the time Ed established himself in the new medium in 1955, but she still attended Sunday-night dinners with Bob. The late 1940s and early 1950s were the primitive years of television, and radio was still very much alive. "In the car on the way home we would listen to Jack Benny, Mortimer Snerd [one of Edgar Bergen's dummies], and Paul Winchell and Jerry Mahoney," says Glenn.

I never thought, until hearing Glenn speak of sitting in the back seat and listening to those voices, how big a part radio must have played in my mother's childhood. She saw television only in its early years, but she lived through the golden age of radio. Her Sunday nights were probably defined by Jack Benny and Edgar Bergen, whose shows aired at seven and eight o'clock respectively. It seems inconceivable that she wasn't intimately acquainted with Amos and Andy, Ozzie and Harriet, Fibber McGee and Molly, and Lum and Abner. I'm sure the boys in the house tuned into *The Shadow*, *The Green Hornet*, and *The Lone Ranger*—perhaps Ruth knew them as well. She was only two when the Hindenburg disaster was broadcast coast to coast and three when Orson Welles spooked the country with *War of the Worlds*, but did she listen, at age six, to FDR give his "date which will live in infamy" speech or to his many fireside chats? Did she follow the soap operas or the game shows?

"You know," says Glenn, after a lull in our conversation gives us a chance to hear about Curious George breaking his leg, "I do have one picture of Ruth I'll bet you haven't seen." After some digging in a cabinet, she hands me an image that strongly evokes Ruth in the era of radio. Ruth, Glenn, their mother, and a friend sit at a breakfast table in California during their Western trip of 1949. In the center of the table is a large microphone labeled ABC. They are attending a live broadcast of a morning radio program—Glenn can't remember the title, but it was probably *Breakfast in Hollywood*. Jack McElroy was the host in the summer of 1949 and perhaps he stopped to quip with my mother and her family, who sat there, in a scene right out of Woody Allen's *Radio Days*, smiling over coffee and eggs at table forty-one while the whole nation listened in.

Glenn remembers not only the Sunday dinners at Callanwolde, but Christmas there too. "In the huge upstairs hall, each grandchild would

Màmà, Glenn, Ruth, and a friend at a broadcast of Breakfast in Hollywood
in 1949.

have a corner, or some other place that was their spot." Glenn talks about the excitement of mounting those imposing stairs and dashing for her own corner. While others in the family will later tell me of a slight disappointment in 1950s Callanwolde Christmases, because their corners traditionally held a rack of clothes, Glenn was enough younger than her brothers and sister that she was still unwrapping toys from her grandparents while the others pulled their new suits and dresses off the racks.

Glenn's phone rings, and I do my best to politely look away while she speaks briefly. The apartment is pleasantly roomy, with a wall of windows looking out into the woods, a fireplace, and cases of books and videos. Lucy stares out the window at the rain.

"It sure is a rainy day," she says.

Glenn hangs up and rolls her eyes. "Màmà heard I was sick and wants to know if there's anything she can do." We both force a laugh—Màmà has not been out of her own bedroom in three years and is attended to by nurses round the clock.

I ask about Cumberland. Glenn has been back recently, for the first time in ten years, she says. She took her boyfriend there to show him around, but says the visit was something of a dud. "There were just too many memories," she says. Memories of her first marriage—of another life. I understand why my father has never gone back to Cumberland since Ruth's death. I imagine some of their happiest times together must have been there. Glenn reminisces about her early days on the island, when teenage Ruth would bring a group of friends from school and her mother would chaperone the gang and play along with whatever schemes they concocted.

"We used to explore the old Carnegie house," Glenn tells me, confirming Wight Crawford's memories. In Ruth's collection of slides I have seen pictures of this house, which has since burned down. During the time Glenn remembers, it had been deserted for years, and looked something like the set for *The Munsters*, with a Victorian tower, peeling paint, and doubtless a haunted interior. "We would hide in closets," says Glenn, "then jump out and scare each other, holding flashlights under our chins to make ourselves look spooky."

Ruth seems to have had no objection to including her little sister in her own activities. "When I was ten to twelve years old," Glenn says, "Ruth was dating Bob, and they were both very active in St. Luke's Episcopal

Ruth's photograph of the old Carnegie mansion of Dungeness on Cumberland Island that she and her friends explored.

church. I sort of tagged along with them for a few years—I'm not sure why. I persuaded the church to let me be confirmed early, so I could take communion, and, I think, so I could be a part of the activities and be with Ruth and Bob. I remember liking the church activities and wanting to be with the older group. I never would go to Sunday School, I wanted to go to church with Ruth and Bob, and I guess I plagued them unmercifully. I never remember feeling unwanted, however. Ruth and Bob always took me with them and made me part of their lives during this period."

"I'm afraid I don't remember much," Glenn tells me for the third time, and then she proceeds to reveal yet another wonderful tidbit. "On that trip to New York, we went to see *South Pacific* on Broadway."

"That was in 1954, right?" I ask. "When you went to the Metropolitan Opera and the Stork Club?"

"That's right," says Glenn, "It was during Ruth's winter break at Sweet Briar." I wonder if Ruth ever saw any other Broadway shows and who she saw in *South Pacific*. I'm enough of a fan of Broadway that I will later look up the 1954 season and discover that *South Pacific* was not running at the time. I will be reminded how often we remember things incorrectly, how fallible many of my sources for this book are.

I have read in a letter from Aunt Betsy that Ruth broke her arm at the elbow as a child and I ask Glenn about that injury. She remembers every detail of the leather-covered footstool Ruth fell over, but can't remember in which house it happened (the family moved when Ruth was twelve). She does remember that a small piece of bone was left over after the arm was surgically reset when Ruth was a young woman, and Ruth kept this in a jar for some time. She also tells me that she had never seen her father as devastated as he was at Ruth's death.

I tell Glenn that no one in my Atlanta family ever talked to me about Ruth or even mentioned her name in my presence when I was growing up. I tell her that no one has ever offered to take me to visit her grave and the first time I saw it was at Grandpa's funeral a few years ago. This surprises her. The family, she says, was never inordinately silent on the subject of Ruth. In years past, she has often spoken to her mother about Ruth, though Grandpa, if anyone, avoided the topic. Glenn feels that my perception of silence might be different had I lived in Atlanta and seen my family there more often. Perhaps, she says, there just wasn't enough time to raise the subject. Perhaps, I think, when your grandson only visits for a week or two every year, you want to spend that time as pleasantly as possible. After all, when I have my all-too-short times with Lucy, don't I want her to be happy?

I thank Glenn for the visit and apologize for imposing while she is sick. As I gather up Lucy and her books, Glenn repeats—"I'm not sure how much help I've been." I don't know how to tell her that I am finally beginning to see Ruth as a sister, and to see Glenn no longer as a rarely visited relative but as someone who has an unbreakable and important connection with me.

"Thank you for coming to see me, Lucy," says Glenn. "You'll have to come back when my grandkids are here sometime."

"OK," says Lucy in a groggy voice that lets me know she'll sleep in the car on the way to lunch. With a hug and a final good-bye I rush back into the rain and the darkness, balancing Lucy, her books, and my notes and splashing through puddles to the chilly confines of our car.

During her high school years and her year at Sweet Briar, Ruth's friend

Betsy Denny probably knew her better than anyone. Betsy became Ruth's sister-in-law when she married my uncle Bo in 1954. Bo, too, was there to observe Ruth's adolescence and early womanhood, and he also remembers her earlier childhood. Not long after Ruth's father purchased Rolling Meadows Farm in 1955, Bo and Betsy built a house there, where they still live. They have invited me and Lucy to spend the night. We leave Atlanta after dinner and continue our catechism in the car on the way to the interstate.

"How many kids did Ruth have, do you remember?"
"Three!"
"And who were those kids?"
"Who?"
"Well, I was the littlest one. I was the baby. Then in the middle came Aunt E, the cousins' mom, and then the oldest was Uncle David. We were all kids together."
"Uncle David, one, Aunt E, two, Daddy, three!"
"Who was the littlest kid?"
"Daddy!"

By the time we have been on the highway ten minutes, Lucy is asleep. At eight-thirty, I pull up to the ranch house at the end of a quarter mile of steep driveway. I haven't been here in ten years, haven't seen Bo and Betsy in almost that long, but when Betsy opens the door and invites me in, everything seems familiar—the portraits on the wall, Coke memorabilia, photographs of children and grandchildren. Everything contributes to a strong feeling of family, not least the familiar softness of Aunt Betsy's welcoming voice. Betsy looks so like her beautiful pictures in the Washington Seminary yearbook of over forty years ago that I wonder how much Ruth might look the same as her teenage self had she, too, lived to see her grandchildren.

Bo's rugged, bearded face appears in the hallway, and we all undertake to move sleeping Lucy into the guest bedroom. I pull off her shoes and slip her under the covers, and she hardly stirs. We tiptoe with whispers down the hall and into the high-ceilinged informal family room where we will talk for the next two hours. Maps of Cumberland hang on the wall, and the room is filled with reminders of the island and of Bo's love for the outdoors—skulls of sea turtles and wild boars, antler chandeliers, a chair made of cow horns, and a carved wooden coat rack in the shape of a life-sized bear.

Whenever I settle in to talk with friends or family after I have put a child to bed, I always feel we are entering into some secret compact. Maybe it comes from all the years of being the child who was sent off to bed, of hearing the murmur of voices filter up through the heating ducts and of wondering what *they* were talking about. Now I am an adult. I am in on the secret. And this night it seems a secret indeed, for we are talking about the one topic that, as a child, I never imagined the voices downstairs discussing.

Betsy shows more enthusiasm for my project than anyone so far. "I just think it's so wonderful what you're doing," she says.

She sits on the wicker sofa across from me and each time silence falls on the room she says, "Let me see. . . . What else can I remember about Ruth?" Unlike others I have talked to, she is not depending on me to ask the questions. Not only is Betsy enthusiastic, she has an astounding memory, as her husband repeatedly remarks. Where others have so often offered generalizations, Betsy provides details. While Bo adds to the conversation, often it is at Betsy's prodding. It seems she remembers stories he has told her years ago better than he remembers the original incidents. "Tell him about the time that . . ." is Betsy's refrain.

In spite of how many stones I have already turned, I discover some completely new information at Bo and Betsy's.

"Did Ruth ever wear braces?" I ask.

"Oh yes," says Bo, "when she was eleven or twelve, I think." Betsy produces a picture of the family in a restaurant and Ruth's smile shows off a mouth full of metal. One more thing she and I have in common.

"Wasn't this taken on that trip to Mexico City?" she asks Bo.

"Yes, I believe it was."

"What year was that?" she asks, and Bo digs up some airline timetables he has saved from the trip to confirm the date—1946.

More than anything, Bo and Betsy help me to fill in details about many things I have already discovered.

"I remember the first time Ruth ever ate meat," Betsy tells me. "We were at a restaurant and she ordered shrimp. No one said anything about it." Like so many personal decisions, Ruth seems not to have talked to anyone about giving up vegetarianism. Most who knew her remember that the change took place about the time she started dating Bob, and no one seems to regard that as a complete coincidence. Recalling Ruth's visits to her house for dinner, Bob's sister, Susan, wrote, "She was raised as a vegetarian, a concept quite difficult for the beef-eating Lovetts. I remember that mother catered to her vegetarian wishes at first and then Ruth began eating (and enjoying) meat at our house, but not her own." Just how much Bob had to do with her conversion, I don't know, but in light of later letters to her father extolling the virtues of one beef dinner after another, it amazes me that she stayed a vegetarian as long as she did.

"She brought cottage cheese and honey to school every day for lunch," says Betsy. Apparently Ruth would add various side dishes to this mixture, but for years the concoction was the mainstay of her lunch-time diet.

Betsy says "Once at Sweet Briar someone asked for a jar and Ruth got up, took the door off the hinges, and handed it to her, and said, 'The door's ajar.'" At the Seminary, she was a ring leader in math class. The teacher was going deaf and the class bell was in the back hall far away from her room. At an agreed-upon time, ten or fifteen minutes before the bell was due to ring, Ruth would give the sign and everyone would start putting away their books and papers as if they had heard the bell. The teacher smiled and said good-bye. And then there was her favorite saying—"Take away my name and call me Ruthless." Maybe it's late and I'm getting punchy, but that gets a long hard laugh out of me.

The evening wears on and the memories flow from both Bo and Betsy as I share with them discoveries I have made. When we try to say goodnight, we find it hard to stop, as if the floodgates, once open, cannot be easily shut against all that pours out. We stand in the hall outside the guestroom, Betsy talking of how Ruth never really developed a taste for coffee (neither have I) and Bo trying to remember which house they lived in when Ruth broke her arm (like Glenn, he remembers the footstool she fell over perfectly). I finally say goodnight and retreat into the guest room. I check on Lucy who has assumed her usual sprawl—flat on her back, arms outstretched, one foot dangling off the bed. I could stare at her like this for hours, listen to her breathing, burn her image into my mind, but tonight I tumble exhausted into the soft folds of the other bed, amazed at how alive her grandmother still is in this comfortable place.

The next morning after breakfast, Lucy finds a plastic car with plastic people that some grandchild has left behind, and spends at least two hours driving it around the house. The adults' conversation is punctuated with her entrances and exits, her "vrooms" and chatter—all so meaningful to her and incomprehensible to us. Betsy has found some pictures of Ruth and her brothers at their first house on Lullwater Parkway—playing outside, posing with the whole family beside a new car, unwrapping Christmas presents. In another box are pictures of the children at the pool at Callanwolde and looking for Easter eggs while Danny and Popee watch. Later, the four Candler children are posed outside Callanwolde, the young men with a Napoleon hand inserted into their jackets. The most recent snapshot is of Ruth outside one of the brick buildings of Sweet Briar during a snow storm. With snow falling around her, Ruth stands in three or four inches, wearing boots, a jacket, a hat, and huge wool mittens. I know she saw snow in Atlanta, because I have seen pictures she took of David and Elizabeth playing in the snow as toddlers. In her life, though, snow was enough of a rarity that it warranted picture taking. On the back of the picture, in blue ink, is written "Rufus," a nickname I have never heard.

"Here's a picture of the Big Six," says Betsy, handing me a large black and white shot of six young women in formal dresses. The Big Six consisted of Ruth, Betsy, and four of their high school friends. Four of the six are still living and still keep in close touch with each other. I'm jealous of those women, jealous of the friendships Ruth would enjoy if she were alive.

"We were rushed by different sororities in high school," says Betsy. Ruth was a Pi Pi, but she and Betsy, a Phi Pi, took little interest in the doings of the sororities. Some of the Big Six were also members of the Youth Group at St. Luke's, and when I ask about that, Betsy puts me in touch with another former member of that group, Don Harrison, now an Episcopal priest in Stockbridge, Georgia. Ruth's older brother, Buddy, has written to me recalling that Ruth dated Don at one point, so I was eager to talk with him. With the smell of bacon, scrambled eggs, and toast with homemade kudzu jelly still lingering in the air, Betsy dials Don's number ("I need to talk to him about something anyway," she says), and introduces us over the phone.

I am nervous talking with a stranger on the phone, but the intimacy of our connection and Don's kind enthusiasm puts me at ease.

"No," he says, "I didn't date Ruth, but I used to double date with Ruth and Bob quite a bit." These dates, he says, usually ended up at Ruth's house on West Wesley Road. He has also been to Cumberland a number of times as a guest of the family.

I ask Don about the Youth Group, and he says that it was large and active. "By attracting people from many different schools, it bridged quite a few gaps," he says. Like others I have talked to, Don seems happy to hear Ruth's name after so many years, and to have his memories valued. Rev. Harrison and I exchange addresses and say good-bye and the circle of Ruth's friends in my mind broadens yet again. More remarkable, though, is the ease with which this all happens—that I can pick up the phone and talk to a stranger about Ruth.

Lucy pulls her car into the kitchen for a pit stop, and before I can offer to take care of her, Betsy lays out a snack of crackers, milk, and apple slices. Lucy will play happily all day as long as you keep feeding her.

Bo and Betsy's daughter Beth, who also has a house on the farm, stops by for a visit and joins our conversation, asking questions I haven't thought of—further prodding her parents. Bo contributes his own memories, but most of the stories come from Betsy, and Beth and I often look at each other as if to say, "How the hell does she remember all that?"

"Ruth had an old worn-out pair of loafers she used to wear all the time at the Seminary," says Betsy. "We all thought they were so cool."

"She got a big doll house for Christmas one year," says Bo.

"I spent a week with her on Cumberland in the fall of 1949," says Betsy. "We flew down on Delta Airlines and Olie took us over on the boat."

"Before Ruth got her license and started driving her blue Ford to school," says Betsy, "she was one of only two people who were brought to the Seminary by a chauffeur. The other girl sat in the back seat and waited for the chauffeur to open the door for her, and all the girls teased her about it. But Ruth sat up front, and let herself out." The car was driven by A.B., the black man who did everything that no one else did at Ruth's house. A.B. was still working at the house on West Wesley Road when I visited as a child, years later—picking up groceries when the store finally stopped delivering, and being kind to grandchildren.

Betsy says, "Sometimes, when she was still living in Atlanta, Ruth would come down to the farm with David and Elizabeth to visit us. She would stay over at Grandpa's house while he was in town. The first time she stayed there alone with the children there was a violent thunderstorm and the lightning kept making the phone ring all night long."

"When she moved to Winston-Salem," says Betsy, "she didn't trust the movers to take care of her harpsichord. So, she took it completely apart, labeled all the pieces, and then reassembled it when they got to North Carolina."

"Seems like she could do anything," says Bo.

Some of Bo and Betsy's memories change between night and morning. "Ruth was right handed," Betsy said during our evening talk, "and she broke her left arm." The next morning, Betsy is sure that it was the right arm that Ruth broke. Whichever arm had been broken, Betsy is amazed at what Ruth could do with her slightly crooked arm—not only play the piano, but play basketball, too.

"Ruth was truly an outstanding person," Betsy says, "smart, talented, steady, thoughtful, loyal, gentle, witty. I knew of no one in our silly and sometimes catty teenage crowd that didn't admire her and call her a friend. I never heard her make an unkind remark about anyone. She had a great sense of humor, yet she was serious in whatever she undertook. She was always calm, well organized, and methodical." Thinking over her experiences with her long-dead friend, Betsy smiles and says, "She was just a regular person who did everything so well," and Bo nods in agreement.

Whether playing a keyboard or building one, doing homework or housework, dealing with her brothers or with her own children, Ruth, in the eyes of her closest high school friend and her brother, approached life with a rare and valuable combination of self-esteem and modesty—a combination that made her both capable and likable.

Lucy and I leave the farm after a hot bowl of chili and a cold Coke. We are quiet for the first few miles—she in her post-lunch daze and me trying to process all the information I have taken in during the past three days. I am most off balance because of the unexpected enthusiasm with which everyone in Ruth's family talks to me. That night, I will talk to my father. He will tell me that he thinks my writing this book, asking these questions, stirring up these memories, is probably the best thing anyone could do for Ruth's family. But even now, I am beginning to sense that.

And do I belong in this family? Certainly more so now than in many years. I feel that in losing Ruth I lost my link to these people, that I am an outsider—but is that feeling the product of losing Ruth or of having moved away from Atlanta or of my own failure to make an effort to stay in touch? Whatever the answer, in the search for a lost mother, I have discovered a family.

The traffic thickens as we approach Atlanta, and Lucy starts to grow impatient with the trip—too much sitting in her carseat the past few days. To distract us, I resume her catechism.

"Who was Ruth married to?"

"Who?"

"Granddaddy."

"Was that a long time ago?"

"You mean when Ruth died was it a long time ago?"

"Yeah."

"It was a long time ago. When Daddy was just a little baby."

"Then how did you quickly get a new Mommy?"

"Well, it wasn't that quickly. I got a new Mommy when I was almost five years old and my first Mommy died when I was two years old, so for three years I didn't have a Mommy, I just had a Daddy."

"And who was your Daddy?"

"Granddaddy Bob was my Dad. He was a good Dad."

"Was he good at cooking, too?"

"He was pretty good at cooking. And later on he got married to Granny Mim—she's very good at cooking."

"That makes me think of the people who have all those doggies. Are those the people?"

"Those are the people."

"Now they live all by theirselves."

"Yeah, now they don't have any kids living with them. But after they got married they had two more kids. Do you know who those kids were?"

"Who?"

"Uncle Peter and Uncle John. That's a lot of people to remember, isn't it?"

"It is."

"Did you know that Ruth and Granddaddy used to live in Atlanta?"

"No way!"

"Yes they did."

"No way, no way!"

"I'll take you by to see some of the places she lived while we're here, okay?"

"Okay."

XII

Memory as a place, as a building, as a sequence of col-
umns, cornices, porticoes. The body inside the mind, as
if we were moving around in there, going from one place
to the next and the sound of our footsteps as we walk,
moving from one place to the next.
                                                —PAUL AUSTER

Lucy does not easily tire of Evans' pancakes. We both slept soundly after
our trip to the farm, and today is my last day with her on this trip. After
lunch, I will meet her mother in the parking lot of a hotel and Lucy will go
with her and I will drive to the airport alone for my return to Kansas City.
So I'm feeding her more pancakes, giving her the energy she will need for
a long day. I eat a plate of them, too.

"Do you want to see some of the places where Ruth and Bob lived
today?"

"I thought we were going to see Mommy today."

"We are, but not until after lunch. Should we go look at some houses
this morning."

"Can we go inside them?"

"We can go inside one of them."

"Well, I think we should walk around in the yards some, so I can find
some nice leaves."

"OK. We'll take a walk before lunch."

Ruth lived in three houses and two apartments in Atlanta. These homes
and one other house played an important role in her life. Lucy and I
won't make it to all of these places this morning, but because most of
them are within two or three miles of Emory, we'll at least drive by all
but one.

After Ruth was born in the Emory University Hospital on June 5, 1935, she was taken a few blocks away to the family home on Lullwater Parkway to take up residence with her parents, five-year-old Buddy, and three-year-old Bo. Lullwater Road begins two blocks from Emory and winds through lovely forest and past homes large enough to be luxurious but not so intimidating as to be called mansions. Lullwater Parkway is a loop off one side of the road that is separated from the main road by the Lullwater Conservation Garden, an area of gardens, trees, and a stream crossed by stone footbridges. The Lullwater Garden Club established the garden in 1931, so while it may have been less scenic when Ruth wandered it as a child, it was nonetheless a protected bit of city, and a buffer from the world for the four homes on Lullwater Parkway.

I don't know the number of the house, but my father said it was the one closest to Emory, so I pull onto Lullwater Parkway and stop across from the first home.

"This is where Ruth lived when she was your age," I tell Lucy.

"Can we go look inside?" she asks.

"No, we don't know the people who live there now, so we just have to look from here." I wish I had the courage to walk up and ring the bell. We sit in silence for a few moments, staring across the street. The house stands well back from the road on a wooded hill. I take some pictures of its Tudor facade through the trees. Though much smaller, it bears a resemblance to Callanwolde, with dark brown timbers, cream-colored stucco, and an arched front door. Ruth's father moved into the newly completed Callanwolde with his family at sixteen, only ten years or so before he had the Lullwater house built a few blocks away.

"Can't we take our walk now?" I turn off the engine, take Lucy out of her car seat, and we stroll through the few hundred yards of the Lullwater Conservation Garden. The pathway winds under thick trees, and I try to imagine little children playing here when the trees were smaller. Ruth lived across the street until she was twelve. For half that time she had only two older brothers. When she was six, Glenn was born.

Lucy distracts me from my reverie with a bright red maple leaf, and I realize I don't have to imagine children enjoying this spot.

As we climb back into the car, I take one more look at the house. Maybe I could get up the nerve to go knock on the front door. But it's nearly ten thirty. Next time, I think.

One of the pleasures of Lullwater Parkway must have been the proximity to grandfather's house, Callanwolde. As a real-estate developer, Asa Candler had planned, with the help of Frederick Law Olmsted, the Druid Hills neighborhood, supervising the construction of many of the homes, as well as the golf and country club that backs up to the Lullwater house. He had also left some areas undeveloped, and some of those spots became the sites for the homes of his descendants.

Five minutes after leaving Lullwater, we pull into the winding driveway of Callanwolde.

"Did your Mom live in this big house?" asked Lucy.

"No. But her grandfather lived here, and she came to visit him all the time."

"Does that make you think of that house we saw in the mountains." She means Biltmore House, and while Callanwolde would look like an outbuilding on the Vanderbilt estate, I'm impressed with Lucy for making the comparison. Druid Hills' designer, Olmsted, also designed the grounds at Biltmore.

"What do you think it looks like inside?" I ask.

"Can we go see?"

"We sure can." I drive past the house to a parking lot that was certainly not a part of the original estate, and we walk back to the side entrance. We hold hands while we climb first the stone steps under the porte-cochere and then the grand staircase inside the house. When the staircase reaches the landing beneath a huge stained-glass window, it splits in half for the remainder of the ascent.

"You go that way," says Lucy, "and I'll go this way." We walk up separately and rejoin each other at the top.

"There's not much furniture in this house," she says.

"Nobody lives here anymore," I say. "They just use it for art classes and things like that." Though the house is empty of most furnishings, it bustles with activity. A painter works on the ceiling of the billiard room, the Callanwolde Guild is meeting in the library, and the offices are a beehive of commotion. In the middle of all this, we still manage to find Sonja, who greets us cheerfully and introduces us to the director and the rest of the staff as descendants of "Mr. Candler."

"Things are a little wild around here," Sonja says. "The Italian Olympic Committee is renting the house next summer." But a few ladders cannot interfere with our exploration of the house and my chance to peek behind those closed doors.

"The Warrens lived in this wing of the house," says Sonja before we leave the offices.

"This is where Aunt Kit used to live," I tell Lucy, who has grown quiet in the presence of strangers. As we wander from room to room, she looks, but does not talk.

Leaving the offices, we pass through several large, empty bedrooms, Sonja identifying the occupant of each. Danny's bathroom is outfitted with multiple shower heads and an array of built-in cabinets graces her dressing room. Popee's bedroom is now a gift shop. As we walk the vast upstairs hall, I try to picture the grandchildren dashing for their special corners on Christmas afternoon, but all I see is emptiness.

Downstairs I recognize the cabinet specially built for Danny's collection of Doughty birds. I saw it in the background of a picture Aunt Kit gave me of Ruth's family. We admire the portrait of Popee over the fireplace in the library where the women of the Guild listen to a preluncheon speaker. In the great hall I take a close look, for the first time, at the three keyboards of the house's built-in Aeolian organ. The organ's console is permanently anchored in the corner of the great hall, and the nearly four thousand pipes are hidden above ceilings and behind walls throughout the house. Here, according to a pamphlet Sonja gave me, Marcel Dupre, the organist for Notre Dame Cathedral, once entertained the family.

"Lucy, look at this organ," I say. "Isn't that big?"

"Is that like the organ Grandma Vail plays at church?" Lucy's grandmother on her mother's side is a church organist.

"It sure is. Do you know who used to play this organ?"

"Who?"

"My mommy, Ruth."

"Really?"

"That's right. So you had two grandmas who played the organ."

"Wow."

I've been told that Ruth played this organ more than anyone else during the 1950s. While her aunts had taken organ lessons in childhood, Ruth had trained only for the piano, but she was able to entertain the family during gatherings. The organ was also equipped with a roll player, like a player piano. Recently the organ was restored, but I have never heard it played. I can only close my eyes and imagine my mother sitting on that high bench, her once-broken arm poised at its strange angle in front of the array of stops and controls, and music filling the house. I long to hear that music. Maybe next time.

For the first time I walk the length of the butler's pantry. On the counter top where Aunt Glenn marveled at Sunday buffets, the lunch for the Guild is being prepared. I glimpse the kitchen, and I imagine that in Ruth's day, too, it was kept out of sight of visitors most of the time.

When we reach the basement, Lucy perks up. What was once a single-lane bowling alley is now a pottery studio and while Sonja shows me where the pins were placed and reminisces about a portable bowling alley the family used on Cumberland, Lucy watches in awe as pots take shape on spinning wheels. One of the potters gives her a ball of damp clay that she will mold in her hands for the rest of the morning.

Sonja has work to do, and I thank her for taking the time to show me around. I have not seen much more than my first time here, but it was important to have these doors open, to know that no great mystery lurked behind them. The sun is back today, so we set off to explore the grounds. Reduced from the original twenty-seven acres to fifteen, they still offer us plenty of opportunity for walking and collecting leaves.

I wonder if the woods in which the fictional Wingo children met the evil "Callanwolde" were behind what is now the back fence of the estate. I imagine horses, gardens, tennis courts, and everything else that once graced the grounds. Several outbuildings still stand—an eight-car garage, the gardener's cottage. These

Buddy, Bo, and Ruth at the Callanwolde pool about 1940.

Little Ruth in the shallow end at Callanwolde; Màmà sits on the bench.

have been restored and are used for arts groups, but one building especially interests me, and Lucy follows me as I turn down a narrow path into
overgrown woods in search of the club house, a stone building next to the
Callanwolde swimming pool.

The grandchildren swam regularly in the chilly waters of the spring-fed
pool. One picture that Bo and Betsy lent me from Ruth's early days shows
a wooden platform that was built into the pool to provide a "shallow end"
for the littlest children. Ruth, who can't be more than two, climbs on the
railing. Soon all the children were swimmers and could enjoy zooming
down the tall slide into the deep water. Many of Ruth's high school friends
told me about pool parties at Callanwolde, and my father said that the
summer after he and Ruth were married, they swam there nearly every
day.

The pool has long ago been filled in, and the land on which it lay is no
longer part of Callanwolde, but Lucy and I find the spot where Ruth
spent so many happy times. A chain-link fence separates the current Callanwolde property from the site of the pool, now a parking lot. Near the

fence is the shell of the club house, which had dressing rooms for swimmers downstairs and a stone-floored game room upstairs where Ruth and
her friends held parties.

I'm not sure whether I'm glad we have found the club house or not.
Lucy won't walk into it with me, and I don't blame her. The windows are
boarded up, but the doors hang off their hinges and I peer into the darkness at piles of rotting timbers and assorted debris covered with ceiling
plaster, cobwebs, and dirt. That the building still stands seems remarkable. The main house and the other outbuildings, though changed, are at
least being used, and I like to think that Popee and Danny, great lovers of
the arts, would appreciate that use. But this building, where Ruth's friends
still remember coming on warm afternoons to swim in one of the few
pools in Atlanta, is devoid of life. Though Sonja told me they hope to
raise the money to restore it, for now this building is as dead as Ruth. Lucy
and I are glad to leave.

What do I gain from this second visit to Callanwolde? Certainly the
new knowledge I brought with me—the images of Ruth playing the organ,
Glenn ogling the buffet, children opening presents—helps me imagine the
house as it was. But ultimately, visiting Callanwolde is not a trip back in
time, but merely a walk through empty rooms. This time the doors are
unlocked, but the rooms are still empty. The Candlers are gone.

I strap Lucy into her car seat with her ball of clay and a few leaves she has
gathered, and we continue our journey into the past.

The newspaper article about my parents' wedding ends, "After a wedding
trip to North Carolina the couple will reside at 1542 Farnell Court." This
is how I discovered the address of their first apartment. After her family
moved out of the Lullwater house in 1947, Ruth lived in another house
until her marriage in 1955. That house, on West Wesley Road, I know
well—my grandmother still lives there. But Lucy and I don't have time this
morning to make the trek across to Buckhead. Farnell Court, however, is
nearby.

Ruth's new home with Bob would be near her old neighborhood, about
as close to the Emory campus as the Lullwater Parkway house had been,
though on the other side. About all that separated her apartment building from Emory was the estate of her great uncle, Walter Candler. The

185-acre estate, called Lullwater, would be purchased by the university in 1958 and the manor house would become the home of the university president. On the other side of the Lullwater estate from Emory is a small development of apartments, now owned by the university. This little neighborhood includes a two-block street named Farnell Court, and here Ruth and Bob spent their first year of marriage. She was still a student at Emory, and he was an undergraduate, too, at Oglethorpe College, a smaller school on Peachtree Road a few miles away.

There isn't much for me and Lucy to do on Farnell Court. We drive its length, looking for building number 1542. The buildings are nearly identical, but I still want to know which one. The last one on the right is the answer.

"That's where Ruth and Bob lived after they got married." I say to Lucy.

"You mean married like my Mom and Dad?' she asks.

"That's right."

"And like you and Janice?"

"Yep. And then they lived in that building."

"Do you think they played in that sand box?" she asks.

"Maybe so," I say, relishing the image Lucy has conjured up for me of my young parents building castles here on Farnell Court. I feel like a private detective, slipping out of my car and snapping pictures, not of a lovely old house, but of an ordinary apartment building. Farnell Court looks like a place where married college students might have lived in 1955. The two-story apartment houses of brick and white siding stand back from the street behind green lawns and large oak trees. Only the addition of an ugly modern apartment tower at one end of the block mars the tranquillity of the street. The tower adds to the mystique of the place for me, though, because Janice spent the early days of her first marriage on Farnell Court as well, on the fifteenth story of the new tower.

I've been in post-war apartments before. I can imagine the hardwood floors and linoleum kitchen, the cranks on the windows and the towel bar on the side of the pedestal sink.

"We had a converted studio," my father told me, "so the common rooms were nice and big. We paid $67.50 a month."

What a change from the sprawling house on West Wesley Road this apartment must have been for Ruth. No formal living room and dining

room, no spacious grounds insulating her from neighbors, no cook, chauffeur, or upstairs maid, no private bathroom and dressing room, no siblings, and no parents. Ruth had spent a year living in a dormitory, and
had taken vacations on Cumberland where living conditions were more
rustic than elegant, but her home had always been Lullwater Parkway or
West Wesley Road. Now, like the graduate students and young faculty
who made up their neighbors, home was Farnell Court. I doubt that the
neighboring students had quite the cache of silver, crystal, and china that
Ruth and Bob had received as wedding presents.

Though Farnell Court was a major step down in luxury from West
Wesley Road, Ruth responded not by pining for more elegant surroundings but, according to some of the notes in the wedding album, by making
her own furniture. Betsy says Ruth was no cabinet maker, but she did
build a couple of end-tables. "Ruth fit into her role quickly when she
married," wrote Betsy. "She was a good cook and learned to sew at some
time." My father has never been what you would call a handyman, but
apparently Ruth took over that role too. "She was always able to fix things
and to do things," wrote Bob's sister Susan. "It seemed that whenever
anything needed to be fixed, someone would say, 'Well, let Ruth do it.
She can do anything.'" She also had her junior year in college to attend to.
During the fall term, she took "Medieval Culture," "The American Novel,"
and "History of Western Thought." She made two B's and a C.

The apartment on Farnell Court is the first of Ruth's Atlanta resi-
dences that can be described as ordinary. I wonder if anyone else in the
building knew that the sweet young married couple that just moved in
was having dinner at Callanwolde every Sunday night.

"Okay," I say to Lucy as I hop back in the car. "Only two more houses to
see and then we can get some lunch."

"That's a lot of houses," she says, and it seems so, but we're covering
twenty-seven years of Ruth's life, after all. It only seems like a lot when you
do it in three hours.

That we can make our next stop is a great stroke of luck. Several weeks
ago, I wrote to St. Luke's Episcopal church, where Ruth and Bob met, and
asked for any records they had about Ruth's baptism, confirmation, and
so on. The church archivist sent me photocopies of the cards for the Candler family, and for Ruth and Bob after they were married. The address

"1542 Farnell Court," had been crossed out and the next address on the list was "1308 Clairmont Circle." Daddy had not mentioned this apartment to me.

"I'd forgotten about that," he said when I asked him about it on the phone. "It was a little bigger than the apartment on Farnell Court. We lived there for about six months after David was born and before we bought the house." So Lucy and I are headed for Clairmont Circle. The distance from Farnell Court isn't much more than a few hundred yards. The street is lined with drab two-story apartment buildings, much closer to each other and to the street than those on Farnell Court. The pale yellow paint is peeling off the concrete sides of the buildings. A step down, I think.

The street has been renumbered since 1956; there is no number 1308. In a way, I'm glad. I'd rather imagine Ruth and Bob at the peaceful end of Farnell Court than in one of these dilapidated buildings. True, they probably weren't dilapidated forty years ago, but it's with no regret that I drive right on by.

In the summer of 1957, with a new baby in the family and Ruth finishing up her college degree, my parents moved into their first house, about two miles from Emory. Black Fox Drive consisted mostly of small ranch homes on large lots with tall pine trees and rolling hills. Behind my parents' house the hill dropped off sharply toward a small lake. Unlike the other houses in the neighborhood, Ruth and Bob's new home was a victim of 1950s "modern" architecture—my least favorite architectural style. The additions my father told me about obscure the original shape of the house, but its modern look still stands out. I pull up across the street and snap a picture, hoping no one will see the lens sticking out of my car.

"See that funny looking house?" I ask Lucy.

"Did your Mom and Dad live there?" she asks.

"They sure did. And do you know who else lived there."

"Who?"

"Aunt E and Uncle David."

"They did?"

"Yep, when they were little kids."

"My age?"

"That's right."

"Did you ever live in that funny house?"

"No, I wasn't born yet."

"Oh."

Modern domestic architecture of the 1950s seems out of keeping with what I think of as my father's traditional tastes—his love of classical music that he shared with Ruth, his professorial affection for the eighteenth century in England, even the more traditional architecture of the house he and Ruth bought in Winston-Salem five years later. I asked Aunt Betsy if she knew what possessed my parents to buy the house on Black Fox Drive.

"Ruth had a change of taste not long before she was married," Betsy said. "She had her pink room painted green, and she traded in the silver flatware she had been collecting—a frilly French looking pattern—for a sleek modern design." Betsy thought Bob influenced this change. I tried to inventory the furniture I knew Bob and Ruth purchased in the early years of their marriage. Sure enough, there it was—Danish contemporary dining room furniture, a similar hi-fi cabinet, and the chair that Ruth would be carried out of her house in. I, too, went through a Danish contemporary phase after I first got married, but I thought I was being hip and modern. It never occurred to me that my parents had done the same thing thirty years before.

They lived in the house on Black Fox Drive for five years, and I have seen almost no pictures of Ruth, Bob, or their house from that period, because they now had something else to photograph—children. My brother David was born during spring break of 1957, shortly before they moved into Black Fox Drive, and my sister, Elizabeth, followed in June of 1958. The children started arriving before college was finished for Ruth, and with these arrivals, Ruth might have felt that her adult life really began.

"One thing Màmà sometimes talked about was Ruth's love of children," Glenn had told me. "She said her one goal in life was always to get married and have children; she also said you children were her whole life when you came along." So, while she no doubt supported her husband in his struggle to make a career choice—he worked for Sears and Roebuck for a while before deciding to go to graduate school in English—Ruth had made her own choice long ago. Even if the house is, in my opinion, less than attractive, Ruth's years in her final Atlanta home were happy and she looked forward to the eventual addition of two more children and to all that raising a family had to offer.

I shake my head as we drive back up Black Fox Drive. How could some-one who grew up surrounded by homes as beautiful as Callanwolde and the Lullwater house end up in a place like this? But before I can speculate on an answer, Lucy sighs a dramatic sigh from the back seat.

"Now can we have some lunch?" she asks.

Some of these houses will one day fall victim to development or decay, but for a long time, probably until long after I'm gone, there will be houses standing in which Ruth lived, though no one may be left to know it.

Earlier in the week, Lucy and I had a chance to visit one other landmark associated with Ruth—St. Luke's Episcopal church in downtown Atlanta.

During the late 1940s and early 1950s, St. Luke's was the largest Epis-copal parish in the South. Ruth's mother had been married at St. Luke's and, despite her Theosophical leanings, was still a member, though she did not attend services. In fact, during Ruth's childhood, her family were not churchgoers. When they lived in the Lullwater house, the children sometimes went to Sunday School, but once the family moved to West Wesley Road, church was not a part of family life. Ruth, like Bob, starting going to St. Luke's because some of her friends told her about the youth group there. In May of 1950 she was confirmed there; she had started attending services the year before.

In 1949, the year Ruth started ninth grade, a young assistant rector at St. Luke's named Wilson Sneed thought it would be a good idea to have a youth group for ages thirteen through fifteen. Ruth's friends invited her to the group, just as Bob's friend would invite him a year or so later. To Rev. Sneed, then, I perhaps owe thanks for introducing my parents.

I wrote to Rev. Sneed and he was kind enough to call me and chat. He was on a break from chemotherapy, he said, and writing a letter was just too much effort. He remembered Ruth and Bob as two of the earliest members of that youth group. "We met every Sunday night," he said, "had a light supper, played parlor games, and then had a talk either from someone in the church or from someone from another church. It was a friendly and casual group. They had a good time, and got some spiritual knowledge." A few months later, I would get a note from St. Luke's telling me that Rev. Sneed had died and I would call my father to tell him the news.

Through St. Luke's, Ruth and Bob became friends. When he was old enough to drive, Bob picked Ruth up on Sunday mornings to attend the eleven o'clock service. Most weeks, the service consisted of Morning Prayer, punctuated by an impressive music program. Though he admitted that spots in the choir were as valuable as "seats on the New York Stock Exchange," my father described the service at St. Luke's in those days as profoundly low-church. "Not a Eucharistic vestment in sight."

Rev. Austin Ford, who came to St. Luke's as a young assistant in 1953, wrote to me, "Your parents gave me their friendship right away and helped me dig in. One says 'they' because they were invariably paired, and it was assumed and accepted that someday they would marry. Bob and Ruth were unusually mature, clearly in love, but in a comfortable rather than an excited relationship. I was a fairly strict and orthodox Anglican, rather High Church which also drew your parents and me together. Defenders of the Faith. We thought it needed defending as the tradition [at St. Luke's] was Broad, tending to lax." I, too, favor the High over the Broad—the outward and visible sign.

With the parish located downtown in an increasingly sprawling city, I wonder what Lucy and I might find there the Sunday after All-Saints Day. Unsure if there is child care available, I decide to try an early afternoon visit, hoping the services will be over but the sanctuary might still be unlocked. Peachtree Road is as empty as it gets on a Sunday morning, and I scan each block for the familiar "The Episcopal Church Welcomes You" sign. As the numbers on the buildings get lower we pass "Nude Dancing" and then, across the street from a giant "Hooters" billboard, we spot St. Luke's.

Its facade is not as imposing as I expected. No great towers or steeples. The brick and stone building is more similar in shape to an Oxford college chapel than to a Cathedral. Inside, we discover the conclusion of a service of Baptism and Holy Eucharist, and Lucy and I slip into the back pew for the final prayer and hymn. The high wide sanctuary is unbroken by pillars or transepts, and narrows only slightly at the choir. Above the altar, a mural of the good shepherd catches Lucy's attention. She draws a picture of it in the pew while I stand to sing the final hymn, "Ye Watchers and Ye Holy Ones." I haven't sung it in years, but still know several verses by heart. As the choir processes to the back of the church their voices lift my own to its full strength and I feel like a real participant in worship. I can almost hear my father's voice, so like my own, ringing out the same words in this same space so long ago. Then, before I can try to imagine Ruth's voice joining his, the hymn is over, and the congregation, which nearly filled the church, begins filing out. Lucy and I stay long enough to look around the sanctuary. She especially wants to see the freshly baptized babies having their pictures taken with family under the pulpit.

We hold hands as we walk back down the aisle and out into the cold day. I'm pleased to have felt so at home in the parish that brought my parents together, to see that, in spite of its immediate surroundings, it is still active (the congregation was white, black, Hispanic, old, young . . .). And, I am pleased to have shared the experience with Lucy.

With my catechisms, our sightseeing, and our family visits, I have been trying to impart something of Ruth to Lucy during this visit. I'm never quite sure if I'm successful in such an effort—never certain how much of what we talk about Lucy remembers.

As we leave St. Luke's, I tell her, "Your grandmother went to that church."

"Ruth?" Lucy asks, and I pick her up and hold her close to me and thank God for every day I'm alive to spend with her.

XIII

I mark this day with a white stone.
　　　　　　　　　—Lewis Carroll

During my visit to Atlanta with Lucy, I assumed there would be a *next time*. Janice and I have friends in Atlanta, Jordan's father lives near Atlanta, my grandmother, though frail, still enjoys short visits. I had avoided my fear of ringing a stranger's doorbell on Lullwater Parkway by saying "next time." I had solved the problem of what to do with Lucy while I dug through the boxes and trunks of Màmà's attic by saying "next time." I had decided to go to St. Luke's on Sunday morning rather than to the church Ruth and Bob attended after they were married by whispering "next time."

Next time came a few months later, in mid-March of the following year, without Lucy, but with Janice. We were on our way to Cumberland Island, at the invitation of Bo and Betsy. I would get a chance to see the place where Ruth spent so many happy times. Two weeks before we left, I wrote to Ruth's childhood house on Lullwater Parkway. Not knowing who lived there, I addressed the letter to "Resident" and added a plea on the envelope—"This is not junk mail. Please open it." I explained myself to whomever might read the letter. "My mother grew up in your house," I said. "Could I possibly take a look inside?"

Five days later, the phone rang, and I met Spencer and Gail King. They knew about the Candler family, knew about the history of their house, and were eager for us to visit. So now, with a envelope full of old photographs loaned by Bo and Betsy, I guide another rental car down Lullwater Road, this time turning not just onto the Parkway, but up the serpentine drive of Ruth's first home.

Some of the pictures in the envelope next to me show the outside of the house and the yard as they were in the 1930s. Save for some growth in the landscaping, the house looks much the same. The driveway curves gracefully up the hill. A stone wall cuts across the incline to create some flatter lawn space. Now this space is filled with shrubs and ground cover. In the old snapshots children play on a playground merry-go-round, pull a "Streak Lite" wagon, and pose in front of the wall in Indian get-ups, Ruth's three-year-old curls emerging from the band of her paper headdress.

We drive under the porte-cochere and pull up in front of the three-bay stone and stucco garage. Spencer King, trim, silver-haired, and smiling, emerges from the stone archway of the back door to greet us. Introductions accomplished, we step into the house. The back door opens onto a landing. Half a staircase leads to the lower level, another half up to the main floor. The banisters are polished wood supported by intricate wrought iron. Spencer points out that the letter "C" is worked into the design.

"Did your grandfather build this house?" asks Janice.

"Yes," I say.

Mrs. King, who has just emerged from the kitchen, says, "We actually have copies of the blue prints. We'll have to show you those."

I hardly have time to take in the cozy splendor of the main hall. In front of me is another arched doorway opening toward the front yard. To my left is a passage leading back toward the kitchen and a large arch opening into the dining room. On the right, several steps lead down into the one oversized room in the house—the living-room. The high-arched

The Candler home on Lullwater Parkway as it looks today.

ceiling is painted white between crosspieces of dark woodwork. The floor, too, is dark wood, and the fireplace carved limestone.

"It was originally mahogany," says Spencer, "but the people who lived here after your family tore it out and tossed it into the woods out back. The next residents found the thing, and had a limestone copy made."

I imagine Mrs. Russell teaching drama lessons to Ruth and her friends in this room, or her seventh-grade class having a dance party here. In the corner by the steps stands a piano. Its design stops me. I have only ever seen one other piano like this—a Mason & Hamlin upright. The carving on the legs, the design of the music stand, everything is identical to the piano I grew up with, the piano I learned to play on—my mother's piano.

"You know," I say to Spencer and Gail, "That's exactly like Ruth's piano."

"You're kidding!" says Gail. She has never seen another one like it either.

We tour the kitchen and breakfast room, Gail showing us how they have modernized without losing the original feel. "We had the cabinet maker copy the cabinets in the butler's pantry when we put these new ones in the kitchen."

The passageway I had spotted earlier leads to a small paneled study, which reminds me of several such studies in homes of my grandfather—from his ranch house at the farm to his last condo in Atlanta.

"Look at this," Spencer says. He reaches behind the curtains and presses a small button recessed in the woodwork. A section of paneling opens up, revealing a deep cabinet with several shelves. "What do you suppose they kept in here?"

I know my grandfather, and Janice knows her American history. We look at each other and say "Whiskey."

The tour continues upstairs, where there are four reasonably sized bedrooms. The largest, excepting the master bedroom, had been the boys room.

"There used to be a mural painted on the ceiling," says Gail. "World War II airplanes viewed from below painted against a blue sky with clouds." I can imagine my uncles lying in their beds and staring up at airplanes—their father was a flyer, Bo would later fly his own plane, and his son Ricky would become an airline pilot some fifty years after his Dad stared at this ceiling dreaming of the sky.

Gail shakes her head. "It's a shame," she says, "somebody painted over it."

"Probably the same people who tore out the fireplace," Janice says.

From the top floor, we go to the bottom—the floor that opens out to the porte-cochere. A low arched hallway leads past a large room filled with bookcases, exercise equipment, and basement clutter.

"We thought this might have been a pool room," says Spencer, but here I am able to enlighten them. Uncle Bo told me that he used the room in the basement as a workshop where he made models—most often of airplanes. At the other end of the hallway, a door opens into the real basement, and Spencer shows us the battleship gray paint on the walls behind the furnace.

"The kitchen and butler's pantry used to be painted like that too," he says. I don't know how many servants worked in this house when Ruth lived here, but every room is equipped with a button that rings a bell in the butler's pantry, and on the pantry wall is a display showing where the summons originated. The Kings have kept the system in working order, as part of the house's history.

Outside, I am impressed by how isolated the house is. Not only is the lot huge, at least an acre or two, but the area beyond the hill on which we stand is part of the Druid Hills golf course. Below us is the Lullwater Conservation Garden. In the summertime, I imagine, it's difficult to see another house.

Beyond the terrace and a swath of lawn is a plain building with brown siding—too big to be a garden shed, too small to be a servants' cottage.

"That's the playhouse," says Spencer. A playhouse probably built originally for Ruth's brothers. I close my eyes for a moment and try to bring those pictures of children playing and Uncle Bo's stories to life.

"We used to play cowboys and Indians," Bo told me, "and take turns storming and defending the fort."

"How old was Ruth when you shot her with the arrow?" Aunt Betsy asked Bo.

"You did what?" I asked. Bo said it was no big deal—he just shot the arrow up in the air and it happened to come down and stick in her head.

"It didn't break the scalp or anything," said Bo, and I rolled my eyes and realized that growing up with two older brothers was not always easy.

The other outbuilding is the garage, which has a large room above it. We walk around to the back of the house and negotiate a series of stone paths, arches, walls, and staircases. In one wall I notice a round white stone, about eight inches in diameter.

"We've always wondered about that," says Spencer. "It has some sort of inscription on it in Latin, but it's too worn to read. I think it might be from the Holy Land, but we don't know if Mr. Candler got it on a trip or how it got here."

The room above the garage is dusty, but still as beautiful as the rooms in the house. High ceiling, dark wood paneling, a fireplace, kitchenette, and bathroom make it a perfect apartment. I have a hard time imagining a room so nice being used as a workshop, but according to Uncle Bo, that's what Grandpa used it for. If I lived here, I think, it would be my library.

"We used to rent it out," says Gail, "mostly to Emory students."

"I wish I'd known. " Janice laughs, and we exchange a glance that communicates all we both remember of her first apartment off campus.

Back inside, Gail pours us all a Coca-Cola and we settle down to look over the blueprints she has spread out and the pictures I have brought.

"House Designed for C. H. Candler Jr." say the blueprints. The dates vary, but it looks as if the house was finished around 1930, just about the time the first child was born. The family lived here for seventeen years.

Only two of the pictures I have to show the Kings were taken inside the house, both showing Buddy, Bo, and Ruth under the Christmas tree. In the first, taken in 1938, Ruth, at two and a half, holds a doll nearly her own size. Her curls have bows near the front and a pigtail in the back and she looks about as much like Lucy as in any photo of her I have seen. The boys are posed next to a set of toy cars, and a dog looks on in a perfect "his master's voice" pose.

"A dog?" I asked Uncle Bo. Yes, a dog. I shouldn't have been surprised Ruth and her brothers had a dog—it was merely one more normal detail of life I had never heard about. The absolute ordinariness of dog owner-ship was driven home by the dog's name—Spot. Looking at the picture, I can see the name was aptly given. Spot was a small short-haired white dog with a prominent black spot over his right eye and another two-thirds of

the way down his back—a near clone of the dog in the Little Rascals mov-
ies. If ever a dog deserved the name "Spot," this was the dog.

The other picture of Christmas at Lullwater is undated, but looks a year
or two later. The children sit behind, what else, a toy airport, complete
with planes. Now four or five, Ruth has grown her hair below chin length
and has it done up in Shirley Temple ringlets.

Spencer and Gail seem genuinely interested in the family. Gail was
active in the movement to save Callanwolde in the 1970s. Spencer is a
doctor working for Emory.

"Where did the children go to school?" asks Gail.

"They went to Druid Hills Elementary," I say. That school has long
ago divested itself of the lower grades, and is now just Druid Hills High

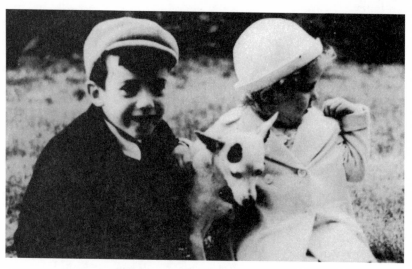

Bo, Spot, and Ruth, in the late 1930s.

School. It's a mile or two away, just on the other side of the Emory campus and across the street from a house Janice lived in during her first
marriage.

"Their uncle Billy's chauffeur would drive over from Callanwolde and
take them to school in the mornings," I say, repeating Uncle Bo's memory.
When they did go to Sunday School, uncle Billy's chauffeur would drive
them there, too, even though Glenn Memorial Methodist church, which

Danny had given the money for and named in honor of her father, was only a few blocks away.

As the four of us sit at the breakfast table, sipping Coke and speculating on what it was like to live in this house during the war, I am overcome with a sense of the immediacy of the place. I have been to many places where Ruth lived, but this is different. The Ruth I know the least, Ruth as a child, did more than live here. She did more that sit on the spot where I sit and rush up and down the stairs I have climbed and defend the playhouse I explored. Her life was shaped here. For twelve years, this was her world, and it's hard to imagine a more protected place to grow up. When she wasn't here, she was at Callanwolde or Cumberland, both even more insulated than Lullwater. True, at school she received instructions on air raid drills, but the war must have seemed far off to a little girl living on Lullwater Parkway.

"Did the murder happen during the war?" asks Janice, and I have to dig through my notes to answer her.

"September, 1943," I say. "Ruth was eight."

In a house a few blocks away, a burglar shot and killed Ruth's great uncle. Until I found it mentioned in a book on local Atlanta history, I had never heard about this crime. Henry C. Heinz was a prominent banker married to Popee's sister. When he encountered an intruder in his house just before ten o'clock that night, he tried to stop the man. In the ensuing struggle, he was shot. Certainly some of Ruth's family must have attended Heinz's funeral. And how could the eventual apprehension of the killer have escaped conversation? I can't imagine Ruth's not knowing about this incident. I wonder how an eight-year-old girl would feel, during wartime, waking to the sound of sirens and then learning the next morning that not a soldier or a sailor, but a gentleman banker who also happened to be a relative had been shot to death less than a mile away. I would have been terrified.

About this same time, when she was eight, Ruth fell and hurt her arm. According to her medical records, her right elbow was dislocated and was set in a cast for several weeks after being relocated. None of her siblings could remember which house this happened in, but when I obtained her medical records from Emory Hospital I solved that mystery—she fell in the Lullwater house. Two years later, in January of 1946, she was back in the hospital with appendicitis, and underwent her first surgery.

"They didn't move until after the war, right?" asks Gail.

"Summer of 1947," I say. "Ruth lived here longer than any other place in her life." This had been Ruth's home on her tenth birthday, and two months later when the war finally ended. On quiet Lullwater Parkway, I suspect the celebrations were more reserved than elsewhere. Ruth's father returned home from his volunteer patrolling duties and the family pattern was never quite the same as before the war.

"I think" I say to Gail, "that for a lot of those years before the war, they were happy here. As happy as they would ever be." Ruth had told my father just that.

"If we had stayed in Atlanta," Daddy told me, "Ruth would have loved to buy that house on Lullwater." It is not hard to see Ruth's adult life as an attempt to recreate the Lullwater days. She had three children and was planning a fourth. By the time she moved to Winston-Salem, the North Carolina mountains seemed on their way to acting as the same sort of retreat that Cumberland had been for the Candlers. Ruth saw Lullwater, my father said, as the site of the happiest times for her family—times when they truly were a family.

"Maybe that happiness was the reason she signed her name on the house," says Spencer.

"I beg your pardon?" I say.

"Come here, I'll show you." Janice and I follow Spencer out the front door, and he points to a strip of mortar between two blocks of stone.

Ruth's signature on the Lullwater Parkway house.

There, in crude but perfectly legible printing, are the words "Miss Ruth Candler Jr." My mother signed her house. How this signature has lasted fifty years I have no idea. It looks as if it is written in pencil, and it looks as if it were written this morning. "This was my home," it says. "I was happy here." Even her sense of humor is there between those stones. "Miss Ruth Candler Jr." she writes. Her mother was also Ruth Candler. If her father could be a "Junior," why not her?

"It will only take us a few minutes," I told Janice when we pulled into the King's driveway to look at the house. Two-and-a-half hours later, we finally head back to our car, still swapping stories as we stand in the driveway. We came here looking for the past, but we found, too, a friendship that has every promise of carrying on to the future. I think Ruth would like the Kings, would like the care and love they have given to her house, and would like the way they took her son and her daughter-in-law into their hearts.

"So," says Janice, "if we could buy that house, would you want to live in Atlanta?" Atlanta is too big for me, now, but it's easy to forget that in a beautiful house on Lullwater Parkway.

"I've fallen in love with that house," I say. "I can understand why Ruth would have liked to live there again." But I can also understand why she wanted to leave Atlanta, and I can't quite forget the traffic and the noise that we're headed for and that keep me from entertaining serious dreams of living on Lullwater even in a house that Ruth had inscribed as her own.

The next morning, we attend services at St. Bartholomew's Episcopal church. Ruth and Bob transferred here in the late 1950s, when the new church was under the rectorship of Austin Ford, their friend from St. Luke's. The last service Ruth attended here was my baptism in December of 1962. Like the house on Black Fox Drive a couple of miles away, St. Bart's is built in 1950s modern style. I-beams and duct work are exposed, and the fact that the entire building is under construction as part of an expansion program only adds to its contrast with the traditional interior of St. Luke's. Try as I might, I cannot feel my parents' presence here the way I did in St. Luke's.

The gospel reading that morning, however, seems appropriate.

> And as Jesus passed by, he saw a man which was blind
> from his birth. And his disciples asked him, saying, Mas-
> ter, who did sin, this man, or his parents, that he was
> born blind? Jesus answered, Neither hath this man sinned,

nor his parents: but that the works of God should be
made manifest in him.

The house Ruth's mother lives in was built in the 1930s by the president
of the Trust Company of Georgia, Robert Strickland. It is a white brick
structure nestled on several acres of trees in the heart of Buckhead.
Strickland died of cancer in the summer of 1946 at the age of fifty-one,
and the house went on the market. It is larger than the Lullwater house
and Ruth's parents decided they wanted it. Ruth's grandfather served on
the board of the Trust Company, so it is likely that he, if not his son, had
already seen the inside of the house. The Candlers were not the only
family bidding but in the end they bought the house for what I'm sure
seemed an outrageous price at the
time and would no doubt seem
like pocket change now.

The house that, to me, has always been "Màmà's house" became the Candler family home in
the summer of 1947. Ruth was
twelve, and the move symbolized
the end of her childhood years and
the beginning of adolescence. She
transferred from Druid Hills Elementary School to Washington
Seminary and left the Lullwater
life far behind. These were the
years when Betsy Denny became
her best friend and her brother

*Màmà and me at the house on West
Wesley Road in the mid-1960s.*

Bo's best girl and the years when she met, befriended, and fell in love with
Bob Lovett.

Janice and I go upstairs to visit Màmà as soon as we arrive. She is awake
and sitting up, something that happens only a couple of hours a day, so
we take advantage of our opportunity. She smiles and remembers us, but
a good visit with her these days consists of ten or fifteen minutes during
which she might say a dozen or so sentences.

I doubt she will know what I'm talking about, but I say, "We went to visit an old house of yours yesterday. The one on Lullwater Parkway. We had a nice time looking around."

She is quiet for a moment, then smiles her knowing smile. "Did they give you the Cook's tour?" she asks.

"Yes, Màmà," I say, "they did."

The front door of Màmà's house opens into a large foyer facing a wide curving staircase. To the left is the formal living-room and to the right the formal dining room. They are the only formal rooms in the house—rooms that I rarely set foot in during all my years of visiting.

"We always ate in the breakfast room and lounged in the library," I tell Janice. For Ruth, though, these formal rooms were a central part of life.

In the French decor of the living-room, according to Aunt Betsy, Ruth gave solo piano recitals for friends and family. The piano she played, a baby grand that sits in the far corner past the fireplace, is now neglected, but in my teenage years, I played it occasionally—my fingers lumbering across the same keys Ruth's had danced over, the same notes ringing off the walls or soaking into the thick curtains.

The dining room, where I have eaten only once, was the site of family dinner each night at six o'clock. "It was not a formal household," Betsy said, but dinner was always at six and always in the dining room. Betsy and I marveled that dinner was kept on such a strict schedule until Bo reminded us that a full-time cook took care of the kitchen, and the up-stairs maid helped with the serving. Dinner consisted of two entrées each night. At one end of the table, where Ruth's father sat flanked by his sons, the meat was served—Betsy remembers roast chicken most often. At the other end, where the vegetarian mother and daughters sat, the meatless entrée would arrive.

I sit down at the head of the table and do my impression of Màmà as Glenn, Betsy, and Daddy have done it for me. Squirming in the chair I stretch a foot far under the table and press a button on the floor. When the door from the breakfast room opens in my imagination, I wave my fingertips over the detritus of dinner and in my best musically southern Màmà voice whisper, "Willie, you can get these things." Janice laughs and the sound echoes in the empty room.

According to Betsy, Emma was the cook in those days, and Willie the upstairs maid was followed eventually by Katie. The full-time staff probably consisted of at least three at any given time, and all three were black. Ruth grew up in a time and place where even modest middle-class homes had black servants. After Ruth's death, Bob, a single working father, decided to hire help. Mary Kimbrough came to work for us when I was four and stayed after Daddy remarried, until after I had gone off to boarding school. I loved Mary. She was bright, a voracious reader, and an assiduous follower of local politics. Years after she stopped working for us, she came to my house for a surprise anniversary party for my father and stepmother. I never saw her alive again, but I went to her funeral. There, I realized how little I had known of her. To me, as a child, her life was her interaction with my family. What went on when she returned to her neighborhood of small, clean houses seemed peripheral to me. Sitting at her funeral, I realized that the opposite was true—that her eight hours a day in our house was only a sidelight to her real life, family, friends, neighbors, and faith.

So I wonder about the lives of those who served the Candlers. I know that the Candlers attended their funerals and remembered them in their wills. They are frequently an integral part of family stories and remembrances. But how did Ruth really view the people who kept her house running? Did she have any insight into their real lives, or did she define them primarily by the roles they played in her own life? And how did they view her and the part of their life that took place at West Wesley Road? Was it merely a job, or something more? The only servant that I knew there, A.B., eventually got too old and infirm to work anymore. When Aunt Betsy went to visit him, he said to her, "If I could only go back to West Wesley Road, I'd be happy." He died shortly after that.

The remainder of the downstairs at West Wesley Road includes the library, breakfast room, the kitchen with its eight-burner gas stove, a large workroom over the four-car garage, a variety of pantries and hallways, a coat closet that brims with sheet music and classical records from the 1950s, and, of course, the powder room. For years it seemed every time I visited that house I found another bathroom I didn't know about. I believe now that there are nine, though I wouldn't be shocked to find others. Oddly only one half-bath offers relief on the sprawling main floor.

The basement is in two separate sections, each with its own staircase. One area was built for the servants and includes a bathroom and rest area. The other houses the pool room, my favorite place as a child. Sometimes

Carl would shoot pool with me, but usually I played in this room alone. As Janice and I descend the narrow winding staircase, a familiar musty smell greets me—stronger than it was twenty years ago, but still recognizable. The pool table is gone, a gift to some grandchild, and the room is damp and dirty, now used for storage. Janice notices a stack of 78 records on a shelf. Pasted onto the label of each is a return address sticker with Ruth's name. I whisk the records under my arm, wondering if, in this era of CD players, I will be able to find a machine that can play them. I'd love to hear what Ruth listened to as a teenager.

I hope that, if we open enough cabinets, look in enough closets, and venture into the attic, we will find some remnants of Ruth's life. Where are her letters home from Sweet Briar or her high school grade cards? Where are her letters from Paul O'Shields and her Valentines from Bob? This is not a house in which things get thrown away, so they must be somewhere.

At the top of the grand staircase, Janice and I turn left, away from Màmà's bedroom and toward the children's wing. On one side of the hall the guest room is followed by two bathrooms in a row leading into the boys room at the end. On the other side, a progression of three bathrooms leads from the master suite into a green bedroom I have never gotten a good look at. For most of my life, this was Carl's bedroom—I remember it only as a vast heap of papers and books obscuring walls, floor, and furniture. Carl died a little over a year ago and the room has been nearly excavated. For the first time I can walk through the door unchallenged and take a good look at what was once my mother's bedroom.

The peeling green paint is probably the same that Ruth picked out forty-five years ago when she decided to change the room from pink. No curtains hang in the windows. A faded rug worn completely through in spots covers most of the hardwood floor. But the built-in bookcase, the fireplace, the sunlit windows, and the door to the dressing room and private bath all speak of what a room this once was. Aunt Glenn, Aunt Betsy, and my father have all described it for me, and their descriptions are surprisingly similar. I walk through the room pointing out to Janice the location of each piece of furniture.

To the left of the door was the bed—a four-poster with swans on the top of the posts and pictures of ballet dancers hanging above it on the

wall. In the corner by the bed, Ruth's collection of miniature glass ani-
mals sat on a shelf. On the center of the left-hand wall is the fireplace, and
beyond it a niche with a window. Set under the window was a chaise—
which Ruth's friends considered the height of luxury. On the wall opposite the bed, another window, a dressing table, and the chest of drawers.
The right-hand wall held the piano that Ruth's grandmother had given
her. Next to the piano was the door to the dressing room, with its built-in
drawers and closet. From there another door led to Ruth's bathroom.
Add to all this the fact that the upstairs maid kept the room clean and the
clothes washed and you begin to get a sense of the style in which teenaged
Ruth lived.

Janice and I begin searching through the bedrooms, looking for anything that will tell us about Ruth. We don't find much. As we peer onto
shelves and through drawers, I dredge up all the stories I've heard from
my aunts and uncles about life in this house.

To begin with, there was Ruth's bed. Before long, the swans started
disappearing off the bedposts. Her brothers, who called them buzzards,
hid them all over the house. Now, nearly fifty years later, those brothers
still laugh about the "buzzard bed."

Betsy talked of Ruth's studying in her room. She would sit on a low
chair between the bookcase and the bed and lay out all her books on the
bedspread. "I would spend a half an hour getting ready," said Betsy, "but
Ruth just sat down and studied. It came naturally to her." I'm impressed
with Ruth's studiousness, but even more so with her nonchalance when
her studies were interrupted.

"Bo would come into the room and pick up one of Ruth's books,"
Betsy told me while her husband cringed at the story of his past foibles.
"'Do you need this page?' he would ask. If Ruth answered 'No,' he would
tear it out and throw it away; if she answered 'Yes,' he would tear it out
and give it to her." Doubtless he often grabbed a buzzard on the way out
of the room. Ruth would roll her eyes, fish the crumpled page out of the
trash, and go on with her studies.

Like so many others—family members, classmates, and friends—Bo and
Betsy say they never once saw Ruth lose her temper. Ruth didn't get angry,
and that trait impressed people so much they remember it thirty years
after her death. Again I wonder if she suppressed her fury, or if she was
able to avoid not only the expression of anger, but the anger itself.

Betsy spent many nights visiting Ruth in the house on West Wesley Road. She would sleep in Ruth's room or, if other friends were visiting, in the guest room across the hall. Each room was equipped with a house phone and the girls could call each other across the hall, or anywhere else in the house for that matter. When I was a child, most of these phones didn't work anymore, but I still loved playing with them, and I can remember the smooth heavy feel their black receivers had in my hand, so unlike the flimsy phones of today.

Our search of the bedrooms yields nothing, so I pull the rope that hangs from the center of the hall ceiling and a staircase emerges that will take us to the attic.

"I think I was up here once years ago," I tell Janice as we climb the ladder, "helping Màmà find a suitcase."

We find the lights and then look across an expanse of boxes, footlockers, closets, and blanketing everything, dust, dust, dust. I know we cannot look through every box, but we begin. In a closet I find a rack of old costume party clothes, including a dress my grandmother might have worn to the *Gone with the Wind* ball in 1939. Janice discovers a trunk of clothes from the 1930s—from hats to underwear. Under the eaves, I find a box of old board games, puzzles, and children's books. Only the "Elsie the Cow" game has Ruth's name on it. The rest look like they belonged to the boys—toy holsters, a copy of *Treasure Island* . . .

There are many trunks, most of them full of Carl's things, but Janice finds *the* trunk. It sits on rollers and is at least four feet high, almost three feet wide. She points to the return address label on the top. "Sweet Briar College," it says. This is the steamer trunk my mother took with her to Sweet Briar. It could have college papers in it, or better yet, letters from Bob.

"The key's taped to the top," says Janice. I turn the key in the lock, open the clasp, and prepare to pull the two vertical sections of the trunk apart. Nothing. Twenty minutes later, after pushing and pulling to the point that we are covered with sweat and dust, Janice looks at me.

"We're not leaving until we get this trunk open, are we?" she asks. I have no desire to keep my wife captive in a dusty attic, but I will not be back in Atlanta for several months, and I want to see what is in this trunk.

"No," I say, "We're not." But I take a break and creep under the eaves to inspect boxes of old letters, tax returns, and Theosophical Society newsletters. Before long I have wandered to the far side of the attic, out of sight of the trouble-making trunk.

"Charlie," says Janice, her voice pushing through the must, "I got it open." I dash past a stack of suitcases, jump over a heap of Christmas ornaments, and arrive in front of her to see the open trunk—space for hanging clothes on one side, and a neat row of drawers down the other.

"It's empty," says Janice. She shows me a travel iron built into one of the drawers, but other than that, there is nothing.

"All I had to do was rotate the clasp, and it popped open," she says. Sometimes you can find what you want by doing something so simple. We leave the attic with three things: a box of letters my grandfather wrote to my grandmother before they were married, a poem that may have been written by Ruth (in pencil on a piece of notebook paper), and Ruth's engagement calendar for the school year 1951–52. When I return home, I'll have something to look at.

We close up the attic, wash off as much of the dust as we can in one of the nine bathrooms, say good-bye to the nurse, and head outside for a walk around the grounds. The fresh air of impending spring and the bright sunshine are welcome after the stifling environment of the attic.

By the time they moved to this house, I imagine Ruth and her older brothers were more interested in dating than exploring the woods of the huge lot of West Wesley Road. Bo remembers coming home from dinner or the movies with Betsy and parking in the lower driveway—more private than any lovers' lane.

Across the back of the house is a wide stone patio looking into woods that drop away behind. Around the corner from that, a screened-in porch with ceiling fan offers some relief from summer heat. The house is not air-conditioned, but with shade from all the surrounding trees it has never seemed to me inordinately uncomfortable even on the hottest Atlanta days—as if the heat didn't dare touch the Candlers.

To the side of the porch, a sunken lawn is bordered on two sides by a low stone wall. Here, according to Betsy, Ruth played host to a "baby party" during high school. Every guest dressed as a baby, complete with oversized diapers and woobies. The regular entrance to the side yard was blocked off and a large sliding board erected. To enter the party, the girls had to climb the ladder and slide into the festivities.

Both the size of the lot and the size of the house meant West Wesley Road offered privacy for its residents. As Janice and I stroll across the side lawn, I feel pleasantly removed from the city. Here Ruth could visit with her friends and they could avoid her brothers. Here, also, her parents could remain under one roof while they drifted further and further apart.

Because Màmà's house is the one I know, I had always thought of it as the house Ruth grew up in. But she spent twelve years in the Lullwater house, and only five years on West Wesley Road before leaving for Sweet Briar. By the time she returned to spend her sophomore year at home, she was an adult. It seems overly simplistic to say that she was a child at Lullwater and an adolescent at West Wesley Road, and yet it's true.

Janice and I put our box with the records from the basement and the letters and papers from the attic into the back seat, and pull away from the house. Two hundred yards takes us over a short hill, through the woods, and back into Atlanta, as busy as ever.

And what of the booty? It turns out I had not one, but two pieces of browned notebook paper with what appears to be Ruth's youthful hand-writing. The first Betsy identified as authentic. "Yes," she said, "we used to play that game." It was a list of titles and authors—

Love's Lost Labor by Miss Carriage

The Broken Bra Strap by One Hung Lowe

Don't Change Yet by I. C. You

Some of the less seemly ones I remember from my own days at summer camp.

The second is a poem in eight stanzas about being stuck in bed with the measles. The poem is childish, with an overemphasis on meter and rhyme, but it has flashes of humor. It is also the only literary creation that I can even attempt to attribute to my mother. At first, it annoyed me that I couldn't be sure Ruth wrote this, but I realized it didn't make any difference. If I believe she wrote it, then she did, and I choose to believe. A stanza should be enough to give a sense of its style.

> One Sunday afternoon real late
> I came home from the show,
> Feeling hot and sort of tired,
> And weary don't "cha" know

My momee said, "You have the mumps,"
And put me in the bed,
Next day I woke up full of spots,
It was measles I had instead.

The engagement calendar promised to be a little more revealing. It covered the year when Ruth went from being the steady girl of Paul O'Shields to being the future wife of Bob Lovett. One would never guess that change from reading her few entries in this calendar, though.

"Paul Gets in, 8:20" on December 21, 1951. Then in following days, "Paul's Party," "Downtown with Paul," "Paul over for Dinner," "Date with Paul," and "Paul leaves." The week of Christmas is the busiest of the year, according to this calendar. Bob makes his only appearances here—she notes his birthday on the 27th and writes "Open house at Bob's" on the 24th. The three days after Christmas she has a dance every night, though one of them has been marked through. In January she goes to see Robert Frost give a reading. In February the Pi Pi formal (her high school sorority) falls on the day after "Paul got home, 6:00." In March, as in other months, she draws a heart around the 17th—this time she writes "two years." Undoubtedly her anniversary with Paul. The entries for the rest of the year are sparse and obviously written in far ahead of time. The heart around the 17th, for instance, continues through September, by which time Ruth and Bob had been having Sunday dinners at Callanwolde for some months. She records dates with "Ralph" and "Marshall," but none with Bob. By the time she and Bob become serious in the spring, she isn't writing in this calendar anymore. Too bad. Still, there is a touch of her teenage self in these pages, and I feel more intimate with that self for having seen them. This is, for all its sparseness, a more personal document of her high school years than any other I have seen.

And the records? Many of the titles and artists are unfamiliar to me, but the ones that are give me an idea of her musical tastes beyond her beloved opera and classical. Hank Williams, "Howlin' at the Moon"; Patti Page, "The Tennessee Waltz"; Perry Como, "Hello Young Lovers"; Gordon Jenkins and his Orchestra and Chorus, "Bewitched"; Randy Brooks and His Orchestra, "Harlem Nocturne"; Henri René and his Orchestra, "I'm in Love Again"; and tunes sung by Doris Day, Arthur Godfrey, Eddie Fisher, Les Paul, Dean Martin, and Mario Lanza.

My other discovery in Màmà's attic was serendipitous—I had hoped to find love letters that Bob sent to Ruth, instead I discovered some hundreds of letters that my grandfather wrote to my grandmother, primarily during the 1920s before they were married.

"I live from one letter to the next." "Are you wearing the pin all the time?" "Letters from you mean so much; if I don't get one tomorrow, I'll die." "Day by Day in every way I miss you more and more." "I hope you won't mind me keeping [your glove] because—well, I suppose it's foolish, but I take it in my hand and imagine that your hand is in it and sometimes it gets so real it hurts."

Hundreds of pages of this sappy stuff, this wonderful stuff, pouring from the pen of my reserved business-like grandfather. How different they are from the letters he would write his daughter forty years later. And what have they to do with Ruth, coming ten years before her birth? I had always thought of Ruth's parents as estranged from each other, of Ruth's growing up in a household without any real affection between mother and father. But Ruth was not born of an unhappy marriage, she was not a child of convenience in a wedding arranged for Society—she was the offspring of an intense and long-standing love that, though it faded away in the years after her birth, lived on in a box of letters that no one ever threw away.

XIV

Cumberland Island should be acquired for public use because no other area of comparable size exists on the Atlantic coast that offers better recreational opportunity. This choice natural resource, examples of which have given way elsewhere to commercial and residential developments, should be preserved as a National Seashore that will ensure its enjoyment by the greatest number of people.

—NATIONAL PARK SERVICE, 1966

A few of the letters from Ruth's father to her mother bear the postmark of St. Simon's Island, Georgia—letters that were written while Grandpa was staying on Cumberland Island. I have visited all of Ruth's homes in Atlanta and Winston-Salem, worshipped in her churches, even worked at her college, but Cumberland remains to be explored. Several members of the family have mentioned to me that guest books at the Candler compound can tell me exactly when Ruth was on the island. Cumberland is a place devoid of fax and copy machines, so the only way to see these guest books is to look at them myself. I have been to the island once before, nearly twenty-five years ago, but I remember that trip only vaguely and my memories have nothing to do with seeking my mother—more with seeing a beach for the first time, building sand castles, and getting knocked over by waves. At the invitation of Uncle Bo and Aunt Betsy, who still have a home on the island, Janice and I, along with my brother David, his wife Ellen, and his sons Lewis and Andrew, step off a small boat onto a weatherworn wooden dock on a cool and windy March day. Janice and I have left our exploration of Atlanta behind and arrived on Cumberland.

Cumberland Island is the largest and southernmost of the Golden Isles that protect the coast of Georgia from Savannah to Florida. The

island is sixteen miles long and several miles wide in places. Despite its
wild and empty appearance, Cumberland has a long history of human
habitation, from its original native American population, through six-
teenth-century Spanish missions, an eighteenth-century fort built by General Oglethorpe, plantations in the nineteenth century, and pleasure
grounds for the wealthy in the early twentieth. Beginning in the late 1920s,
the Candler family owned two thousand acres and some old clapboard
buildings, the remains of the Cumberland Island Hotel, at High Point
near the north end of the island.

We toss our bags into the back of a white pickup truck that an employee will drive to the house, and we load ourselves into the back of
Uncle Bo's purple pickup, which he has outfitted with wooden benches
for children and grandchildren. The ride to High Point takes about fifteen minutes bumping along a road that, like all the roads on the island,
is no more than a narrow strip of white sand and shells cutting through
trees dripping with Spanish moss.

The High Point compound is now an inholding in the U.S.
government's Cumberland Island National Seashore. The compound consists of a wing of the original hotel, now over a century old, that the family

Ruth's picture of the "Old House," probably taken in the late 1950s.

calls the "Old House"; a house that Popee had built in 1941 out of wood from the island (the "New House"); and four other houses fashioned from outbuildings. At the end of another generation, it will revert to the Park Service and the houses that my family has cared for and loved for so long will be abandoned and fall into ruin—like the Carnegie family's mansions at the other end of the island.

Bo and Betsy's house was a guest cottage of the hotel, and looks out over the tidal Christmas Creek and a wide saltwater marsh toward Little Cumberland Island. The small room Janice and I settle into was last occupied by Jimmy and Rosalynn Carter when they visited Bo and Betsy here a few months ago. Now Betsy jokingly refers to it as "The Presidential Suite." A rocking chair, chest of drawers, and bed with end tables comprise its furnishings. The windows look inland, and the wide painted floorboards have frequent gaps between them.

David and his family stay at the New House, a rambling affair with a huge living and dining room and several upstairs bedrooms. In front of the house the azaleas are in bloom. Despite their size both the old and new houses are simple and rustic, if not primitive. Although there is something inherently extravagant in owning 2,000 acres of a wild island, the Candlers' lifestyle on the island was far from luxurious.

After dinner, we settle into Bo and Betsy's living room, a cozy room with a screen porch on either side. On the walls hang postcards of the old hotel; pictures of children and grandchildren with Loggerhead turtles, alligators, and strings of fish; and various relics of nature on the island—a turtle shell, a barnacle-encrusted alligator skull, a deer trophy. The evening is cool enough that Bo lights a fire in the wood stove, and I start to narrate our adventure visiting the Lullwater house. Bo hasn't been back since the family moved out.

"He keeps wanting to go," says Betsy.

"Now that I know who lives there," says Bo, "Maybe I'll give them a call." It hadn't occurred to me that by opening doors for myself, I might leave them open for others in the family.

I ask Bo about the round white stone in the wall behind the Lullwater house.

"I wonder if Daddy brought that back from his trip to Egypt," he says. But he's not sure. Not sure, even, when Grandpa went to Egypt.

It doesn't take long to get Bo talking about childhood summers on

Cumberland in the 1930s. The only electricity was what they generated themselves. Cooking was done with wood or gas; refrigeration was provided by ice they brought over from the mainland in three-hundred-pound blocks.

"We used to chip pieces off the blocks so we could have iced tea," says Bo.

The well water had so much sulfur in it the ladies would save rainwater in a barrel to wash their hair. They had no telephone. In addition to Olie, the boat captain, the family had other employees—George and Audrey Merrow worked for the family for years as did various other islanders. And then there was Jesse Bailey, an alcoholic who spoke Gullah, loved to read, and was fired and rehired by Olie more times than either could count. Jesse caught whatever seafood the family needed, spending his days working the waters of Christmas Creek and living his life to the rhythm of the tides. In later years, he even took Jimmy Carter fishing. Jesse couldn't swim, and when he drowned in Christmas Creek, the family put a memorial stone next to the dock that read "He died where he lived, doing what he loved." Staring down at that gleaming white stone the next day I will wonder if the same epitaph might be applied to Ruth.

Jesse and Olie and George and Audrey are all gone now, but they were as much a part of Ruth's life on the island as her own family, and Bo's memories of them slowly start to shape my vision of what that life must have been like—a strange combination of primitive living (few modern conveniences, rustic living quarters) and wealthy luxury (plenty of servants, big houses, and a wild island of your own to explore).

In spite of the National Park Service's buying the island, in spite of the deaths of Jesse and Olie, in spite of the fact that nature is constantly reshaping the shorelines, Cumberland has changed less in the thirty years since Ruth's death than any other place she knew. The wild horses and pigs still roam the island, although the wild burrows of her day are gone. The live oaks strewn with Spanish moss still stand between the Old House and the New House. The beach is still a mile from the houses—a lovely walk through forest and across dunes. And people are still scarce, especially at the island's north end, far from the Park Service ferry and campground.

The next morning, Janice and I take a walk on the beach. At low tide it stretches at least two hundred yards across—wide and flat enough to

Ruth on the beach at Cumberland with her cousin Alfred Eldredge, Jr.

land an airplane, which Bo told us he has done on occasion. On the island's windward side, the beach is uninterrupted for sixteen miles. We walk for two or three of those miles and gaze along two or three more without seeing another soul. To Ruth, this was what the word "beach" meant.

Chilled from our walk on the windy shore, we congregate with Bo and Betsy and David's family in front of a fire at the New House and I gather up four old guest books in which I will search for my mother's name. Unfortunately, the family practice of writing lengthy descriptions of a visit in the guest book did not begin until after Ruth's death. During her lifetime, little was written beyond names and dates, but even these are illuminating. Ruth first came to the island in August of 1936, when she was just over a year old. The summer before, her family had come without her.

"She probably stayed in town with a baby-sitter," says Aunt Betsy.

From 1936 through 1940, Ruth spent at least part of every summer on Cumberland. During these years, her whole family was with her—there is no indication of the rift that would eventually separate her parents. It is difficult to tell exactly how long these stays lasted, because the signatures usually only bear one date, but in 1940, for instance, she came for two visits of about ten days each. She is described in 1937 as "Little Ruth Candler," but by 1939, at age four, she signs her own name.

In the spring of 1941, the family spent a long weekend on the island, Ruth writing her name in cursive, though she was still two months shy of her sixth birthday. That visit ended Ruth's early childhood on the island. On July 12, 1941, the final entry appears in the first guest book. For the next four and a half years, there would be no vacationing on the island. Cumberland would be, as it had been centuries before, a military outpost.

Most of the few pictures I have of Ruth on the island are from the pre-war period. About all that these pictures show is that Ruth did, as Sonja Kinard remembered, have curly blonde hair, and that she seemed to consider clothing optional. The pictures show her wading in the water and walking on the beach. In one where she is a little older, perhaps five or so, she wears a bandanna tied over her hair and, with her head tilted ever so slightly, cracks that glorious smile that would distinguish so many of her pictures as a young woman.

The war ended and Ruth returned to the island for Easter of 1947. She was now twelve years old, and would visit the island every year for the next eight years. She would soon be old enough to bring her friends with her to Cumberland, and as I turn the pages of the guest books, I see many familiar names from Washington Seminary. Ruth's house parties started in the spring of 1948, just shy of her thirteenth birthday. In the summer of 1949 I spot not only familiar names, but familiar nicknames.

Ruth at Cumberland.

"Anne Stewart Morris (cat woman), Wight Crawford (zombie), Ruth Candler (Voo Doo) . . ." The girls were about to begin their freshman year in high school, but Wight would write these Cumberland nicknames in Ruth's senior annual four years later.

"April 8, 1950 Laughing Party. Patsy Cathcart, Ruthe Yeargan, Ruth Candler, Jane Howard, Barclay Coggan, Paul O'Shields, Bill

Emmonds, Bob Lovett . . ." The first time my father came to Cumberland. He was one of the gang.

"I heard about that party," says Betsy. "They laughed for three days. All they had to do was look at each other and they'd start laughing."

Comparing the date to Ruth's record of her anniversary with Paul O'Shields in her engagement calendar, I realize this party happened just three weeks after Ruth and Paul became an "item."

Later in 1950, Betsy made her first trip to the island and met her future husband. The house parties and family visits continued and then in the summer of 1952 Ruth visited the island with Patsy Cathcart, Patsy's date, and Bob Lovett. No more Paul O'Shields. Bob was visiting the island as the boyfriend. By Thanksgiving, when the Candlers spent the holiday on the island, Bob was nearly a member of the family. He and Betsy were the only nonfamily members to sign the guest book that weekend.

"It was a family house party," says Betsy, "and they invited us because we looked like we might end up being family. I remember we had the table stretched out all the way into the hall and I remember Aunt Lou and Popee singing 'We Gather Together' before our Thanksgiving dinner."

After that, Ruth never came to the island without Bob. The next two summers they vacationed there, always with some chaperone, of course. In late August of 1954, one of the first narrative passages appears in the guest book.

"9:00 P.M. Had to take refuge at the beach as fire was threatening and smoke was so thick impossible to remain as sparks were showering houses. As fire got to within fifty feet of cattle guards [at the edge of the compound] the rain came putting out fire. Uncle Nelson [an island resident] said it was the largest fire ever on Cumberland island. Today, 29th, Hurricane Carol reported 200 miles east of Cumberland."

"We were sure the houses were going to burn down," says Betsy. "Everybody was trying to save something. Màmà came out of the house with a armful of belts! But Bob was the only one who kept his head. 'If we're going to save something' he said, 'save the guest books,' and he went inside and got them." The houses survived, but even if they hadn't, I might still be able to read these books thanks to my father.

What fear Ruth and the others must have experienced in that thick smoke and shower of sparks. It was not the only frightening experience

Ruth had on Cumberland. Uncle Buddy, Ruth's older brother, wrote to me of being on the island during another hurricane. "Ruth was very much afraid," he wrote. I have been in storms and even near fires, but I have never experienced what Ruth must have felt in such extreme situations in such an isolated place. Did that fear prepare her for the fear to come, the fear of her own death?

The next summer, for the first time since the war, Ruth didn't visit the island. It was 1955, and she was busy planning her wedding and writing those 151 thank-you notes. The following spring, she and Bob came to the island for the first time as a married couple. That summer they stayed on Cumberland from July 13 through September 9, about as long a stay as any recorded in the guest book by any family members.

Ruth did leave the island at least once during that summer—to visit a doctor in Atlanta who would confirm her pregnancy. But 1956 was Ruth's longest visit to Cumberland. She had been married less than a year and was looking forward to starting a family.

I imagine she spent the summer in much the same way as I spent my three days on the island—walking on the beach, watching the sunrise, exploring the woods, swimming in sparkling blue fresh water of Whitney Lake, spotting wildlife in the woods, and eating seafood. Above all, I imagine she enjoyed the chance to share the quiet and isolation of this peaceful place with a loving spouse.

Other vacationers came and went, including Bob's brother Chip for a few days. Ruth and Bob were rarely alone, but they were the constant on Cumberland for those two months. Standing by the shores of Christmas Creek at high tide as the sun sets over the marsh, I can imagine my parents here forty years earlier. They can smell the smoke from the fire where Jessie is baking oysters behind the Old House. They watch the fading evening light glitter off the ribbon of the creek winding through the marsh. A heron rises from the water, its great gray wings slowly taking it downstream. Ruth and Bob stand hand in hand, completely in love. They don't need anything else.

Despite a couple of opportunities, my father hasn't been back to Cumberland since Ruth died. "Too many memories," he told me, and I suspect many of those memories must come from the halcyon summer of 1956.

The next summer, with a new baby in the house and Ruth finishing her course work at Emory, my parents didn't make it to Cumberland. They visited for a few days in 1958, this time with year-old David in tow, but their visits after 1956 were few and short. Three days in 1958, five days in 1959, and ten days in 1961—Ruth's final visit to the island. David and Elizabeth (who first came to Cumberland at age two months) were along for these final visits, and in 1959 Bob's mother, whose husband had been killed in an accident the year before, and sister Susan also joined the growing family.

In the summer of 1962, Ruth was pregnant with me and busy moving. In the summer of 1963, she and her family were getting used to their new home and limited Georgia visits to Atlanta and Rolling Meadows. In the summer of 1964, she was dying. I never visited Cumberland with my mother or my father. In April of 1971 I wrote my name in the guest book alongside my grandfather, Mim, David, Elizabeth, and assorted other family. Now I write it again, but I am not even signing the same volume that contains Ruth's name.

I came to Cumberland to discover Ruth, and I have discovered her in the pages of the guest books and in my own imaginings as I wander the island, but my mind is soon distracted from that search by what else I discover. Bo and Betsy welcome Janice into their hearts with genuine love and kindness. The search for Ruth has led me back to her family, and I silently thank her for that. I discover, too, this unique island, which affects me in so many ways. It recalls my childhood summers of wandering the woods of the North Carolina mountains. It instills in me a sense of history of both nature and humanity and of the ability of those two to live together harmoniously. It elicits a sense of pride that my family was partially responsible for establishing this island as a National Seashore, permanently preserved. At the same time, I feel sadness that my family, who had preserved their own part of the island so carefully, were essentially forced to sell to the government and will eventually be evicted—the houses filled with so much history left to decay.

On our last day, we take a long walk through the woods with Betsy and David's family. We pass the remnants of The Settlement, a black community started by freed slaves, and Betsy points out where an Indian village once stood. We find shards of ancient pottery on the beach and watch wild horses grazing by the marsh. I stand in the wind that bends the marsh grass and look at Hushamouth Island a few hundred yards away—the tiny island where Ruth once dreamed of having a home is still wild, unchanged since she and her husband stood on it forty years ago. We visit the grass airstrip where my grandfather used to land his plane, and where Bo's son, Ricky, still lands. Finally, we come to the graveyard, hidden among the trees. Most of the stones are old, but some are more recent—some of the last residents of the island who needed special permission from the government to rest here. Betsy takes Janice over to a spot beneath a live oak where the Spanish moss hangs thick.

"That's where Bo and I are going to be buried," she says. "I hope you'll come visit us."

Janice smiles and says, "I hope we have a chance to visit you again before that!" And I know that we will.

XV

*Real life . . . presents us with questions marks, censored
passages, blank spaces, rows of asterisks, omitted paragraphs, and numberless sequences of three dots trailing
into whiteness . . .*   —Steven Millhauser

The discovery of someone's life does not take place in chronological order. I began with Ruth's letters to her father during the last two years of
her life. I end with the beginning—a small box that Glenn found filled
with the mementos of Ruth's early childhood, along with a few documents from later in life. I find the box waiting for me when Janice and I
return from Cumberland near the beginning of April. The contents raise
as many questions as they answer, and even cast doubt on the most basic
facts.

My mother's birthday. For thirty-three years, I did not know the date
of my mother's birth. Then, reading birthday greetings in a letter from her
father, I discovered the date—June 5, 1935, the date I would later see on
her grave stone. June 5 is the official, legal date of her birth. I had started my
journey looking for facts about my mother. What could me more factual?

In her baby book, I find her hospital birth certificate—not a legal document, but the card with footprints that the nurses prepare as a keepsake.
"Born 11:59 p.m., Wednesday, June 5" it says. So close to midnight, I
think. How could they be sure? How quickly did someone look at the
clock? How accurate was that clock? Who's to say, within a minute one
way or the other, when one day ends and another begins? Flipping the
pages of the baby book, I make a more surprising discovery. Under "Time
of Birth," Ruth's mother has scratched out "Wednesday the 5th at 11:59"
and replaced it with "Thursday the 6th at 12:08." In a pile of notes and
cards is an unsigned poem written for Ruth's fourth birthday. At the

bottom it is inscribed "June 6th 1935-1939." Does it matter to me whether my mother was born on the 5th or the 6th? Of course not, but I am humbled by the knowledge that even the most straightforward of facts can be clouded by uncertainty.

Ruth's baby book tells me in excruciating detail the story of Ruth's first few weeks on the planet—the only time of her life for which I have such a complete record. But these details are meaningless in terms of discovering Ruth as a person. The first six weeks of life are fairly similar for most members of the human race and, in spite of their overwhelming importance to a parent at the time, they quickly pale to insignificance. Occa-

Little Ruth reading in bed—a photo from her baby book.

sionally, though, Màmà has written something that touches me, though it does so most by calling forth memories of Lucy.

Speaking in the voice of her baby, Màmà writes, "On August 30, I had hysterics nearly, laughing and chuckling out loud for the first time at Buddy and Bo playing with a yellow and blue balloon. I nearly jumped out of Mama's lap with excitement." The final entry in the baby book gives Ruth's age as two years and one month. "Knows lots of nursery rhymes—'Little Miss Muffet,' 'Six Little Rabbits.' Carries on good conversation over telephone. Knows Màmà's number [*her* maternal grandmother] and calls her."

Now I start to see Ruth as a person, not just a biological machine. I can almost hear her two-year-old voice and of course in the comment about her phone skills I see the future and my own relationship with Lucy.

The documentary evidence of Ruth's childhood is here too—documents with significantly more charm than college transcripts, tax returns, and medical records of adulthood.

A program for National Music Week, May 7–13, 1939. On the cover in her mother's handwriting, "Ruth's first 'public appearance'—age 3, nearly 4." In a production of *The Enchanted Princess* on May 9, Ruth was one of eleven bunnies.

A program for a Dance Recital by the Atlanta and Marietta Pupils of Marian Bailey Springer, June 9, 1939. Written on the front cover "Ruth's first dance recital—4 years old and was she cute!!"

Atlanta Journal (ca. 1941?): "The Johnny-Jump-Up Garden Club hasn't gotten around to attending state garden conventions yet, but they have been very busy this past week practicing arrangements which they will enter in the Peachtree Garden Club's annual show Tuesday. From left to right are Ruth Candler . . ."

Notes passed back and forth from mother to daughter:
"Dear Ruth, You are being a very sweet girl. We will get a coca-cola before we go home. Love, Mother."
"Dear Ruth, Please write me a letter. Do you like this meeting? I'm so glad you won a blue ribbon in the flower show. Love, Mother."
"Dear Mother, When are we going to take my ribbon home."

Atlanta Journal, March 14, 1943: "Pallett [sic], Brush, Paints and Canvas are the favorite instruments of Ruth Candler, right, and Ann Brantley Clare, left, pictured here at their easels at the High Museum of Art."

On a homemade staff, a sixteen-bar "Lullaby" by Ruth Candler. Judging from the handwriting, Ruth must have been about twelve when she wrote this piece. At the same age, I started composing music. Janice plays the piece, in 6/8 time and the key of G. It is pleasant and unsophisticated, hummable and simple, but still beyond what I would have done at that age—sticking to 4/4 and C and never writing anything down.

Violin Recital by the Pupils of Ruth Dabney Smith. Saturday Evening, May 28, 1949 at 8 o'clock . . . Ruth Candler—"Pastourelle," Norden; "Ase's Death," Grieg.

The largest collection of papers from Ruth's childhood comes, like so much else, as a surprise. On yellowed paper in envelopes with three-cent stamps are a stack of letters that Ruth sent home from summer camp in 1945. At ten, she spent eight weeks at Camp Carlyle for Girls in Hendersonville, North Carolina. I had no idea she had ever been to summer camp, much less for such an extended period. Here, I think, is the beginning of Ruth's love of the North Carolina mountains. All her children would eventually spend five-week sessions at Camp High Rocks, not too far from Hendersonville and Camp Carlyle.

Betsy later told me that Ruth claimed to have hated that summer, but I suspect she may have hated being away from home for so long more than the camp itself.

While much of this correspondence is typical "kid away at camp" material, I find some telling things here. On June 25th, Ruth writes, "Dear Dad, Since I have written Mom a letter now it's your turn. But I am writing both of you a letter on the same day." Only once during that summer does Ruth address her parents together. Most of the letters are only to her mother. In one case, she uses a piece of carbon paper to send two identical letters in one envelope—one to Mom and another to Dad. Even at ten, Ruth realized that some degree of separation already existed between her parents.

Ruth writes of learning to swim, having fun riding horses, and missing her parents, grandparents, and little sister, Glenn. Other passages give some indication of activities she was involved in—"I need my tap shoes and ballet shoes very much. Will you please see if you can find them anywhere and send them to me?" Many of the letters, like those I wrote home from camp thirty years later, communicate nothing—"Dear Mom, I have to write this for supper and it is time for supper now, so, Goodbye. Love, Ruth." Considering the number of letters and postcards, Ruth says very little. Was she miserably homesick as I was the first time I went off to camp? And did she also genuinely enjoy the activities, as I did? Like her later letters to her father, there seems to be a thin barrier of pretense in these notes. If there are any letters or diaries Ruth ever wrote in which she drops that barrier and truly spills forth her innermost thoughts, they are lost.

I realize now that Ruth was not in Atlanta on V-J Day. On August 8, the day the United States dropped the second atomic bomb on Japan, Ruth writes, "Dear Mom, I have made up my mind to come home with you on the 14th instead of the 15th. I received your letter today about coming up here Sunday. Please come to camp before 11:30 so you can be here for church and come for supper if you can and stay for the campfire (vespers). Well, good-bye. Love, Ruth." I remember how cut off from the outside world I felt at Camp High Rocks, an isolation that was relaxing. Ruth, I suspect, may not have known the details of what had happened on the other side of the world. But certainly someone at Camp Carlyle announced that the war was over. Did the church service that Sunday give thanks for the end of hostilities?

Also in the box from Glenn are a few items from beyond Ruth's childhood. Two grade cards from Washington Seminary, for seventh and ninth grades, confirm Ruth's academic abilities. More interesting than her grades, though, are the other areas evaluated on the report card. In Deportment, Attendance, Promptness, Neatness, and Attitude, Ruth scored A's, though I do wonder about that 'D' she received in Deportment for one marking period in the seventh grade. One section of the report card lists "Good Traits" and "Traits Needing Correction." Teachers initial those traits that apply. In the seventh grade, Ruth received initials in only two "Traits Needing Correction"—"Posture," and "Is a disturbing influence in class," and even those were initialed by only one teacher in one marking period. By ninth grade, her "Traits Needing Correction" section is blank. A part of me wants her not to have been so well-behaved. Her "Good Traits" grid is filled with initials both years, though more so in the ninth grade than in the seventh. She scored best in "Takes an interest in work," "Is attentive," and "Is Courteous." I am impressed by her grades, and also glad I never had to be rated on my posture or neatness. Every new fact I learn about Washington Seminary tells me that even in the 1950s it was an old-fashioned school. I mourn its loss all the more.

In an envelope marked "Junior League—Ruth" are a collection of notes on Ruth's qualifications for joining that volunteer organization that held an important place in Atlanta society. Apparently assembled by Màmà in 1958 in order to put Ruth up for membership, the notes include a rough draft of a résumé and recommendations from friends. The file is a testament to Màmà's effort to get her daughter into the League. That her acceptance would ever be in doubt seems almost silly, but I admire her mother's work nonetheless.

On the résumé I discover the details of Ruth's employment. In the summer of 1953, after graduating from Washington Seminary, she worked as a sales clerk for Davison-Paxon, a department store. Janice would work for its descendant, Davison's, a few months after I first met her. The following summer, before enrolling in Emory, Ruth worked as a clerk in the Emory Alumni Office. In the first half of 1955, she worked at the Public Relations and News Bureau at Emory, though in what capacity, I have no idea. Perhaps she wrote news releases? These were the only paid positions she ever held. I wonder how much these jobs had to do with her desire to experience something of the world and how much had to do with encouragement from her parents. Her father, I imagine, would want all his children at least to know what it was like to hold a job.

Under "Volunteer Positions Held," her résumé lists "Red Cross, Summer 1951, played piano at St. Luke's Sunday School Chapel, 2 years, and Young People's Service League, St. Luke's, 5 years."

The brief recommendations written by other League members tend towards generic praise, like so many other evaluations of Ruth's character:

"Ruth's background, many talents, and creative ability will be a definite asset to the League. She is dependable and conscientious about any job she undertakes. Ruth knows the true meaning of 'service,' and her admirable qualities and experience in many fields will make her an invaluable Junior League member."

"[Ruth is remarkable for] her outstanding loyalty, reliability and consideration of others, her adaptability and congeniality with various age groups. She has the poise and "know how" that seems to be a special mark of the Junior Leaguer."

She was accepted into the League, serving in both Atlanta and Winston-

Salem. Among other placements, she acted in that children's theatre production of *The Wizard of Oz*–frightening David in her Tin Woodsman costume–and worked with Marge Sosnik on those lost radio programs for schoolchildren.

There is little else in this final box of remnants–a couple of childish pictures drawn for her little sister, a homemade Valentine given to her mother. These and all the rest I place back in the box that I will send to my sister, next in line to view the relics. I have pursued these mementos and their ilk for nearly a year now, pursued the people who knew Ruth and found the places that made their mark on her and where she made her mark. Now I place notebooks full of letters, transcripts, photocopies, and documents on a shelf in the closet. Next to them I place a new photo album–now instead of nine I have dozens of pictures of Ruth. A few of these I leave on my desk, ready to take to the frame shop and hang in the upstairs hall. The faces of Ruth from childhood to marriage look up at me, yet still I am left alone–alone with my thoughts, my memories, and my unanswered questions.

Thoughts:

Ruth was delivered by Dr. Bartholomew. I was born on St. Bartholomew's Day and baptized in St. Bartholomew's church.

Ruth was born in the "Lucy Elizabeth Pavilion" of Wesley Memorial Hospital at Emory–the wing named after Popee's mother. Ruth's granddaughter, though not named for a specific ancestor, keeps the name Lucy in the family.

For seven years, Ruth was educated at all-girls schools. Then she entered Emory that, until the year before, had been officially all-men.

For seven years, Ruth and Bob lived as husband and wife in Atlanta, in houses and apartments that are still essentially unfamiliar to me. She lived only two years in the house I think of as home, a house I have spent more nights in than any other, a house that she only ever thought of as new.

What did I fear would happen if I sought out Ruth? That someone would cry? Or that I would–that once I learned exactly what I had lost, I would then ache because of its absence? Why didn't I understand that coming to know Ruth was the one way I would be able to let her go?

Things that happened:

A child at Jordan's elementary school is accidentally killed over the weekend. On Monday the teachers must explain what happened to 500 children. I wonder how the teachers at Summit School dealt with the fact that two students, David and Elizabeth Lovett, lost their mother three weeks into the school year.

I used to be afraid to ask my father about Ruth. Now, when I call him on the phone, I can mention something about her or ask a question with almost no hesitation.

Every time Lucy comes to visit, I show her some pictures of her grandmother or tell her a story—trying not to overemphasize the importance of this lost relative, but to familiarize her with the past, and to make sure she will never be afraid to ask.

My father says I am the perfect person to write about Ruth. Since I was so young when she died, he says, I have little emotional involvement. This is not as true as he believes and not as false as I would like to think, but writing does serve to both capture and release my emotions.

Found Objects:

A two-and-a-half dollar gold coin that Ruth's maternal grandmother gave her at the time of her birth. I am having it made into a key ring.

A lock of hair from her first haircut at age two. It is a tight reddish blonde curl—almost exactly the same color as Lucy's. It smells of must and dusty forgotten places but feels soft against my cheek and contains the genetic code that created, and perhaps destroyed, Ruth.

Her Christmas stocking with her name embroidered across the top. The fabric is brittle from too many years in the bottom of some box. I put my hand inside and find nothing. What did Ruth once pull out of it?

Dead Ends:

I located her piano teacher from her high school years. She remembered nothing of Ruth or her ability.

Paul O'Shields died several years ago. I was too late to ask him about his high school sweetheart.

And how many others I tried to contact were lost, or didn't remember, or didn't reply, or had died? I lost count.

Missing Objects:

Her letters home from Sweet Briar. What did she say about life away from home? Did she mention Bob? Did she feign happiness, admit loneliness, or discuss what she would do the following year?

Her correspondence with Paul O'Shields. How deeply in love was she with Paul—or how deeply did she believe herself in love? How did she feel without him when he went to Tulane? Did they contemplate marriage? Did she put on a facade when writing Paul, or was he one with whom she could drop all pretense? And what exactly was in the letter she mailed on the way to Sunday dinner at Callanwolde with Bob?

Her letters to and from Bob Lovett. Daddy has told me that he and Ruth threw them away after they married and he remembers little of their content. How often did they write while she was at Sweet Briar? Did they profess love to each other in every way possible, as Ruth's father had done to her mother three decades earlier? Or were they more reserved and quiet in their affection, the way Austin Ford remembered them? Did they discuss plans for the future, how many children they wanted to have, where they wanted to live? Were these letters the place where she was most honest in recording her feelings?

Things I will never know:

The sound of her voice.

The smell of her hair when she's just rushed inside after being caught in a summer rain storm.

The look on her face when her youngest child cuts his hair with a pair of safety scissors or rides his bike in front of a moving car or graduates with honors from college or gets married or gets divorced.

The feel of her hand on my arm when I'm frightened by a movie or she's frightened by a roller coaster or we're both frightened by the evening news.

Her true feelings about being a housewife, about her parents' marriage and divorce, about God.

The sound of her playing the piano.

What she would say to me.

And in spite of all I've learned, I'll never really know what she was like, how I would feel being with her.

The most recent item in the box Glenn found is a letter from Ruth to her mother sent on February 5, 1964—the same date she sent a similar letter to her father. It is the only letter to her mother that she wrote as an adult that survives. In spite of Ruth's nonchalant attitude, she must have found the idea of giving her mother this news over the phone frightening. I understand. I dread few things more than spreading bad news to those I love. So she wrote a letter.

> Dear Mother,
>   I am writing to report the latest medical findings of the family. I have a sizable lump in my breast which must be removed. I don't know when exactly it will be. I am on call to go to the hospital in probably 2–3 weeks, whenever there is a bed available. The doctor says he believes it benign and there is nothing to worry about. I will probably be in the hospital only one day. I just thought you would want to know about it. . . . Will let you know when I go so you can "think" about me.
>   Love, Ruth

The last sentence is a reference to Màmà's practice of meditation, and I wonder if Ruth viewed this practice with at least a bit of distaste to refer to it thus. I can recall as a child visiting Màmà and waiting for her in the mornings while she meditated. Afterward she would tell me all the things she had "thought" about, right down to the family dogs of her grandchildren.

Was Ruth trying to break bad news to her mother slowly, or did she really believe that there was nothing to worry about and she would only be in the hospital one day?

XVI

*It is thus, if there is any rule, that we ought to die—nei-
ther as victim nor as fanatic, but as the seafarer who can
greet with an equal eye the deep that he is entering, and
the shore he must leave.*

—E. M. Forster

The beginning of the end came, or so I thought, on Tuesday, February 4,
1964, when Ruth's doctor felt a lump in her right breast. The following
day she wrote a brief note to each of her parents informing them of her
need for an operation. The week before, she had written to her father,
"Bob and I got the Atlanta paper yesterday and were shocked to learn of
Charles Thwaite's death last week. I know it must have been a blow to all
of you down there. It seems such a waste for such a fine *young* man to go
at that age." Thwaite, the chairman of the board of the Trust Company of
Georgia, was fifty-two. Later in the same letter she writes, "All goes well
here."

   I had some hope her medical records might tell me more than letters
to her parents, so I wrote Baptist Hospital in Winston-Salem asking for a
copy of her file. "Could I provide her Social Security Number?" they asked.
A month later, after writing to the lawyer that settled her estate and the
bank that served as co-executor, I finally obtained a copy of her estate tax
return and sent her number to the hospital. "Was her spouse still living or
was I the eldest surviving child?" they asked. "Yes and no," I replied, and
provided them with the address of my father and older brother. Finally
they wrote back that they would only release the records to my father. I set
their letter aside, not giving up, but putting the matter out of my mind
until the next time I visited Daddy. Two days later, without explanation, a
thick envelope arrived in the mail.

   The first dozen or so pages of her records from this hospital detail the course of my delivery into the world. A letter from her doctor in Atlanta written to her new doctor in Winston-Salem says, "I know you will find Mrs. Lovett a lovely person to take care of, and certainly an easy person to handle," and gives her expected "date of confinement" as August 16, 1962. I was born August 24 and Dr. Linton, who delivered me, wrote to Ruth's Atlanta doctor, "thank you for referring this very interesting and fine lady to us."

I flip the pages and keep looking.

October 31, 1963. A painful right eye is diagnosed as conjunctivitis and she is sent home with eye drops.

January 22, 1964. At the top of the sheet, her name. On the "Signature" line, the typed name of Dr. Linton. Weight: 142 1/2 lbs. And then, part way down the sheet: "Ten days ago she noticed a hard mass in the right breast which is a little bit tender. . . . I would suspect this will necessitate biopsy." My assumption was wrong. The beginning of the end came on January 12, nearly six months before Ruth's twenty-ninth birthday. There is nothing different about this page that I now stare at. It is typed on the same form as her diagnosis of conjunctivitis and her "routine postpartum checkup."

On February 4, another record of examination by Dr. Linton. "The mass in the right breast is approximately the same, maybe a little larger than the last visit. She was referred to Dr. Cordell, who will take the mass out as soon as possible." In his report the same day, Dr. Cordell writes that Ruth had had a small mass in her breast during a previous pregnancy that disappeared spontaneously. Under "Implications" he writes "mammary dysplasia, malignancy?"

I cannot read between the lines of what these doctors write, but Dr. Henry Valk, the family friend who looked after Ruth during her final days, reviewed her records for me and wrote that the lump was "thought to be nonmalignant." Still, there is a family history of breast cancer, and Dr. Cordell feels the lump should be removed and examined. Ruth is placed on the waiting list for a bed in the hospital and told her surgery will probably be scheduled in two to three weeks. She goes home and writes letters to her parents.

The wait for surgery must seem interminable to Ruth and Bob—a wait for a verdict from an unseen jury. Ruth's father writes that "we would like to have you here at Emory [Hospital], but I understand your feeling of wanting to stay there with the family and I suppose they have excellent doctors there just as we do here."

Two weeks later, the wait continues, and Ruth writes to her father, "Dr. Cordell assures me there is absolutely no danger in the slight delay. We hear he is just about tops in surgery here. We know him personally. His wife is president of the Junior League and his son is in David's class at school."

On February 25, the wait for space in the hospital ends and Ruth is admitted at 4:10 in the afternoon. Is she nervous about undergoing anesthesia and surgery? It is certainly nothing new. The medical records I obtained from Emory Hospital in Atlanta show several surgeries—her emergency appendectomy at age eleven, the removal of an impacted tooth just before she turned fourteen, surgery to correct the faulty setting of her childhood broken arm a year before she was married. She has also given birth three times. I have never been under a general anesthesia or spent the night in a hospital but, though she is only twenty-eight, hospitals are nothing new to Ruth.

The following day, she undergoes four hours of surgery. I have watched doctors on television dictate the progress of a surgical procedure into a tape machine, but, until I saw Ruth's medical records, I had never read one of these documents. The account of the surgery she underwent at the hands of Dr. Cordell runs two single-spaced typed pages.

Dr. Valk's wife wrote to Bob after Ruth's death, "A doctor—from necessity—is a little cold-blooded—dealing in death daily." I understand that necessity. Still, there is a difference between understanding the need for a doctor to give himself emotional distance from his patient, and coming face to face with a surgical report that objectifies my mother.

"The patient was placed on the operating table in the supine position," begins the report. This is the closest this report comes to indicating that a human being is involved in what happened that day. The lump was removed from her breast and "thought to be malignant, on gross section, at the operating table." Following the surgery Dr. Cordell writes in a letter to Dr. Linton, "I must say that I was somewhat surprised to find that the mass in her breast was malignant." But he confirms this finding at the pathology table and proceeds to perform a radical mastectomy of the right breast. And even now, with this report in front of me, I find myself slipping into clinical objectification. "*The* right breast," I write, not "*her* right breast." Reading this report, I cannot think of my mother—one doesn't think of a mother in terms of "subcutaneous tissue," "auxiliary fat pad," and "thoracocervical nerve." What lays supine on that operating table is not my mother, but merely a body—a body that has begun to betray her.

From this body, "the entire breast was removed, along with the pectoralis major and minor muscles," which, my dictionary tells me, are muscles used in the movement of the shoulder. The final paragraph notes that "the patient seemed to tolerate the procedure well." How, I wonder, can the doctor possibly know this? A huge section of tissue and muscle have just been removed from her, a malignancy has been found, and "the patient" is still asleep—how can anyone hazard a guess as to how she will tolerate the physical and emotional scarring that those four hours have caused?

I have a friend who's a surgeon. I sent him a copy of Ruth's surgery report and he called to discuss it with me.

"We understand so much more about the disease now than we did then. We know that it becomes systemic much earlier than we thought." He asked the question everyone asks. "How old was your mother?"

"Twenty-nine."

"The prognosis for breast cancer in someone that young is just terrible," he said. I had wondered if Ruth's chances would have been any better if she had had the benefits of 1990s medicine. The only difference may have been how long she knew she was dying.

At the bottom of the second page of her surgery report, just above Dr. Cordell's signature is the "Postoperative Diagnosis." "Adenocarcinoma of the right breast." Breast cancer. The bad news. The good news will come the next day when the pathology report is completed. No cancerous tissue in any of the twelve lymph nodes that were removed nor any indication of spread of the disease in the breast tissue.

So read the medical records. The official, objective version of the events of February 25-27, 1964. But this is Ruth they are writing about. My mother. The same woman who played Miss Willie in the school play, who played piano for children's radio, who camped in the mountains, who fretted over her son, me. On a day when spring is in sight and most of Winston-Salem goes about its business, an ordinary Tuesday no different from the one that came before or the one that will come after, this woman lies unconscious on a table while a sizable piece of her body is sliced off of her. If the prayers of her husband and family are answered, she will live a long life with only one breast and with substantial physical and psychological scarring. Yet the words on the paper in front of me—written by good men who tried to save her life, who knew her family, who still write eloquently about her death—these words convey nothing of her humanity to me. Mastectomy. Adenocarcinoma. Lymph node. Pathology. From the child hypnotized by the power of the angel-photo to deny the humanity of his mother I have become the man distracted by the language of medicine to do the same.

When the report from the pathologist comes back saying that Ruth appears free from cancer, there is no reason not to be optimistic. After all, others in the family who suffered from breast cancer made full recoveries. Ruth appears on her way toward doing the same. But she has had a major operation and it is 1964—she will spend a month in the hospital before doctors allow her to go home.

This leaves Bob with a full-time job, two children in school, an eighteen-month-old baby, and a wife in the hospital whom he wants to visit as much as possible. The first order of business is to hire someone to take care of me, which he does.

"She looks like Ma Kettle in the movies," Bob writes to his father-in-law. "She has worked in a nursing home, has three children of her own, and has recently taken in the children of working mothers. I am hopeful that, in spite of her general lack of culture, she will be just what we need. She understands that Charles is to be her first concern."

Ruth "did very well after surgery," Dr. Cordell wrote to me. Her medical records track her progress from department to department in the weeks following her operation. Chest film from radiology. An examination in radiation therapy ("No established indication for radiation therapy. Have discussed this with patient"). Back to radiology for a mammogram of her remaining breast ("breast appears to be within the normal limits"). From her hospital bed to the "progressive care center," and then back when a mild infection of her surgical wound develops. More chest film. Dr. Cordell writes to Dr. Linton. "in general we were pleased with the results of her radical mastectomy. . . . We certainly hope she will not have any recurrence of the tumor." In the eyes of her doctor, her wounds are healing.

Her psychological wounds seem to be healing well, too, or else she's successful, as always, in not showing her fear and grief.

"Today she is very chipper and asking for company," my father writes about a week after the surgery. "Bill and Fritzi Herring went to see her and found her willing to talk about the operation, which I think is a good indication that her mental condition is good. In short, she seems to be relaxed and natural with people other than the family and her doctors."

Bob writes because Ruth is as yet unable to. "I got her to write a check . . . today, and it was a considerable effort." Only this one letter from her time in the hospital survives. In time of crisis, most communication is done by telephone.

Ruth has short visits with her children in the lobby of the hospital, but still it must be a tremendous relief for her to get home on March 23. Two weeks later, she is back to writing her father, with the same cheerful tone as always.

"I actually took a real bath yesterday for the first time in six weeks. I still won't feel *really* clean until I can get under a shower, but that will be another week or two. I cut my own hair the other day and it helped the spirits tremendously. I didn't really *need* them, but four new dresses make me feel good too!"

By the end of April, two months after the operation, her life seems back to normal. For the second year in a row she and Bob go to the steeple-chase at Tanglewood Park, an excuse for everyone in town to have an elegant picnic. They spread an old oriental throw-rug from Callanwolde across the hood of their used Mercedes. "It was great fun," writes Ruth, "our menu: caviar canapés, vichyssoise, pressed chicken, Liebfraumilch, avocados, roast beef and French bread, strawberries, and champagne." In a hurried note to her father, she encloses a newspaper clipping that shows Dr. Valk sitting on the roof of his car watching the horses. "See you in June," she concludes.

On May 5, while many of her Atlanta family and friends are enjoying Opera Week, the hospital records indicate that Ruth returns for her second monthly postoperative checkup. "Her wounds have all healed well and she has excellent arm and shoulder motion," writes Dr. Cordell.

With Ruth well, a trip to Atlanta is in order, and there's plenty of reason to go. Her sister Glenn will graduate from Emory on the eighth of

June, and her cousin Howard Warren will be married in Macon, Georgia, on the thirteenth.

On the morning of the eighth, Elizabeth, Ruth, and I fly from Winston-Salem to Atlanta. We children stay at Bob's mother's house while Ruth goes to her sister's graduation. The next day we all converge on Grandpa's farm, Bob and David having driven down.

That three-day stay in June of 1964 was the longest my whole family spent at Rolling Meadows during those brief years when there were five of us, and they must have been happy days. From later visits I remember Rolling Meadows as a peaceful place where the days moved slowly as I rode my wheel toys around the flagstone walkways that ringed the house, swam in the pool, picked cat tails, fed Camel cigarettes and vanilla wafers to the donkeys, and occasionally flew in my grandfather's plane above the entire spread.

The only picture I have of Ruth at the farm is from the previous summer, but as I look at it I emotionally transfer the image to a year later. It's the one showing Ruth, me, and David in the pool. Only I am looking at the camera, but the others are smiling. Ruth looks well, her upper arms

Me, David, and Mommy in the pool at Rolling Meadows in the summer of 1963.

just a little bigger than she might want them, but speaking of her health. It is a moment of innocence and happiness. Its glossy color seems incompatible with the harsh black and white of the hospital records.

The peaceful days of rest on the farm soon give way to the usual frantic schedule of Atlanta visits, complicated by the grownups' jaunt to Macon for the wedding of Ruth's cousin. All the Candler family is there—for most it will be the last time they see Ruth. We spend a few more days in Atlanta after the wedding. Ruth has missed Opera Week, and hasn't seen Atlanta family and friends since Christmas, so there is much catching up to do.

When all the visits have been paid, the car is loaded up with everyone but David and Elizabeth, who will stay visiting grandparents for another week or so, and Bob eases into traffic, leaving the city of Ruth's birth and his courtship behind. It is the last time Ruth will see Atlanta. The next gathering of the family will be for her funeral.

June 5, 1964—Ruth's twenty-ninth birthday. The patient returns for postoperative checkup. "Asymptomatic—no evidence of recurrence. Return 6 mos. Get chest film then."

Late June, 1964. Ruth lies awake in the double bed in the master bedroom at the house on Robinhood Road. Bob sleeps beside her, occasionally snoring lightly. The pain in her back that has come between her and a good night's sleep for several days now is throbbing with each beat of her heart. This can't be a pulled muscle from lifting the baby. It's getting worse not better. She will call Dr. Valk in the morning.

July 2, 1964. Dr. Valk makes a general exam of Ruth and then sends her for X-rays of her chest and spine. Her physical exam reveals no abnormalities. The films "show no change in the appearance of the chest."

Life goes on. In late July, Ruth's father and stepmother, Pete, come for a visit. "It certainly was nice to be right in the house with you and I hope it didn't inconvenience you too much. Our visits together are not near often enough and I am glad to be able to spend every minute possible with you and the children."

Bob, still working toward his Ph.D., learns Spanish in order to pass his foreign-language requirement. "I am so proud of his teaching himself enough Spanish in five weeks to get through the exam," writes Ruth.

Plans are discussed for Ruth and Bob to make a trip with Grandpa and Pete to the Canadian Rockies, one of Grandpa's favorite places. "We are really looking forward to next summer," Ruth says in a letter to her father, "I'm practically packed. I have wanted to go back up there for fifteen years, and I know Bob is going to love it." Ruth's first trip to those mountains in 1950 was cut short by the death of her grandmother.

On August 9, Ruth writes her last letter to her father on brand-new personalized stationery.

"Do you remember that Charles had a high fever the night before you left? I took him to the doctor . . . and he had the beginnings of a throat infection. . . . It took him about three days to get back to really being himself again. But he sure is now! He is really full of pep, energy, and mischief. Sometimes I think it might be nice if he would get just slightly sick for a couple of days, so he wouldn't be so wild!"

She writes of plans to take a trip to coastal North Carolina and Virginia without the children sometime in September and sends best wishes to her little sister Glenn who is expecting her first baby. ("She told me what kind of diapers to use," Glenn told me, "and she was right, too.") As so often before, she signs her letter merely, "Affectionately, Ruth."

Grandpa writes her back a few days later. "We were glad to learn that Charles is well even though he is so full of pep and energy. I sure would like to see him and all of you again, but I guess it will be about Christmas time before we can do that." He will visit her for the last time in a little more than a month.

Among the people I wrote asking for remembrances of Ruth were a couple from Winston-Salem who wrote back, "I'm afraid we're not much help as we only met your mother once." I mentioned this note to my father. One of many dead ends, I said.

But Daddy told me this couple met Ruth at least twice, the second time at a dinner party they threw on Friday, August 21, 1964. Why have they forgotten this episode after thirty-one years? A better question might be why has Bob remembered. To him, that party began the last weekend of innocence he would spend with his wife, a weekend that has stayed frozen in his memory. Few of us remember the details of any particular

weekend from three decades ago, but few of us have had such a weekend.

After the dinner party on Friday night, Ruth and Bob throw a dinner
party of their own on Saturday. She has not been feeling well. The pain is
now in her abdomen, but she decides she can make it through the party.

Ruth's "gift for making people feel at home" that Rand Lee spoke of
helped her through the evening. Those few gathered around her dining
table that Saturday night are the last to fully experience Ruth as hostess.

Sunday is Ruth and Bob's ninth wedding anniversary. They rest at
home, but she still does not feel well. The pain in her abdomen grows
worse as the day wears on and they finally call Dr. Linton, who lives a few
blocks away. From the location of her pain, Dr. Linton tells Bob that he
suspects she might have a gallbladder disease, and he admits her to the
hospital at 10:40 that night.

Monday is my second birthday, but is not marked as such. The records
I have of that day are not snapshots and birthday cards, but more photocopied sheets from the various departments of Baptist Hospital.

The radiology department looks for gallstones, but detects none. Dr.
Meredith decides to perform exploratory surgery, but the preoperative
diagnosis is "acute cholecystitis." Translation: inflammation of the gallbladder. The operation lasts an hour and twenty-five minutes.

In one hour and twenty-five minutes, Ruth goes from a mother with a
pain in her stomach to a woman under sentence of death. As soon as she
is opened up, the problem becomes obvious. "A somewhat enlarged liver
was noted, which was riddled with innumerable whitish nodules, varying
in size from a few mm. to 3 cm. With the patient's history of adenocarcinoma of the breast, this was assumed to be metastatic disease." Cancer
has spread to her liver. Lots of cancer. Terminal.

What did the surgeon and his assistant think? They were not previ-
ously acquainted with Ruth. Did they suspect the worst? Assume the best?
What did they say when they cut this young woman open, hoping to solve
her problems, only to come face to face with something beyond their powers. I have been told by surgeon friends that there is a saying in that profes-
sion—"a chance to cut is a chance to cure." Dr. Meredith would not cure
Ruth. All he could do was sew her back up, fill out his form, and go tell
somebody. Was he upset? Disappointed? Was it business as usual? How

does a surgeon, who has so much power, feel when rendered helpless?

At the bottom of the form describing this operation, the postoperative diagnosis is given. "Metastatic adenocarcinoma of the breast to the liver." But those words are not the ones that claw at me. No, the word that leaps off the page for me, that tells me what is really going on, is "riddled." She is riddled with cancer. It is her youngest child's second birthday. She is going to die.

"I know you've heard of cases where a patient with this type of cancer can go into remission and live for several years," Dr. Linton says to my father, "but I'm afraid this isn't one of those cases." In one weekend she has gone from uncomfortable dinner party guest to terminal cancer patient.

The question that must be on everyone's mind, though no one seems to voice it, is "How long?" Bob at first takes comfort in her overall good health and strength, until he realizes that, because cancer kills by growing, this very health will help the disease flourish. The doctors look for ways to stem the tide. Four days later, they operate again, removing both ovaries "in hopes that the removal of this endocrine source might slow the spread of her disease." It does not. At the bottom of the report of that operation, Dr. Linton, who performed the surgery, writes, "The patient was sent to the Recovery Room in apparently good condition."

"It's a shame," says her mother after the operation, "she did so want another child." Still, the realization has not sunk in that, even with ovaries, Ruth will not live long enough to see the birth of another child. She and Bob had planned to have four. Without my telling him this, Rand Lee told me that if she had lived she would have borne another son.

Ruth and Bob's friends Ed and Emily Wilson return from their honeymoon about the time of this operation to find their apartment decorated with funny pictures placed there by Ruth and some co-conspirators. It is "all a little sexy," writes Emily, "and I was rather impressed that your mother was such a sport. I believe that your mother may have been the one to plan this, and I was extremely touched and pleased." When she finds out about Ruth's prognosis, Emily is "just devastated." She visits Ruth in the hospital. "We talked about my wedding and honeymoon and I remember that she had just had a prescription filled for 'the pill' and we laughed when she asked if I wanted it. . . . She seemed so much more mature than I felt." Ed and Emily also visit Bob in his office on campus, and find him "beside himself with anxiety and grief."

In the file of letters from Ruth's father, I found a letter from her older brother, Buddy. The date is August 26, two days after her diagnosis. "Just a note to let you know Claire and I are thinking about you. Needless to say we were distressed to learn that you were back in the hospital, and sincerely hope that you will be up and about shortly." He goes on with a bit of small talk, and it's difficult to tell if he has heard the bad news. But he must have. Why else would he have written this letter, the only one in the file? But nothing is stated directly. "You can rest assured that if thoughts and well wishes are what it takes, you have all of ours. Bo and I will probably fly up for another visit shortly." But of course, he cannot say, "we're sorry there's nothing we can do to save you, Bo and I will come to visit before you die."

On September 3, Ruth's father writes her a final time. "I was glad to hear from Bob last night that you are continuing to improve and hoping to get home from the hospital any day now." She returns home that day. There is nothing more the hospital can do for her. "I was sorry to know that you are still having those pains in your back," her father writes. "Bob says the doctor is going to prescribe treatment for that and hopes to clear it up." My hindsight is so clear that it is difficult to understand how, at this point, Ruth's father can talk of her improving. Dr. Valk, who has been on vacation, returns to her case, but his task is merely to make her death comfortable. Morphine will help mask the pain. Nothing will clear it up.

"Remember," writes her father, "we will be pulling for you and praying for you."

The next three weeks see a progression of family and friends pass through the master bedroom of the house on Robinhood Road. The words "last respects" are not uttered, but Ruth feels at times, I imagine, almost as if the funeral has already begun. Though she is beyond being able to look after a household, she tries to hang on to the two roles she values most—wife and mother. Few may remember the days that preceded her terminal diagnosis, but many remember the time that followed.

"Daddy and Bo flew me up there late that summer," wrote Glenn. Ruth "had always had, not a weight problem, but a tendency toward being a few pounds overweight and I remember being so shocked at how thin she was. We tried to joke that she could eat whatever she wanted now." Betsy was on that trip as well. "We knew she was bad" Betsy wrote, "but didn't realize that the end would be so near."

"I do remember" wrote Ruth's friend Fritzi Herring, "that when she was bedridden, toward the end, we went and visited and took a game called 'What's That On My Head?' It is a game of deduction, and Ruth beat us all as sick as she was."

"I visited her at home," Emily Wilson wrote, "and I felt a certain closeness, not so much in what was said as just the ease of being in her presence." In spite of all I've been told about her talents as a hostess, it seems remarkable to me that Ruth can engender this kind of ease during her last weeks. How uncomfortable most of us feel in the presence of someone who is dying.

Does anyone realize how fast it will happen? Does Ruth even suspect? As the days slip by and her condition worsens, she must understand there is not much time left, but the morphine is being administered in high doses—doses that affect her mind. By the time she realizes her remaining time on earth is not a matter of months or weeks but days, she may be past the point of being able to realize anything. Would she do anything different in those last three weeks at home if she knew she would have only three weeks?

There is one thing that I wish she had done. I can forgive her for not doing it; I can understand that the time may have brushed past her more quickly than she ever guessed it would, but I wish she had written me a letter. It is a selfish wish, I know, but I wish it nonetheless—to have in tangible form words spoken by her directly to me and only to me, telling me whatever she wished. All the evidence I have of our connection seems secondhand—reportage of a relationship as viewed from the outside. How I wish I had even one sheet of paper that spoke of that relationship from within its bounds. It is a wish that drives me to write letters to Lucy, so that even if I am hit by a bus tomorrow and I fade from her slate of memory, she will be able to look into those words in ten or twenty or fifty years and know that I love her, not because someone else said that I did or because of how I looked at her in a photograph, but because I told her so. I know Ruth felt tremendous love for me, but I still wish she had fought off the pain for a few more minutes one night, and written it down.

By Wednesday, September 23, much of Ruth's family has migrated to Winston-Salem. The Candlers stay at the Howard Johnson's just off I-40. Ruth's mother has driven up from Atlanta with her husband Carl. Her father and two older brothers, Buddy and Bo, have flown up in Bo's plane.

The morphine takes its toll on Ruth's brain. No longer rational, she tries to climb out of bed to get more drugs. At home there's no way to restrain or relieve her. My father makes what he calls the most difficult decision of his life. At 10:00 that morning, he phones the hospital and asks them to send an ambulance for Ruth. He knows it will take her out of her home forever. Because her case is not an emergency, the ambulance does not arrive until 3:00 that afternoon. Ruth is carried out to the curb in a chair, because the stretcher cannot negotiate the turn at the top of the stairs. Màmà rides in the ambulance with her, and Daddy stays home with me. I am upstairs taking a nap.

It is an agonizing time for the family, but perhaps it is a blessing that the agony of dealing with a young wife, mother, or daughter dying is replaced so quickly with grieving for one already dead.

On Friday night, just over two days after Ruth returned to the hospital, my neighborhood seems at peace. Grandparents and uncles have retreated to Howard Johnson's for the night. Far into an evening thirty years later my father will tell me of that night. He cannot sleep. Alone in his room, he does the only thing left to do. He prays.

At the hospital, Ruth slips into a coma, brought on by her liver failure. At 10:30, her heart stops beating. At 10:35, Dr. Valk pronounces her dead, signs her death certificate, and goes downstairs to his car. Our house is a five-minute drive from the hospital. It is no later than 11:00 when my father hears the knock and, knowing full well that only one thing could bring a visitor at this time of night, opens to the door to Dr. Valk who says, "She's gone."

And she was gone.

On the last page of her medical file: "Admitted 9/23/64, Discharged

9/25/64, Result: expired." On her death certificate: "Immediate cause of death—ventricular standstill. Interval between onset and death—5 minutes. Due to—carcinomatosis. Interval between onset and death—4 weeks. Due to—cancer breast. Interval between onset and death—7 months." But none of this carries the impact of those two simple words. She's gone.

At times of death, families enter a world where time on a clock or days on a calendar have no meaning. All time is measured from the moment of loss. The events that normally mark the passing of our days—arriving at work on Monday morning, attending church on Sunday, relaxing or celebrating on Saturday night—give way to the particular progression of the calendar of death: obituary, funeral, burial.

Early the next morning, Bob Lovett gathered his children together in the den of the house on Robinhood Road. "Mommy was too sick to get better," he told us. Then after a long pause, "she died last night."

"I cried," wrote David, "and I don't remember crying again for the rest of my childhood."

The late hour of her death was no impediment to the rapid unfolding of the expected events. Next morning *The Winston-Salem Journal* carried her obituary.

"Mrs. Ruth Candler Lovett, 29, wife of Robert W. Lovett . . . died last night at Baptist Hospital. She had been ill six months . . . The funeral will be conducted at 4 P.M. today at St. Paul's Episcopal church by the Rev. Dudley Colhoun. Burial will be at Atlanta Monday."

The house that had been so quiet the night before now rang out with noise and commotion. "I can still see you the day I came to the house because we had received word that your mother had died," wrote Emily Wilson. "There were many people . . . and great confusion, and I remember thinking the calmest person—your mother—was gone and that it would be a long time before the house could settle back to normal again."

Bob's sister Susan wrote to me of a similar time, when Ruth had been there to be that calming influence. "When my dad died [in 1958], it was Ruth who kept things running smoothly at the house with literally hundreds of letters, phone calls, and visitors to deal with. She kept records of all this, made sure that the huge amounts of food that were brought were stored and served, etc."

Did those hours of visits from friends who could not possibly utter any words of comfort pass quickly or slowly, as if a dream or in ultra-clear vision? I imagine both. And how, during that same time, were arrangements made for a funeral to be held that afternoon, a casket chosen, the Atlanta newspaper notified, and all the other details of death attended to? The human organism is prepared for these crises. The body goes on auto-pilot and the thousand details that cry for our attention avert us from the magnitude of our loss. Sooner or later we are left alone with our grief, alone to face the stretch of our lives without the one who has left us, but that time of grief cannot come in the first day after death. There is just too much to do.

Upstairs in his room, David wrote his mother a letter. "When I tried to mail it," he told me, "somebody said that Mommy couldn't get any letters where she had gone. I thought maybe I didn't have enough postage on it, so I covered the whole envelope with stamps. I wonder what became of that letter. I wonder what I wrote."

Is it morbid of me to wonder about such things as funeral arrangements— the embalming of the body, the purchase of the casket? I have never liked open-casket funerals, but thinking about my mother's corpse, I begin to understand some people's need for them. We cannot let go if we do not know what we are letting go of. After Ruth's death, her body was released by the hospital to Voglers funeral home. I called them to see if they had any record of her.

"Certainly," the gentleman on the other end of the line said, "we have records of every client back to 1905. What would you like to know?" What I really wanted was a copy of her file—I didn't know what questions to ask. "I'd like to know everything you can tell me," I wanted to say. But his voice somehow encouraged specific questions.

"Can you tell me about the preparation of the body," I asked, wondering if I had chosen an appropriately euphemistic term, "and what type of casket was used."

Ruth's body was embalmed at Voglers, dressed in her own clothing, and placed in a Turner White silver half-couch casket with an ivory crepe interior. The man on the phone described the shiny hardware and square corners of this coffin.

"They don't make that model anymore," he told me. "The old half-couch coffins had sides that folded down, for viewing." But there was no viewing of this body. I imagine that was simply the coffin that was available.

"Is there any other information you can give me?" I asked.

"There's really not much else here," he told me. "Nothing else of interest. Just the names of the pallbearers."

Nothing of interest! "If it's not too much trouble," I asked meekly, "could you tell me those names?"

He read a list of seven names, leaving me to ponder the asymmetry of seven pallbearers. The names that I recognized were colleagues of my father in the English department at Wake Forest. "The pall was sent to St. Paul's church," he told me, "and no flowers were ordered." And that was all, but it was more than I had known.

Four o'clock neared, and the house gradually emptied as family and friends repaired to the funeral—some leaving early enough to change clothes or freshen up, others driving directly from the crowded curbs of Robinhood Road to the church a mile and a half away. Bungy Valk, whose husband Henry had signed the death certificate the previous night, wrote in her condolence letter to Bob, "I selfishly elected to stay with the children rather than attend Ruth's funeral. . . . We laughed and talked and Mommie was mentioned many times—and I marveled at what you have given them—and what they are. If you were to follow Ruth tomorrow—you have given the world so *very* much." Years later, her memory jarred by a letter of inquiry I had sent to her husband, Bungy reminisced with my father on the telephone about playing blocks with me on the floor that afternoon. In the six months between the onset of Ruth's illness and her death, I'm sure I experienced many baby-sitters—strangers who played blocks with me and became friends. Did I grasp the fact that that day was different, that something was wrong that had never been wrong before and could never be put right?

Under the vast stone columns of the nave of St. Paul's church Ruth's funeral was held. The church dominates the tallest hill in town and looks

out over the trees of the city. Rev. Colhoun used the standard rite from
the 1928 *Book of Common Prayer.* "In those days," he wrote to me, "it
was not customary to have a eulogy." The funeral service was a short one
of prayer and scripture reading. At its end, Rev. Colhoun faced the casket
containing the shell of Ruth and said, "Unto God's gracious mercy and
protection we commit you. The Lord bless you and keep you. The Lord
make his face to shine upon you, and be gracious unto you, and give you
peace, both now and evermore. Amen."

The family began its return to Atlanta. Màmà and Carl drove back. Ruth's
father and brothers flew the plane they had brought up a few days before;
Lovetts were tucked in available spaces, my father and I riding on the plane.

"Graveside service for Mrs. Robert W. Lovett, 29, of Winston-Salem,
N.C., and formerly of Atlanta will be at 11 A.M. Monday in Westview
Cemetery," said the notice in *The Atlanta Constitution.* Her family's assumption that she would not stay away from Atlanta for long had turned
out to be correct. Did Ruth choose to be buried in her home town? I don't
know. But in Winston-Salem there was no other family member buried,
no plot purchased, not even a burial area next to the downtown church
she attended. Westview Cemetery in Atlanta held the Candler family plot,
and into that family she would be received in the end.

Despite the short notice, friends and family converged from all over
the South to attend this final service. Mrs. Olie Olsen, wife of the boat
captain who had been best man at Grandpa's second wedding, came from
North Carolina where she had been visiting family. Ruth's Aunt Lou,
who had moved to Florida after her marriage in the 1930s, had come to
town to see a football game and stayed for her niece's burial. Judson Ward,
who had been Dean of Emory when Ruth graduated in 1957, attended,
though he did not remember Ruth as a student. Death made Ruth stand
out from the crowd.

The service was short and simple. One of Ruth's Washington Seminary
friends who attended with another classmate wrote, "We had lost a beautiful loving friend, and part of us, too. The day was bright and sunny and
the service was sweet but untimely tragic." Afterwards, Ruth's grandmother
remarked that it was exactly what she wanted for her own funeral. Four
years later, she would join Ruth at Westview.

One friend wrote in his condolence letter to Bob, "Sam Cobb conducted a very fitting and appropriate service. I wish that I could find one
of the prayers that he used, but I have looked in vain. It's the one in which
he said that when God had given Ruth to us he lost something and now
we were losing something in giving Ruth back to Him. This impressed me
on two counts. First, that both God and we had lost something in turn;
and secondly, that we are only on loan, so to speak, from God. This is
something that many of us are inclined to forget."

Ruth's body was buried. Embalmed, sealed in a casket and vault, the
body of the mother I cannot remember still lies six feet beneath the orange clay of Georgia. It is an odd thing. Someone once told me how hor-
rified he was when a funeral director assured him in a sympathetic tone
that he could guarantee the body of his loved one would maintain its
beauty for fifty years. I asked the gentleman from Voglers about this, but
he would only say he didn't know how long a properly embalmed and
entombed body would last.

"We don't check our work," he said. In the file of papers relating to the
settlement of Ruth's estate that my father loaned to me is a Burial Vault
Guarantee from the Wilbert W. Hasse Company. The guarantee assures
the purchaser that if any defects in the vault lead to damage within fifty
years, the company will replace the vault and pay up to $500 for damage
done to the "casket and clothing." No mention of the body.

This potential survival of Ruth's body is contrary to my own desire to
come to terms with her death, to accept that she is gone. Were her body
reduced to ashes or dust I could let her go, remember her only as she was,
but our strange obsession with preserving what was never intended to be
preserved allows that one dark corner of my brain to nag at me. I cannot
remember my mother's physical form, "but there it is," whispers my de-
mon, "nothing between you but a few feet of earth." I pray some nights
that that funeral director was wrong—that Ruth's corpse is present now
only in the grass and the trees and the flowers, that all the precautions
failed and her body has been allowed to return to the earth.

The mourners dispersed, leaving the fresh plot alone in the autumn sun.
For most of those who left, it would become one of many funerals, each
followed by a short period of introspection and sadness that would quickly
give way to a return to life as normal. For a few of us, life would never be

the same again. Any group of mourners is so divided, and today the divisions still exist. As eloquently as her friends and distant relatives write about Ruth thirty years later, I know they were not affected by her death in the same way as my siblings, who have no strong memories of her; my father, who even now wipes away a tear when relating the story of his wife's death; Ruth's father, whom I never heard even utter her name; her mother, who might have been willing to talk to me had I undertaken this journey a few years earlier, when she still had the strength for a conversation ("She believed in reincarnation," wrote Austin Ford, "and claimed she would never sorrow, even at the death of those closest to her"); and me. Everyone who knew her suffered from losing Ruth's, but we six lived the changed lives. A few days later, the Lovetts returned to Winston-Salem, their link to the Candlers both more and less than it had been a week earlier, and began the long climb out of darkness.

No one ever took me to visit the grave. I might attribute this to my father's belief that we could not live in the past, that we had no choice but to forge a new life without Ruth, but he was rarely in Atlanta with his children. We usually visited grandparents in ones and twos during the summer months, but the first time I ever went to Westview, ever even glimpsed my mother's grave, was almost twenty-five years later at my grandfather's burial. Perhaps at first my grandparents felt I was too young, and later the habit of avoidance had established itself. I did not know if Ruth's parents or siblings visited her grave, but none of them ever mentioned it to me, and it seemed sad to me that a woman who was loved so much in life should be neglected in death. I dislike myself for feeling that way, for I know we all kept Ruth in our hearts, which is the true tribute. Visiting the site of the disposal of her remains has nothing to do with honoring her memory, does it? Our society's attention to graves and memorials has made me believe it does. It is the outward and visible sign of the inward and spiritual grace, and I wanted someone in the family to have visited that grave and remembered Ruth in that tangible and outward way.

One of the many wonderful letters I received from family in the past few months was from Aunt Kit. "Until recently," she wrote, "I went to Westview Cemetery every Christmas and I put fresh flowers on Ruth's grave." What a relief to read those words, to know that the ritual had been honored.

XVII

eulogy, *n.* 1. a speech or writing in praise of a person or
thing, esp. a set oration in honor of a deceased person.
                    —RANDOM HOUSE UNABRIDGED DICTIONARY

Ruth Candler Lovett died today. She left behind very little and the tangible things that do remain after her death will gradually disperse and cease to be recognized as hers as the years go by. Those things of least value to the world—photographs, letters, a yearbook, a wedding album—will reside in a trunk, unopened for many years, but eventually cherished by her children and perhaps her grandchildren. Tiny bits of her will remain carefully preserved but hidden from light in the file drawers and computer databases of colleges, hospitals, and banks. She did not, in her life, create those things that, in this world, make one live beyond death—no paintings, symphonies, novels; no brilliant career in the public eye; no heinous crimes. Someone who did not know her will see very little evidence, in a few years, that she ever walked the earth.

Except.

Ruth Candler Lovett died today, leaving the memories of those who knew her. Even thirty years from now, many of these memories will remain. Her friends and family will describe her as wonderful, lovely, sweet, quiet, happy, brave, shy, gentle, smart, silly, gracious, unassuming, attractive, graceful, musical, polite, friendly, and an angel in disguise. They will recall that she never showed anger and never spoke of the things that pained her most. Some will wonder how she expressed her pain and anger, but most will see the absence of these expressions as signs of contentment and kindness. They will remember that she was never beguiled by the wealth of her family and she never looked upon money as a measure of character. Today her friends, teachers, brothers, sister, parents, grandmother, aunts, cousins, husband, and children all mourn her death. But

Ruth will live on in each of them and in the lives of so many she touched. For many years, some may forget her, but a time will come when a sunset or a painting or a string quartet or a ringing phone reminds them, though they are not sure why, of Ruth, and for a moment they will stop and smile at her memory.

Ruth Candler Lovett left us today and not all that she left behind was pleasant. Into the hole left by her death many members of her family will pour pain, confusion, emptiness, frustration, and, above all, silence. The sound of the piano as she plays it on a spring afternoon—gone. The lilt of her voice as she talks with her mother on the phone—gone. The sound of her beating heart as she clutches her youngest child to her breast—gone. Ruth has been silenced, yes, but her family has been silenced, too, and they will struggle for years to find a way to speak of her, a way to cherish her memory and her gifts without tearing open the terrible wounds left by her death. Her children will have dreams that frighten them—dreams of helplessness and hopelessness they cannot begin to understand. Her father will be so devastated by the loss of his daughter that his wife will suffer a mild heart attack from the stress of supporting him. Her husband will suffer most of all, in spite of his strength and faith, for he knew her best and loved her most. He will wonder, during sleepless nights, if he can ever love again.

Ruth Candler Lovett passed today from the world she knew into a world she believed in. Behind her she left her gift to the world, her legacy, her chance at immortality. She left three children who, because they are only seven, six, and two years old, may never realize how much she gave them. She gave them her love of music—one will become a professional musician and all will have music as an important part of their lives. She gave them her love of the written word—one will become a writer and all will be passionate readers. She gave them her love of learning—one will be a teacher and all will be successful students. She gave them her love of family—all will be parents, caring for her six grandchildren. Even in death she continues to give to her children. Her death will hurt them. At times it may make it difficult for them to form strong bonds with others, difficult for them to talk openly with their own grandparents, difficult for them to make a doctor's appointment when they have an odd pain. But her death will also make it easier for them to believe in a world beyond this, to believe in angels, to develop into independent beings, and to value each day of life, to appreciate the tenuousness of our existence.

Ruth Candler Lovett died today, leaving behind a widower and three children, each of whom will find, in the decades that follow, their own ways of dealing with her absence. Her youngest child will not remember her. He will have in his mind no image of her smiling face leaning over to tuck him into bed. Because of this lack of memory, he will be able to make of her whatever he wants—even an angel. Or, he will be able to forget her entirely, to dismiss her life as unrelated to his own. "It's okay," he will be able to tell people, "I never knew her." But the time will come when he will want to know her, when he will depend on those long-held memories of her friends and family to replace his own empty past. He will come to see, among the other gifts she has given him, the lesson that a parent can be an indispensable influence on a child even if his time with her is limited. He will look into the face of his own daughter and see the mother he never knew, the mother he will finally come to know, the mother whose life and death he will not ignore but accept.

Ruth Candler Lovett died today, and today her loved ones begin to put her to rest. It will not happen in a day or a week. It will not be accomplished in the simple acts of funeral and burial. For many of her family and friends, the process will take years, decades. But they will succeed. They will one day be able to say that Ruth rests in peace. And one day, those whom she has left behind will share that peace.

XVIII

O Lord, support us all the day long, until the shadows lengthen, and the evening comes, and the busy world is hushed, and the fever of life is over, and our work is done. Then in thy mercy, grant us a safe lodging, and a holy rest, and peace at the last.

—Book of Common Prayer

Thirty-one years and five weeks after Ruth's funeral, on a cold day in early November 1995, Lucy and I drive down Interstate 20 on the way to Westview. I try to reinforce the conversations we have had about Ruth in the past few days.

"Remember that my Mommy had the same middle name and the same last name that you have?"

"She did?"

"That's right, her name was Ruth Candler Lovett."

"My name is Lucy Candler Lovett."

I get Lucy to repeat Ruth's name a few times, and then it's time to explain the concept of a cemetery. This is difficult for me, because I'm still not sure I understand it myself. So, I opt for a simplistic explanation that fits my own idea of what a cemetery should be and my hope for what I might find at Westview.

"A cemetery is a special place where we go to remember people who have died," I tell Lucy. "They have lots of pretty stones to remind you of those people and we are going to visit the stone where we go to remember Ruth and all the nice things she did."

"With you?" Lucy asks.

"No, I was too little to remember her. But lots of her friends and people in her family have told me all about her and what a nice person she was."

We are off the interstate now, and only a few blocks away from "the largest cemetery in the South." I marvel at how easy it was to get here. It makes it all the more surprising that no one ever took me.

"Sometimes," I say, "it's nice to take flowers to the cemetery and put them on the stone of the person you came to remember to show that you're thinking of that person." I scan the roadside for a florist and spot one next to a vacuum cleaner repair store. We pull across the cracked pavement of the parking lot and head up to the barred door where we press a buzzer to be admitted. Five minutes later, we climb back into our car with two red roses lying on the back seat where Lucy keeps careful watch on them.

"Now we can put those pretty flowers on Ruth's grave," I tell her.

"What's a grave?"

"It's the place where they bury a person after that person has died." Okay, now I've said it, and I don't know how I will explain it when Lucy asks me why.

"You mean their bones?" she asks. I breathe a sigh of relief.

"That's right. A grave is where they bury somebody's bones. The stone they put there is called a gravestone and the place where all the stones are is called a cemetery."

"It's silly to have a stone on somebody's bones," says Lucy, and I can't argue with her.

Westview is to our right, separated from us only by a fence. The land closest to the street is empty, just open fields and occasional trees, but a few hundred yards in the distance, gravestones dot the hillsides.

"Do you see some of the stones over there, Lucy?"

"Oh, I see some flowers!"

We turn in through the tall stone pillars and drive into a different world from the noise and hurry of fast-food joints and Atlanta interstates. Hills rise and fall around us—some speckled with graves, others empty. We wind our way down the main road with no other cars or people in sight. All is silence and peace. I hope I can drive around for a few minutes and recognize the spot where my grandfather's funeral was held. As I recall, the plot was at the bottom of a small hill under a large tree. But this place is filled with hills and trees and stones—stones memorializing the prominent and ordinary men and women of Atlanta. Atop one hill is a statue of a Confederate soldier above which flies the battle flag of the

Confederacy. Beneath those colors are buried several dozen Confederate veterans, their small stones radiating in concentric circles from the statue.

We pass a sign telling us that "cut flowers are permitted during any time of the year." Around the next curve Lucy exclaims, "look at that big tower." The tall stone structure looks more like a castle keep than the water tower it is.

"I've never seen a tower that big," says Lucy, "it touches the sky." We drive through the cemetery. I turn down narrow lanes and scan the names on the stones. On one corner, I spot someone with the middle name "Candler" and another stone with my great-grandmother's maiden name, "Glenn." Doubtless these are distant relatives, but we pass them by and continue our search.

"Where's your Mom?" Lucy asks.

"I don't know. If we can't find her pretty soon, we'll go back to the office and ask."

"Hey! There's someone who has a statue on top!" One thing I love about Lucy—she is always excited by new experiences. Some three-year-olds would be whining about having no toys and nothing to do but look at boring old stones, but she is in rapt attention, looking for anything that catches her interest.

"Look at that tree. It's dead. Can you imagine a tree like the tree that I saw . . ." Her litany of discovery continues as I give up my search and head to the front office. "It's quiet out here . . . I saw a couple that have flags in front of them . . . How many stones do you think there are? . . What do you think your mother's looks like?"

"It's white," I say. "Kind of plain and square, I think. Simple."

We park in front of the flat modern building by the gate and go in through the glass doors to the reception area. The woman behind the counter smiles and I tell her I am looking for the Candler family plot. I expect that this might impress her slightly—the fact that I am associated with such a prominent Atlanta family. Her response both puts me in my place and shows me how much Atlanta has changed since Ruth left in 1962 believing her children could not lead normal lives here as Candlers.

"How do you spell that?" the woman asks. I smile and tell her and two minutes later we are back in our car with a map of the cemetery. In spite of all our wanderings, the map shows that we haven't glimpsed more than about a third of the total developed area of Westview, besides which, more than 300 acres remain for "future generations." Lucy and I are headed for Section 4, Lot 83, a short drive from the office.

After one right turn and one left turn, we pull up across the road from a well kept plot nestled between a large magnolia and a fir tree that has lost its top in a storm. At the head of the plot is a large, but not ostentatious, headstone, engraved simply, "Charles Howard Candler." Ruth's grandfather. In front of it are five small stones nearly flush with the ground. Here Ruth probably attended the burial of her grandfather in October of 1957. To the right of his small marker is that of his wife, whose death in 1968 I vaguely remember; my grandfather, whom we buried here in 1988; and my grandfather's second wife, who is still alive and whose marker bears only a date of birth. On the far left of the row of five markers is what we have come to see.

Identical in size and design to the other four, the rectangular stone is made of white granite, curves up slightly in the middle, and has an engraved leaf and flower pattern on its lower corners. "Ruth Candler Lovett Wife of Robert William Lovett June 5, 1935 September 25, 1964." I remembered it as being square with no ornamentation, but already that faulty memory is fading, being replaced by reality. The edges of the stone

Lucy lays roses on her grandmother's grave.

are scratched from the lawn mower. The recent rain has left a few pine needles across the engraving, and Lucy leans down and brushes them off. We stand together in the silence and cold wind and look at the stone for a moment. The grass is still wet from the afternoon's rainfall, and the sky remains gray.

"Would you like to put the flowers on Ruth's stone?" I ask Lucy.

"Okay." We return to the car and retrieve the roses from the back seat. Lucy walks toward the markers carefully holding the roses. As she reaches the row of white stones, she turns to me.

"Which one is it again?"

"The one on the end," I say, pointing. She leans down and places the flowers gently across the width of the stone, arranging them carefully to fit her taste. Then she runs back to me.

"Look at those pretty flowers over there," she says, spotting an elaborate arrangement across the street.

"Do you think," I ask, "that if you see flowers on somebody's grave it means somebody came to visit—that somebody loves that person?"

"Yes," says Lucy, "and we loved her, so we put flowers on her." How quickly, how effortlessly, yet how earnestly the love of a three-year-old is bestowed.

"Now can I go play?" she asks. We are alone. Only the sound of distant traffic betrays that we are in Atlanta. Lucy has been sitting in the car all day.

"Just stay where you can see me," I say, and she enters her own world of play, walking among the memories of the dead, exploring a new landscape, leaving me standing by the grave of my mother. For the first time ever I can see it clearly, and I have the time to look and think.

What do I expect to find here? Do I expect mystical revelations or psychological closure? No. I don't know what to expect or what to want. I only know that I needed to come here. Perhaps I thought I would feel closer to Ruth here, and in a way I do, not because her body lies beneath my feet, but because, as I told Lucy, this is a place designed for the memory of those who have died. I can wander the halls of her houses or drive around her old neighborhoods, but there my remembering of her is somehow secret. Here, if there were anyone to see me, he would expect that I am remembering someone.

Do I think that my muttered words to Ruth are more likely to be heard here than anywhere else? Not really. I do not know if she can hear me, if she is a guardian angel looking over my life. But if she is, I know she would not limit her listening to words spoken at this place.

Do I think that my prayers for the peace of her soul will have more power spoken here? No. God, too, would not place such limitations on His children.

Perhaps I expected that my visit to Ruth's grave would be life-changing, that it would come to symbolize the end of my search for her. Perhaps I expected to finally feel a flood of grief and tears. But what I feel is peace. Visiting Ruth's grave is, of all things, pleasant—and not just in the sense of finding a quiet refuge in the midst of a loud city. Looking down on this simple stone makes me understand that her life was real and her death was real and she has been laid to rest. I believe she is at peace and that she would want me to be at peace, too. I feel sadness at my mother's grave, but I do not cry. I smile. I smile because coming to her grave represents, for me, breaking down one last barrier of the silence that has characterized my feelings about her life and her death. I realize I can come here whenever I want. I don't need to fear that this place will change my life, but I can find some quiet contemplation here. I can, as I said to Lucy, take a few moments of my life every once in a while, and be alone with thoughts of my mother in a place where it is expected and encouraged.

Did my visit to Westview bring me closer to Ruth? No. But it enabled her to give me yet another gift, for it did bring me closer to Lucy. It gave me a way to let Lucy participate in my most private of journeys and it further opened a door between me and her that had, for so many years, been shut by me and members of my own family. Talking about Ruth to my father or her sister or her friends has been important to me—it has taught me what kind of person and what kind of parent my mother was. But in talking about Ruth to Lucy I begin to discover what kind of parent I want to be. The longer a door between parent and child remains shut, the harder it is to budge, but once open, it easily stays open.

When we meet her mother the next morning at a hotel in Buckhead for the changing of the parental guard, Lucy will happily show off her new knowledge of Ruth with breathless excitement.

"We went to the graveyard, Mommy, and we saw the stone for Ruth and that's Daddy's mommy who died and she's my grandma even though she died." Lucy is blessed with a host of wonderful grandmothers, none of whom is related to her by blood. I'm glad that she will grow up thinking of family as something other than a genetic connection, but I'm also glad that she won't be afraid to talk about the other grandmother, the one who died.

As I turn to leave Ruth's grave site, I call Lucy and she comes running to me. "Look what I found for you, Daddy," she says, and holds a dried magnolia seed cluster out to me. Lucy, in collecting leaves, has been doing the same thing I have been doing—grasping after what is dead and hoping to take some comfort from it. She has been accumulating images of the past—artifacts that remind us of the cycle of life. I take the seed cluster from her, this spiny, ugly thing that looks so dead and yet is so full of life. Lucy, I'm sure, does not realize that, in giving me this gift, she is telling me that in death there can be life, in loss there can be reward, and in pain there can come peace. Who would have thought that the lesson of the search for a mother would come from a daughter? But the loss of each generation, whether at twenty-nine or ninety-two, is inevitable, and we have no choice but to turn to the next.

And so I turn to Lucy, sweep her into my arms, and leave my mother's grave in peace, as the white light of the afternoon sun finally breaks through the clouds and falls warm and soft on our faces.

About the Author

CHARLES LOVETT is an author and teacher who has written six previous books on topics ranging from book collecting to the Olympic Marathon. He has written extensively on Lewis Carroll, and has one of the largest collections of Carroll materials in the world. He holds a B.A. from Davidson College and an M.F.A. in Creative Writing from Vermont College. He recently moved back to Winston-Salem, North Carolina where he lives with his wife Janice and daughter Jordan, and enjoys frequent visits with his daughter Lucy.

If you enjoyed

LOVE, RUTH: A SON'S MEMOIR . . .

Why not tell a friend?

A portion of the proceeds from the sale of this book will go to The Callanwolde Guild in support of Callanwolde Fine Arts Center. The Guild thanks you for purchasing this book, and asks that you consider recommending *Love, Ruth: A Son's Memoir* to a friend. Additional copies my be ordered by phone, mail, or on the World Wide Web.

Additional Copies of
Love, Ruth: A Son's Memoir
May be ordered for $17 plus $3 shipping and handling from:

The Callanwolde Guild
Callanwolde Fine Arts Center
980 Briarcliff Road NE
Atlanta, GA 30306

Credit card orders call: (404) 872-5338

Or visit our Web site at
www.callanwolde.org

A Book Club Guide to *Love, Ruth: A Son's Memoir* is also
available from or Web site or by sending a SASE
to our mailing address.